GW00500414

WOKING
LIBRARY

- 6 JUN 20

19/2/

S
C

GREECE

A GUIDE TO THE ARCHAEOLOGICAL SITES

WOKING
LIBRARY

2000/2001
SURREY LIBRARIES

ARC/938

WHITE STAR
PUBLISHERS

THRACE

Edessa

Amphìpolis

Abdera

Maroneia

Pèlla

Saloniki

Verghìna

MACEDONIA

Olynthos

Corfu

EPIRUS

CORFU

Dodona

THESSALY

Làrissa

Nekromanteìon

Volos

AETOLIA-ACARNANIA
and PHOCIS

EUBOEA

Orchomenòs

Stratos

Delphi

BOEOTIA

Thebes

Eretria

Patras

Oropòs

ACHAIA

Corinth

Eleusis

ATHENS

CORINTIA

ELIS

Mycenae

Cape Soùnion

DELOS

ARGOLYS

MESSENIA

ARCADIA

KEA

Epidauros

AEGINA

NÀXOS

Messene

Sparta

MELOS

LACONIA

THIRA

2324

CRETE

Knossos

Aghia Triàda

GREECE

A GUIDE TO THE ARCHAEOLOGICAL SITES

TEXTS
FURIO DURANDO

TRANSLATION
C.T.M., MILAN

EDITING OF THE ENGLISH TRANSLATION
DOUG LLOYD

EDITED BY
VALERIA MANFERTO
DE FABIANIS
FABIO BOURBON

GRAPHIC DESIGN
CLARA ZANOTTI

CONTENTS

FOREWORD	page 6	OINIÀDAI	page 85	AIGEIRA	page 148
		NEA PLEURON	page 86	OLYMPIA	page 150
INTRODUCTION	page 8	KALYDON	page 86	KAIÀFAS	page 158
The Art of Ancient Greece		DELPHI	page 88	VÀSSES	page 158
ATHENS	page 22	BOEOTIA AND EUBOEA	page 98	PYLOS	page 158
		CHAIRONEIA	page 98	MESSENE	page 160
EPIRUS AND CORFU	page 46	ORCHOMENOS	page 98		
NEKROMANTEION	page 46	GLÀ	page 99	ARCADIA	
KASSOPE	page 48	THEBES	page 100	AND LACONIA	page 162
NIKOPOLIS	page 50	LEFKANDI	page 102	ORCHOMENOS	page 162
DODONA	page 51	ERETRIA	page 102	MANTINEIA	page 162
IOÀNINA	page 52			TEGEA	page 162
CORFU	page 54	ATTICA AND AEGINA	page 104	MEGALOPOLIS	page 163
		CAPE SOUNION	page 105	LYKOSSOURA	page 163
THESSALY	page 56	THORIKOS	page 106	GORTYS	page 163
NEA ANKHIALOS	page 56	BRAURON	page 106	SPARTA	page 164
DEMETRIÀS	page 57	MARATONA	page 107	VAFIO	page 165
VOLOS	page 58	RHAMNOUS	page 107	GYTHION	page 165
SESKLO	page 58	OROPOS	page 107		
LÀRISSA	page 59	PHYLE	page 107	ISLANDS	page 166
PHERAI	page 59	ELEUSIS	page 108	KEA	page 166
		ELEUTHERAI	page 113	MÉLOS	page 167
MACEDONIA	page 60	AIGOSTHENA	page 113	DELOS	page 168
DION	page 60	AEGINA	page 114	NÀXOS	page 182
VERGHINA	page 63			SANTORINI	page 183
VERIA	page 66	CORINTHIA		RHODES	page 186
LEFKADIA	page 66	AND ARGOLYS	page 118	KOS	page 190
EDESSA	page 66	PERACHORA	page 118	SAMOS	page 194
PELLA	page 67	ISTHMIA	page 120		
SALONIKI	page 70	CORINTH	page 122	CRETE	page 196
OLYNTHOS	page 74	SIKYON	page 128	GORTYNA	page 196
		NEMEA	page 129	AGHII DEKA	page 198
THRACE	page 76	MYCENAE	page 130	PHAISTOS	page 198
AMPHIPOLIS	page 77	ARGOS	page 140	AGHIA TRIÀDA	page 199
PHILIPPOI	page 78	LERNA	page 140	KNOSSOS	page 200
KAVÀLA	page 81	TYRINS	page 140	MÀLLIA	page 210
ABDERA	page 82	NÀFPLION	page 141	GOURNIÀ	page 211
MARONEIA	page 82	EPIDAUROS	page 142	KÀTO ZÀKROS	page 211
ACARNANIA, AETOLIA		ACHAIA, ELIS		GLOSSARY	page 212
AND PHOCIS	page 84	AND MESSENIA	page 148	INDEX	page 213
STRATOS	page 84	PATRAS	page 148	PHOTOGRAPHIC CREDITS	page 216
THERMOS	page 84				

AMOS

KOS

RHODES

1 On the famous Lions Terrace at Delos, one can observe nine of the marble lions still preserved.

2-3 The temple of Athena Aphaia at Aegina is one of the most elegant Doric cult buildings from the Archaic period (510-

490 BC). Its pediments are kept in the Glyptothek in Munich.

4 bottom This amphora from the first half of the 6th c. BC is a wonderful example of black figure vase painting, an art at which the Athenian

and Corinthian artists excelled.

4-5 This sequence of mountain chains, hills and small plateaus that faces onto three seas — the Mediterranean, the Ionian, and the Aegean — formed the birthplace of western civilization.

© 2000 White Star S.r.l.
Via Candido Sassone, 22-24
13100 Vercelli, Italy

All rights of translation, reproduction, and partial or total adaptation, by any means whatsoever, are reserved for all nations

ISBN 88-8095-504-7
1 2 3 4 5 6   05 04 03 02 01 00

Printed in Italy by Grafedit
Color separations 3F Fotolito, Milan

FOREWORD

Maurizio Forte
Archaeologist and Head Researcher at the Institute of
the Application of Technologies to Cultural Heritage
at the National Research Council, Rome.

*U*nderstanding of the ancient past is based on visual, cultural, emotive and, above all, geographic comprehension. When we visit an excavation site or we examine an archaeological landscape, we anxiously ask ourselves the same questions: how is this to be interpreted? Who built it? Who lived here? How has the environment changed? How long ago was it used? Next we often make conceptual associations with our own daily life such as, "at that time they also did this, said that, fought and built ..." Our interpretation of the past always passes through the present because we need a cultural, typological and topographical grammar with which to form our cognitive notions, above all in the difficult intellectual synthesis of giving a face to what no longer exists or only partially remains. This operation of interpretive "anastylosis" is not just a capacity of modern man but inherent in human thought; the sight of places prompts us to reconstruct them, to recognize them, to identify first the memory of a site, then a context, and, finally, a territory. When our understanding is saturated, thought becomes cognitive and we are able to orient ourselves perfectly in the geography of the landscape; our walk through it becomes engrossing, culturally rich and, more than anything else, packed with visual information.

This need was well represented and attested by the Greek geographer, Pausanias, who, between 160 and 177 AD, drew up a proper tourist guide to the places and monuments of Greece, or, rather, a guide to the territorial understanding of ancient Greece. This record allows us to fully comprehend the spirit that has moved man since antiquity to describe himself through places and to recognize himself in the evolutionary dynamic of historic geography but especially, to set out on the itineraries magnificently presented by Furio Durando. This superb "Guide to Greece" by Durando is a work of great cultural and topographical awareness that combines excellent descriptions of the past with fascinating and instructive accounts of the present in a continuous narrative that intertwines archaeology, myth, ancient topography and modern thought. The detailed topographical descriptions cover all of Greece in 22 itineraries that embrace the regions of Attica, Argolys, Laconia, Boeotia, Thrace, Macedonia and Epirus, and the islands of Corfù, Aegina, Kea, Milos, Naxos, Delos, Santorìni, Crete, Rhodes, Cos and Samos. And bound up with the artistic and cultural elements recounted, we are treated to the smells and flavors of the Mediterranean: thyme, oregano, juniper, and maquis: nothing will escape the careful and curious traveler.

In addition to the highly informative historical accounts, the first part of the volume is dedicated to the history of Greek art, a useful and outstanding prologue that discusses the literacy of the cultural contexts, their symbolic and representative formalization, the archaeology of power and materials, and the syncretism of artistic, political and artisan expressions without ever forgetting that the distinction between arts and handicrafts was absolutely unknown in Classical Greece. This preparatory knowledge gives us confidence to embark on our explorations, and we happily observe the advanced elements of expression used in Classical art, architecture and thought — in a word, the Greek "logos".

We should be aware that no interpretation exists that is not first of all a narrative event: we see, examine and interpret on the basis of our own knowledge (recognition). And indeed, this magnificently illustrated guide is also a multimedia work, a hierarchic container of information and links; there is not a single paragraph or description that does not refer to numerous other levels or approaches to the text, intriguing the reader to inquire into the descriptions, to examine and gather further information in other chapters for a full understanding of the cultural anthropology of this complex artistic civilization that was fundamental to the entire history of the Mediterranean. The best definition that I can suggest for this book is "A guide to the cognitive archaeology of Greece" by which I mean that cognitive archaeology analyzes understanding of the past through ancient memory and thought. Comprehension of the Greek world in the topological narration is projected through the eyes and horizons of the Greeks themselves. The places illustrated are never desolate "ruins" but are living, inhabited territories, proper conceptual maps of the anthropology of the landscape.

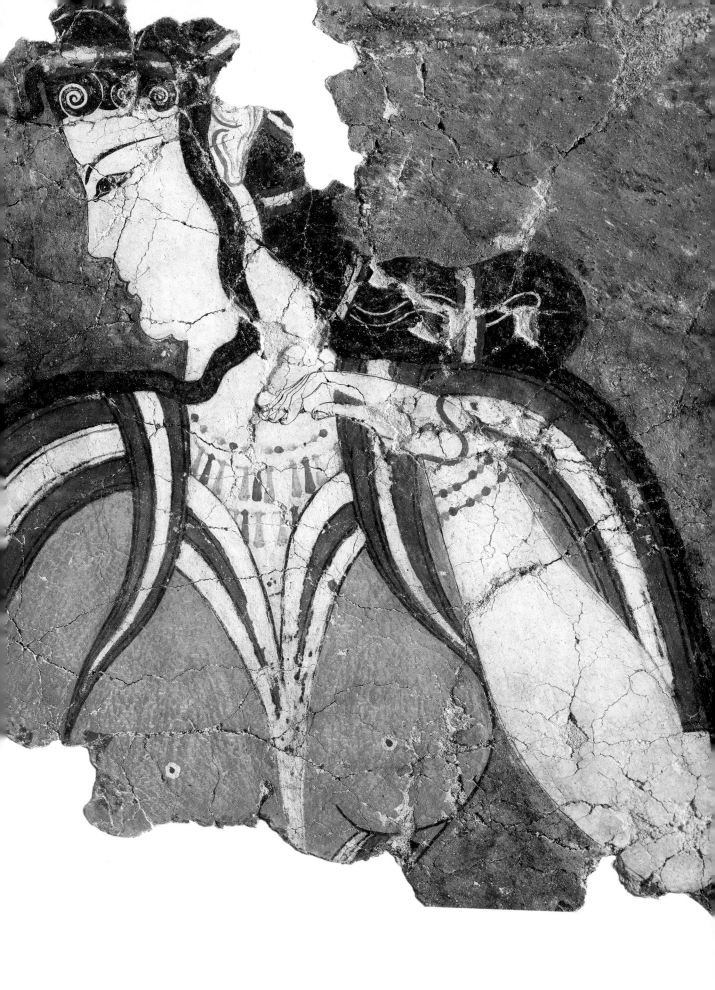

This 8th-century BC fragment of a fresco of a dancer comes from Mycenae and reveals the influence that Cretan art had on the city (Athens, National Museum).

*8 bottom Numerous
jars with small but
strong ring handles to
facilitate harnessing
and transport have*

*been found in the
workshops and
storehouses of
Knossos, the city
palace on Crete.*

THE ART of
ANCIENT GREECE

Greece initiated the pattern, common to all of Mediterranean Europe, of extensively borrowing from the artistic expressions of the prehistoric and protohistoric cultures that developed on its soil. Archaeological evidence from such periods suggests an artistic trend that was later picked up in the rest of Europe: the magical naturalism of Paleolithic art (up to 7000 BC) was followed by the symbolic synthetic abstractionism of the Neolithic and the Calcolithic periods (from 7000 to 4000 BC). It was during the Calcolithic period that the very first settlements of considerable demographic and structural scale (Sèsklo, Dimìni), were founded.

During the Bronze age, with the arrival and settlement of the first Indo-European Hellens, the Helladic civilization soon developed on both the mainland and the islands. Cycladic sculptures, with their amazingly synthetic formal expression, are the most interesting artifacts of this period, the ancient forebears of the masterpieces of Modigliani and Brancusi.

The Minoan thalassocracy (named after Minos, the mythical king of Knossos), that fully controlled the Aegean sea during the first half of the second millennium BC, left splendid artistic evidence in its wake, as it swept through the islands of Crete, where it originated, and nearby Thèra (Santorìni). The Cretans were the first to conceive and develop grandiose architectural structures serving as residential complexes and administrative centers, as well as cultural and production hubs, all at the same time. These were the "palace-cities," featuring a complex layout and structure reminiscent of the Near East and Egypt, from where the Cretans also borrowed the generalized naturalism that underlies all their art, from jewelry to sculpture and mural paintings. While the Cretans freely adopted and adapted Egyptian mural-painting techniques and certain aesthetic canons, the figurative naturalism of Cretan art is further enhanced by the keen sense of color and greater graphic fluidity of Cretan artists.

The Mycenaean civilization (17th-20th century BC), named after Mycenae, its most significant historical and archaeological site, that swept through the Peloponnesos, Attica, Boeotia, and Thessaly to reach Crete and the islands from the 15th century BC, produced an art that, despite its Cretan origins, was far less inclined towards naturalism. The jewelry, bronze work and ceramics of this period feature dampened aesthetic keenness and awareness mainly as a result of a newly developed concept of art as a summarily ideological expression of the powers-that-be. Lastly, unlike the undefended Minoan "palace-cities," the Cyclopean wall architecture of Mycenaean fortified cities with their austere ramparts were designed with functionality uppermost in mind, although the royal palaces, organized in several wings around the focal nucleus of the *mègaron*, feature decorative artifacts, pottery and furnishings worthy of Minoan luxury. Similar luxury and grandiosity also permeated the false-domed Mycenaean royal *thòlos* (round chamber) tombs, that supplanted the ancient cist tombs featuring a grave and burial chamber, towards the 15th-14th century BC.

Mycenaean civilization and art went into decline (12th-11th centuries BC) as a result pirate raids by the "Sea Peoples" and the emergence of a new Hellenic branch, the Dorians, on most of the peninsula and some islands (Crete and the Dodecanese archipelago), that caused the Aegean Diaspora of the Hellenic populations that settled there earlier (Ionians and Aeolians). Nearly everywhere, the Greek Middle Ages, a period of demographic and economic crisis, marked the transition from the Bronze Age to the Iron Age. The aristocratic clans, warriors, land owners, cattle farmers and those who controlled the supply of raw materials, entrusted power to a *basileùs*, an elected sovereign seconded by a council of elders. With economic recovery well on its way during the 10th and 9th centuries BC, this period saw the establishment of the earliest modest settlements that would later develop into flourishing cities. It was, however, in the figurative arts that a radical shift was most for Athenian workshops introduced new ceramic shapes and a new "geometric" language, expressed in the abstract decoration of vases using flat, linear geometrical elements and shapes that coexisted with aesthetic canons symmetry, harmony and elegance. Geometrical art was a product of a worldview in which nature was seen as an infinite and complex reality, not to be merely imitated and reproduced in a purely descriptive fashion, but to be appreciated in its essence and in its inner laws, apart from the variety of its changing contingent forms.

From the 9th to the 8th century BC, *pòleis*, or city-states were formed, in which craftsmen, merchants and businessmen flourished, bringing increasing amounts of circulating wealth. In later centuries, the interests of these classes conflicted with the ruling aristocracy. This gave rise to the phenomenon of Greek colonization that interacted and competed with the

Pheonician colonial effort. During the geometric period, private homes of the common people were based on stone foundations supporting a superstructure built of unfired bricks in a timber frame. The layout alternated between the Mycenaean *mègaron* type, used in noble residences and temples, and a new rational layout of space. Artistic metalwork that was boosted by renewed demand, as witnessed in small plastic votive objects and the production of bronze lebes decorated in relief with embossed motifs and sometimes plastic appliqués, followed the thematic stylistic trends of ceramics. Especially in Athens, the art of ceramics reached the highest levels of elegance and decorative complexity, featuring extremely stylized human and animal figures within small spaces or frames that were not covered by the usual abstract motifs.

The boom in trade, a consequence of Greek and Phoenician mercantile and colonial interdependence, had a deep impact on the artistic civilization of Greece.

9 left The column between the two lions in the relief on the famous Lion Gate at Mycenae (circa 1259 BC) may have symbolized the palace as a center of power or a deity in aniconic form.

9 right This 7th-century BC fresco in the West House in Akrotìri on Santorìni is a lovely example of Cretan painting. It shows fishermen making an offering to the gods (Athens, National Museum).

From 750-725 BC up to the end of the 7th century BC, massive supplies of oriental artistic and luxury products reached Greece and its colonies. These were generally objects bought by aristocrats as signs of economic prestige and majesty or as gifts that sealed trade agreements, and sometimes even political pacts between Western and Eastern nobility. The precious nature of the materials, the wealth of decoration and thematic imagination, rendered Levantine art much more attractive than the geometric style with its austere rules. Levantine art ended up becoming a model for local artists, giving rise to an oriental-leaning style (from about 725 to 610 BC) that tried to adapt the themes and iconography of Eastern art to the need to represent reality or abstraction on the basis of balance of concept and form, already highly developed and seen as the corner-stone of art during the three preceding centuries.

The most immediate consequence of this can be seen in early Corinthian, early Attic and Greco-oriental ceramics, featuring functional and elegant forms and a figurative ornamentation closely linked to the principle of compositive order, often exuding great expressive force and a solid balance of form, especially in small molded bronze objects.

The 7th century BC also saw the development of the most ancient Greek stone statuary tradition: the "Daedalic" figurative scheme, inspired by Oriental art, with a stiff frontal view, accompanied by limited decorative stereotypes. This period saw the emergence of images of Gods and humans in the form of *koùroi* ("boys") and *kòrai* ("girls") that were increasingly distanced from their Egyptian and Mesopotamian origins and gradually assumed credible proportions and an intimate, albeit latent, vitality.

This century also marks the independent development of early Greek stone architecture, especially in temples, that adopted worthier proportions and nobler and more durable materials as well as increasingly graceful and harmonic forms, borrowing only a few technical solutions from the East. The second half of the 7th century BC saw the earliest ground plans of temples and the emergence of the Doric and Ionic architectural orders. The innovation of paneling timber pediments with polychrome clay tiles featuring religious, mythological or epic themes indicates a desire to weave typically Greek motifs and values into the entire structure and its ornamental elements.

In the 6th century BC, the Greece of the city-states or *pòleis* and colonies became the cultural reference point for the entire Western world, and man's rational thought, as expressed through philosophy, the thirst for theoretical and applied knowledge that constantly tended towards totality and perfection, was also applied to artistic, architectural and town planning theory. This was the century of "Archaic" art, so called only to underline the fact that it predated the formally perfect Classical art that was to emerge in the following century.

The Greeks' constant preoccupation with the rational organic unity of technical solutions was also felt in town planning. Greek colonies in Southern Italy and Sicily were the first sites featuring grid-planned cities, with a logical and functional layout. Special care was taken in selecting the locations and appearance of temples and sanctuaries both within and outside the city walls. Quite like the colonies, even the Greek metropolises that grew at a tumultuous rate between the 9th and 7th centuries BC, were subjected to town planning and face-lifting operations. These works were often the result of the largesse of tyrants who, in many cities, rose to power with the support of the rich merchant, business and craftsmen classes as well as small landowners. Public works focused especially on prominent city districts considered important in the eyes of the population: the *acropolis* or "high city" that represented the culmination of the religious identity of the community and the *agorà*, that was its administrative and economic-commercial hub.

Temples increasingly featured a wealth of magnificent and refined ornaments. Temple designs commissioned by the tyrants on Ionic and Asian islands perfected the development of the Ionic order and influenced the lines, dimensions and proportions of the Doric order, especially in the colonies. The question of the sculptural decoration of temples was also faced and resolved: the triangular space (tympanum) created by the slopes of the roof on short sides induced artists to experiment with techniques and themes. Pediments were thus made to bear ethical, political or historical-celebratory messages, through motifs borrowed from mythology or the epics.

The 6th century BC was also the golden age of highly artistic regional and local (of the city-state or *pòleis*) Panhellenic sanctuaries of monumental proportions, including huge stadiums and theaters that were used for religious gatherings and feasts featuring sports, literary and music competitions. The sanctuaries, especially, were centers of religious power that provided the city-states with a forum of discussion to debate issues of prime importance. In an attempt to acquire political influence over the clergy of major Panhellenic sanctuaries (Delphi, Olympia, Delos), the city-states often competed with each other in constructing splendid buildings, commissioning works of art and earmarking percentages of war booty for the sanctuaries.

In the meanwhile, Archaic Greek sculpture irreversibly departed from its remote oriental origins and themes and started focusing on life-size human images. Initially static and clumsy, *kòrai* and *koùroi* developed to become an ideal representation of the human form in terms of naturalism, organic unity, harmony and beauty, totally ignoring, however, individual physical or psychological traits. In the figurative convention that required *koùroi* to be totally naked while the *kòrai* had to be represented dressed in elegant local costumes, each image expressed the concept of youth as the symbol of the perfection of Being.

11 Ionic gracefulness pervades one of the most beautiful works of the Athenian sculptor, Antènor, the kòre no. 680 (circa 530 BC.) in which much of the original pictorial decoration is preserved (Athens, Acropolis Museum).

The early *koùroi*, with a heavy outline and hands and feet added like the limbs of a puppet, and the early *kòrai* that seemed like humanized tree trunks with carved drapery, made way for images that could express a concept of beauty that was both ideal and real. However, while the representation of the physical features and vitality improved and the carved drapery of the clothing became more natural, the faces remained expressionless, in keeping with the Archaic style. This gradual evolution was generated by several currents of sculptors linked to well-defined regions, each featuring its own distinctive elements. The vigorous interpretation of the Doric, Peloponnesian and Cretan "schools" and the tendency to enhance gracefulness found on the Ionic islands and in Micro-Asia, were combined to become one within the Attic current that perfected the Archaic artistic language, as in the works of Anténor. This process paved the path leading beyond the Archaic age towards the sculptures of the magnificent eastern pediment of the temple of Athena Aphaia at Aegina.

An identical quest for artistic independence as well as the affirmation of a well-defined ideal and artistic features that departed from their original oriental inspiration, took place in vase painting. Vase decorations outline the history of the great Greek mural and tablet-painting tradition, of which no trace has survived. After over a century of uncontested artistic and commercial hegemony, towards the second quarter of the 6th century BC, the production of Corinthian workshops declined in the face of the technical, qualitative and figurative superiority of Attic black figure vases, widely exported throughout the ancient world. The vases were actually transformed into many splendid illustrated pages of mythology and

12 The statue of
Apollo taken from the
western pediment of
the temple of Zeus at
Olympia (circa 460
BC.), shown in the
center of a
centauromachy, is a
masterpiece of proto-
classical sculpture
(Olympia, Archaeological
Museum).

the epics. Over the last 30 years of the
century, the introduction of the new red
figure technique by certain avant-garde
workshops allowed artists to indulge in even
greater expressive freedom: the figures
became increasingly detailed in their anatomy,
dress, ornaments and weapons, more credible
in their poses and more realistically spread
over the available space. As against the black
figure technique that involved the use of a
burin, the red figure technique employed
fine brushes that allowed for increasingly
minute detail. Apart from very elaborately
decorated vases created by artists who were
aware and proud of their skill at least to the
extent of signing their work, more affordable,
medium-to low-quality vases targeted at the
general public, were mass-produced in
craftsmen's workshops.

In the first quarter of the 5th century
BC, the Greek world went through a
dramatic series of upheavals: precarious
political balances were upset by the growing
expansionist ambitions that led to rivalries
between the larger pòleis (Athens, Sparta,
Corinth, Argos); the Greeks of Asia Minor
had already lost their independence to the
growing threat of Persian imperial
expansionism, and as the Western colonies
broke away from the metropolises, the
already feeble Greek political uniformity
was further weakened.

At Athens, in the meanwhile, a form
of government that featured surprising
novelty took root. Athenian democracy was
based on the assumption that the State
equals the citizens, and entrusted the
governance of the pòleis to the assembly of
the dèmos ("people") and its freely elected
representatives, but the aggressive military
stance that Athens had to assume in order to
maintain its economic primacy and its
power of political seduction incited the

13 left The austere
grace of the art of
Exekìas can be seen in
this Attic amphora
(circa 540 BC.) showing
the duel between
Achilles and Penthesilea,
the queen of the
Amazons (London,
British Museum).

13 right The band
on the neck of this red
figure cup from the end
of the 6th century BC
is decorated with a
scene showing the duel
between Hector and
Achilles.

hostility of the oligarchic aristocracies and tyrannies that ruled over the rest of Greece. The Attic metropolis, however, greatly increased its prestige and political as well as economic weight in the Mediterranean, since this young democratic *pòlis* succeeded, almost single-handedly, at twice resisting Persian attempts at overrunning Greece (490-480 BC).

These victories marked the dawn of the "golden age" of Greek art and culture.

Greek art in the first half of the 5th

century BC, referred to as "severe" by some art historians and "proto-Classical" or "Early Classical" by more modern scholars, followed in the footsteps of Greek philosophy, from which it took both sustenance and inspiration. The aim was to find the ideal and perfect expression of Being, united yet multi-faceted, dynamic, immense and eternal. At the same time, an attempt was made to develop a form in which all this would appear as a harmonic and rational whole. It was at this time that the concept of "Beauty" as a perfect balance between form and substance was first developed, leading to the inference that aesthetic "beauty" always and necessarily expressed inner or moral beauty.

In the field of town planning, the quest for harmony was championed both in theory and practice by Hippodamus of Miletus,

who established the town planning criteria of increasingly populous urban areas that involved complex functions and needs. His scheme, based on a grid plan and functional elements determined on the basis of logical criteria, that are still in use today, codified a variety of ancient and contemporary experiments. They have since been incorporated into the town planning regulations of famous cities such as Miletus, Rhodes and Piraeus.

This period featured intense architectural activity throughout the Greek world. Where there was no real innovation as such in structural design, the mathematical and proportional criteria of temples were more detailed and implied a prevailing sense of dimension. The grandiose Doric temple

to Zeus Olympios, built in the Panhellenic sanctuary of Olympia where the four-yearly games held in honor of the god assumed huge importance and became an occasion for political dialogue, is especially noteworthy, not only because of its impressive size but more especially for the sculptures that adorn it.

The new style of proto-Classical sculpture was already heralded in the statues on the eastern pediment of the temple of Athena Aphaia at Aegina. By around 480 BC, *koùros* statutes tended towards representing ideal beauty as an expression of the unity and perfect harmony of Being, as depicted in certain works from the Athenian workshops of Kritios and Nesiotes, such as the famous Ephebus and the group of the Tyrannicides.

14 right The Auriga of Delphi is a rare example of proto-Classical bronze statuary (478-474 BC). It was offered by the tyrant Polyzelos of Gela to Apollo to commemorate the victory of his horse (Delphi, Archaeological Museum).

Side by side with marble statuary, the great bronze sculptural tradition also spread. Only copies of these masterpieces executed by skillful imitators commissioned by the large number of collectors of Greek and Roman art down the ages, survive today.

The largest bronze art schools were at Argos, Sicione and Taranto. The rapid spread of the innovations of the proto-Classical style throughout Hellenized Italy with its florid tyrannies, can be clearly seen in the high artistic value of the works created at the time, such as the famous group of the Auriga at Delphi, a votive offering by the tyrant Polyzelos of Gela, and most probably the work of an artist from one of Greece's colonies in Italy. Just before the middle of the century, further progress along the path towards perfection was made by the anonymous artist who created the bronze Zeus of Cape Artemìsso (Artemision). The work marks the "discovery" of the movement and also shows that the

14 left Found in the Persian Expiation the famous Ephebus of Krìtios (490-480 BC) is the first example of the breaking of the rigid conventions of Archaic statuary (Athens, Acropolis Museum).

15 left A lovely marble Roman copy perpetuates the fame of one of the most innovative and admired ancient bronze statues: the Diskobolos by Myron (450 BC), (Rome, Roman National Museum).

15 right Created to incarnate absolute perfection by means of mathematical proportions: this was the Doriphoros by Polykleitos (circa 450 BC), the author of the first treatise on sculpture in history (Naples, National Museum).

frontal vision of the human body in space had, by this time, been surpassed. Even more significant are the works of the Master of Olympia, the anonymous sculptor of the pediments and the metopes of the magnificent temple of Zeus. Only very recently, one of the two frontons has been tentatively attributed to Hageladas of Argos. The imposing figures, now stationary, now in agitated movement, are pervaded by a mood of tension similar to that reflected in the best pages of the great tragic poetry of the time. Proto-Classical art reached its zenith towards 450 BC, in the masterpieces of the great Myron, who sculpted the acclaimed Diskobolos, or discus thrower, in which body movement seems to synthesize the forms so dear to the Heraclitean philosophy of the period. Polykleitos was another great proto-Classical bronze sculptor, the first to have theoretically drafted and practically applied (in his statue, the Canon) a model of the perfect mathematical and proportional representation of the human form. He ingeniously illustrated his model in his renowned sculpture, the Doryphoros, or spear-bearer. Attic red figure ceramics of the time indicate that the great proto-Classical mural and tablet-painting tradition, now completely lost, evolved along similar lines, in terms of content, technique and form. What we do know with certainty is that the great artist of this tradition, Polygnotos of Thasos paid great attention to space and perspective.

The second half of the 5th century BC saw the absolute cultural supremacy of Athens, as the theoretical and practical research successfully carried out by the architects, sculptors, painters, and ceramic artists of the period, culminated to blend into the universal Greek philosophical worldview, as expressed in the inimitable form that we call "Classical." Athens was home to the

16 top *The ten tribes – the basis of democratic Athenian order – are symbolically represented in the festive cavalcade of 60 riders on the north side of the Ionic frieze of the cella on the Parthenon.*

perfection, enhanced by awareness in both thought and action.

The art of Phidias was carried on for several decades, in spirit and in style, by excellent and very skillful pupils of the master, but near the end of the century, there was a tendency toward a closer examination of the human universe in its contingent aspects. The inclination toward representing sentiment is not only evident in the works of Alkamenes, Agorakritos and Kallimachos, not to mention the

greatest philosophers, scientists and artists of the period. They flocked to the cradle of democracy to exchange ideas and gain experience, in their quest for public recognition and success.

In the contrasting climate in which the economic and cultural supremacy of Athens reached its height and democracy perversely regressed into imperialistic ambitions, culminating in the tragic Peloponnesian war, the great statesman Pericles wished to give the city a new face, combining the functional needs of a total review of city planning with an ambitious, unparalleled project for beautifying the town. He wanted the identity as well as the political, ethical, religious and cultural values of the free people of Athens to be fully translated into an adequate architectural and artistic language so that they could be exalted before all the world. Huge resources were invested in the *agorà* or city center, as well as in residential city districts and port and road construction, but it was the *acropolis* that was the focus of Pericles' project. It was placed under the supervision of Phidias, the greatest artist of the ancient world, assisted by a team of highly learned collaborators, including the most brilliant architects of the time, as well as a host of young, talented artists.

The Parthenon, the temple dedicated to Athena Parthénos (Athena the Virgin), universally considered the most magnificent example of Greek architecture, was designed by Callicrates and Ictinus, whose refined mathematical calculations and proportions provided the city's patron goddess with a dwelling unrivaled in harmony and elegance. The Parthenon also introduced, for the first

time, an ingenious combination of Doric and Ionic orders, that would influence architectural aesthetics for centuries to come. The graceful Ionic temple of Athena Nike was based on an old drawing by Callicrates while Mnesikles was placed in charge of building the Propylaia, the mammoth gate building at the entrance to the sacred hill. It is widely believed that Mnesikles also designed the Erechteion, a complex of temples dedicated to Poseidon, acclaimed as a jewel of the Ionic architectural order. The architects of the Parthenon influenced the construction of a large number of sacred buildings, both within Athens and elsewhere, as can be seen in the splendid temple of Hephaistos that is still intact in the center of Athens, the temple to Poseidon at Cape Soùnion, the main core of the renowned sanctuary at Eleusis and the magnificent temple of Apollo Epikoùrios at Vàsses (in Arcadia).

The artistic genius of the century was the Athenian Phidias, who executed memorable, colossal chryselephantine (gold and ivory) cult statues for the cellae (main inner shrines) of the Parthenon and the temple of Zeus at Olympia. Unfortunately these wonders of ancient art are now lost. The rigorous proportions introduced by Polykleitos were enriched by a vast variety of lines and rhythms, accentuating the "idealized realism" that is the essence of Classicism. The perfect bodies and the splendid draperies of the statues on the pediments and the Ionic frieze of the Parthenon, as well as the large number of his other works, reflect an absolute beauty, divorced from any contingent restraints, so as to become an expression of both inner and outer

others, but also in Attic funerary stelae produced between the middle of the 5th and the end of the 4th centuries BC.

Painting made giant steps forward. Realism received theoretical support: two great philosophers, Anassagoras and Democritos, wrote theoretical treatises on perspective that inspired not only the painters Agatharchos, Panainos, Apollodoros, Zeuxis, and Parrhasios, but also Phidias, who besides being a sculptor and architect was also an accomplished painter. No trace of these paintings, however, remains today. The use of perspective lines, foreshortening, shading and touches that gave substance and dynamism to the figures, can, however, be found in the Attic ceramic art of the time, especially in works by the unknown painter of Achilles, the artist Polygnotos the Younger and the great Meidias, whose work was referenced by the great "pictorialist" sculptors of their age, such as Paionios of Mende.

16-17 The pediment on the west side of the Parthenon still has two figures, though badly damaged, probably from the court of Poseidon, and the metope showing scenes of a battle between Greeks and Amazons.

In the 4th century BC, Greece, just emerging from the Peloponnesian war, was torn between old and new, incessant local conflicts that were not resolved under the transitory hegemonies of Sparta, Thebes, or Athens. The political ascendance of certain regional leagues also failed at providing stability. In 338 BC, by winning the battle of Chaeronea, the Macedonian Empire under Philip II put an end to the independence of the Greek *pòleis* and above all, to their rivalry, triggering a process of unprecedented political and cultural unification.

The Peloponnesian war and the constant conflicts between *pòleis* that followed, contributed to the crisis of absolute values that was at the heart of the Hellenic soul for centuries. The loss of the sense of belonging to a community, that is to say, the city-state, total disillusionment and the certainty of the precariousness of man, led to a myopic world-view, individualism, the cult of personality, and a darkening of reason in a sea of irrational "sentiments" that no philosophy could dominate.

As far as religion was concerned, wars, famine and epidemics had placed man face to face with his own solitude: the gods were no longer the superhuman reassuring, logical projection of the perfection of Being, but – reflecting the fragility of all things in the wake of Destiny – became objects of ritual homage, gullible superstition and faithless terror.

During this late phase of Classical art and architecture, town planning above all, reflects the lengths to which philosophers, politicians and town planners went to ensure a harmonic relationship between the city and its environment, while respecting the economic, social and cultural needs of both the community and the individual. Philosophical thought turned towards universal and "scientific" models such as those that emerge from the writings of Hippocrates who underlined the importance of health, and Plato who dealt with what would now be called environmental impact. An excellent example was Aristotle, who through his in-depth understanding of the changing realities of Hellas, theorized a town-planning model that combined the Hippodamian grid plan with empirical principles gleaned from the colonies, on the basis of logical functionalism. Town planning was mainly based on the Hippodamian model with certain variations, depending on the nature of the land, and a tendency toward public buildings that were deliberately spectacular and theatrical.

Residential structures reflected greater attention to the private dimension of human life and were based on a rational and functional standard form that was inserted into modular residential city districts. The public and collective dimension, on the other hand, continued to be centered around the theater, a constant feature of Greek cities, ever more frequently built in stone, accommodating thousands of spectators and incorporating perfect acoustics and elaborate scenic elements. Monumental architecture continued along the lines that developed during the last 30 years of the previous century: elegant forms, refined harmonies, intricate proportions, almost eclectic stylistic combinations, indicating an attempt at producing a seemingly picturesque suavity, more concerned with the effect of an ephemeral notion of Beauty than at the affirmation of an absolute concept of Beauty.

The existential disorientation of the Greeks was also reflected in sculpture and

painting. Greek sculptors started expressing aspects of the human existential experience, the changing manifestations of the unconscious, the irrational inner universe that marked the increasingly deep and painful distance between the human and the divine. Pàthos was the dominating feature of the art of great masters such as Kephisodotos, Praxiteles, Skòpas, Timotheos, Bryaxis, Leochares and Lysippus. These artists, with their roots in the post-Phidias tradition, went further into trying to render changing effects. They tried to freeze passing moments, symbolizing the transitory nature of everything. They molded and sculpted drunkenness and pain, tenderness and anger, no longer following ideals or faiths. But this was not yet the last stage of Greek art.

Philip II, assassinated in the theater at Aigaì (335 BC), was succeeded by his young son Alexander III (who ruled from 335 to 323 B.C), who after the exceptional and very brief historical feats known to all, earned the title of *Mègas* ("the Great"). Alexander the Great, in fact, after inheriting his father's political heritage, transformed the original plan to liberate the Greeks of Asia Minor from Persian domination, into an overwhelming conquest of the thousand-year Empire of the King of Kings, with his

This gold làrnax was ~ied containing the bones ~Philip II of Macedonia ~335 BC (Saloniki, ~chaeological Museum).

~-19 This crown made ~m sheets of gold in the ~m of myrtle leaves and ~wers (350-340 BC) ~onged to Cleopatra, ~ilip II's last wife ~aloniki, Archaeological ~seum).

19 The bust of Alexander the Great is a Roman copy from the first century BC; the original was created by Lysippus for the city of Ephesus around 330 BC (Copenhagen, Ny Carlsberg Glyptotek).

furnishings, is extraordinarily beautiful, with highly refined figurative and ornamental combinations. The funerary paintings of some of the tombs of the region as well as polychrome mosaics made using river pebbles from Pella, reflect the great Greek painting tradition of the 4th century BC, brought to Macedonia by great masters such as Zeuxis and Apelles, the first tending towards lively realism, the second inspired by the visionary and sentimental spirit typical of the period. The greatest sculptor of the period was Lysippus, who owed most of his immense fame to his works at the Macedonian court. His statue of Alexander the Great was the first authentic portrait of Western art, depicting the mortal semi-god in whom willpower and sentiment, divine grace and reason are combined in an ephemeral, wondrous balance. All Lysippus' works, however, happily combine his quest for *pàthos* with the "heroic" celebration of humanity on the basis of Polykleitos' carefully measured harmonies, creating a form that would influence a large number of the artists of his time.

huge provinces from Egypt to Syria, from Ionia to Mesopotamia, going so far as to conquer the remote regions of the Caspian Sea and the Indus, founding dozens of cities named "Alexandria" on the way. Alexander's real greatness, however, lay in his new political idea of a universal Greek empire that was Greek not because of ethnicity, but because of a common civilization and culture!

With Philip II and Alexander the Great, Macedonia had equaled the cultural and artistic levels of the rest of Greece. Macedonian architects had given new life to the ancient type of monumental architecture applied to the royal palace, the center and symbol of monarchical power, located at Aigaì. The spectacular grandeur of the palace is in fact based on a meticulous, rationally ordered design by the architects who also introduced a new funerary structure. The tomb complex contains about 70 of these tombs, including the tomb of Philip II at Verghìna. The tombs feature round chambers and a corbel-vaulted ceiling, outer mural paintings and monumental decorative façades that harmoniously combine architectural ornaments, sculptures and paintings, as well as Doric and Ionic elements, in keeping with the eclectic, especially, pictorial tastes of the time. The splendid goldwork of the period, especially Philip II's precious funeral

20 The sculpture of
Aphrodite of Milos by
an unknown artist
commemorates the
work of Praxiteles and
Lysippus and is a gem
of Hellenistic art
from the second half
of the second century
BC (Paris, Musée du
Louvre).

21 The figure of
Nike (circa 190 BC)
stood on the prow of a
stone ship in the
center of a fountain
in the Sanctuary of
the Great Gods at
Samothrace which
celebrated the victory
of Rhodes against
Antiochus III of Syria
(Paris, Musée du
Louvre).

The period between the death of
Alexander the Great (323 BC) and the Rom
conquest of Egypt (30 BC), the longest of al
the florid and culturally rich kingdoms that
resulted from the breakup of the Macedonian
Empire, is known as the Hellenistic Age.
"Hellenism" was the name given by the 19th-
century German historian J.G. Droysen, to t
imposing and durable phenomenon of the
universal spread of Greek civilization and
culture, expressed through the spread,
absorption and re-elaboration of the Greek
language, religion, political models, custom:
culture and art throughout the regions
covered by Macedonian expansionism.
    While Hellenistic art, in particular, had
unique spirit, it gave rise to as many formal
languages and expressions as the areas covered
by the great Greek cultural koiné, exported k
Alexander the Great and later developed by h
successors. The architectural and artistic
creations of this period no longer celebrate t
civic values of the pòleis, but the absolute an
almost "divine" powers of ruling monarchies
the politically harmless and less extravagant
ostentation of a flourishing business class in a
age without politics. These creations were no
longer products of the mind and meditation, b
rather the fruit of learned intellectualism that
alternated with and complemented a
hedonistic appetite for entertainment and
consumer products. Despite this, great
progress was made in the philosophical,
scientific and literary fields, not to mention th
arts that often produced works of the highest
quality. The virtues of this period would
certainly include a humble attitude towards
the past, openness towards study and
knowledge, vitality, and great mobility that
led to an exchange of ideas, cultural models
and works of art on an unprecedented scale.
Furthermore, artists were neutralized as
political vehicles and dominated as subjects,
becoming professionals of visual
communication, serving customers whose
social company and ideologies they were not
necessarily obliged to share. Hellenism's mo:
important revolution was brought about
however by the fact that Greeks and Hellenize
Barbarians began spreading a universal cultu:
through the use of a common language (koin
diálektos) through which various cultural
traditions could interact, so as to enhance
borrowed concepts and unify cultural
processes without doing away with pre-
existing regional peculiarities.

In town planning, the Hippodamian model was adapted to suit the taste for spectacular, theatrical and monumental buildings so as to exalt the illuminated philanthropy as well as the absolute power of the monarchies that inherited the Macedonian empire. Hellenistic cities were, in fact, huge theaters of ostentatious architecture, with their fortified walls that seem almost too thick, vast areas reserved for public use, and artistic masterpieces of monumental proportions that still enjoy pride of place among the Wonders of the World. Having departed from the austere essential model of the centuries of the city-states, private residences took on fully conceived forms to become units unto themselves, adorned with mosaics and mural paintings, as well as sumptuous furnishings. Hellenistic art has raised a problem of criticism still debated today. Modern critics have long surpassed the notion, put forward in the 1920s, by the German W. Klein, who took the terms "Baroque" and "Rococò" from the history of art and tried to apply them to Hellenistic art as it developed between the 3rd and 1st centuries BC. From this perspective, Baroque was supposed to imply the heroic grandeur and passion of the art of Pergamus while Rococò referred to the artistic creations from the island of Rhodes and Alexandria, featuring a certain thematic "frivolity" and exasperated attempts at obtaining color effects.

Even if schools – or tendencies – may be identified and associated with major centers of Alexander's fragmented empire, they must be considered in light of the effects of cultural and artistic polycentrism. Another factor to be taken into account is that there were thousands of artists and they freely borrowed from both past and contemporary sources, combining their personal creations with "citations" from the great masters or the consolidated styles of the 5th and 4th centuries BC, especially since there was a free flow of ideas, models and experiments throughout the Hellenistic world. Furthermore, and perhaps most especially, one must remember that Hellenistic art has, always and more or less everywhere, had the tendency to alternate between periods featuring great passion, lyricism and calligraphy that were typical of the Hellenistic style, and periods during which works tended towards an original, unexpected sobriety, worthy of the Classical age.

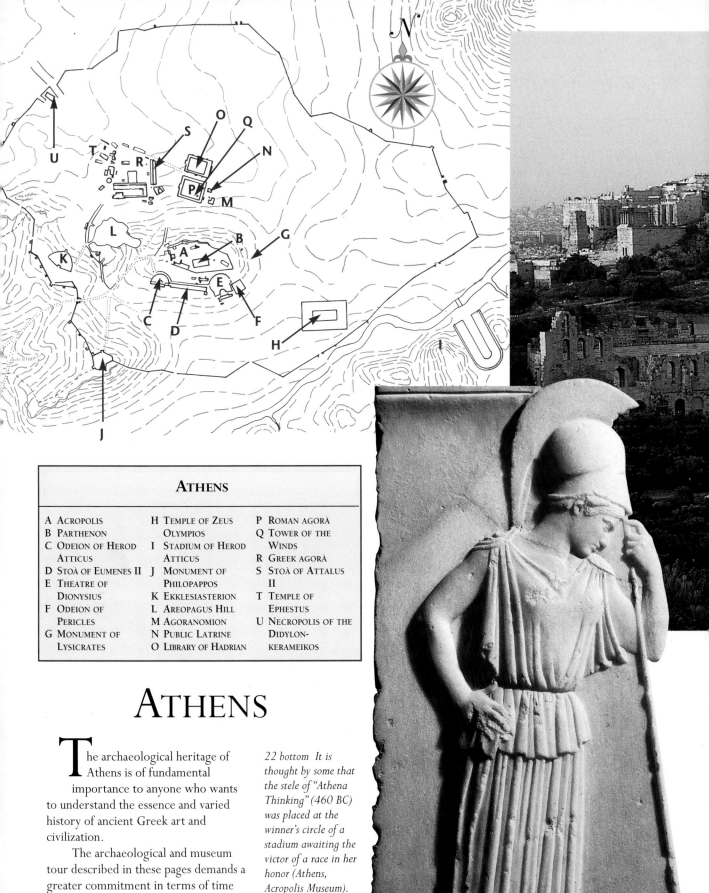

ATHENS

A ACROPOLIS	H TEMPLE OF ZEUS	P ROMAN AGORÀ
B PARTHENON	OLYMPIOS	Q TOWER OF THE
C ODEION OF HEROD	I STADIUM OF HEROD	WINDS
ATTICUS	ATTICUS	R GREEK AGORÀ
D STOÀ OF EUMENES II	J MONUMENT OF	S STOÀ OF ATTALUS
E THEATRE OF	PHILOPAPPOS	II
DIONYSIUS	K EKKLESIASTERION	T TEMPLE OF
F ODEION OF	L AREOPAGUS HILL	EPHESTUS
PERICLES	M AGORANOMION	U NECROPOLIS OF THE
G MONUMENT OF	N PUBLIC LATRINE	DIDYLON-
LYSICRATES	O LIBRARY OF HADRIAN	KERAMEIKOS

ATHENS

The archaeological heritage of Athens is of fundamental importance to anyone who wants to understand the essence and varied history of ancient Greek art and civilization.

The archaeological and museum tour described in these pages demands a greater commitment in terms of time and effort than most mass-tourism itineraries that generally feature a quick visit to the most easily accessible and popular sites. Anyone who knows Athens well will find it difficult, after a few days immersed in the city's chaos, to resist the innumerable more leisurely delights that archaeology, art and nature have in store for true lovers of Greece.

22 bottom It is thought by some that the stele of "Athena Thinking" (460 BC) was placed at the winner's circle of a stadium awaiting the victor of a race in her honor (Athens, Acropolis Museum).

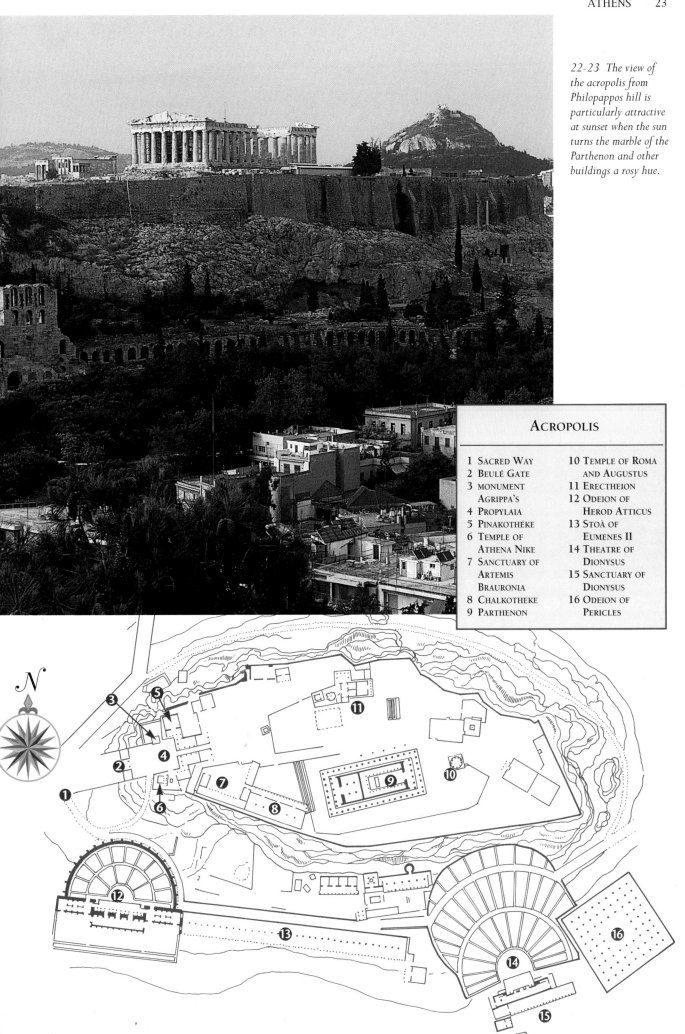

ATHENS 23

22-23 The view of the acropolis from Philopappos hill is particularly attractive at sunset when the sun turns the marble of the Parthenon and other buildings a rosy hue.

ACROPOLIS

1 SACRED WAY
2 BEULÉ GATE
3 MONUMENT AGRIPPA'S
4 PROPYLAIA
5 PINAKOTHÉKE
6 TEMPLE OF ATHENA NIKE
7 SANCTUARY OF ARTEMIS BRAURONIA
8 CHALKOTHEKE
9 PARTHENON
10 TEMPLE OF ROMA AND AUGUSTUS
11 ERECTHEION
12 ODEION OF HEROD ATTICUS
13 STOÀ OF EUMENES II
14 THEATRE OF DIONYSUS
15 SANCTUARY OF DIONYSUS
16 ODEION OF PERICLES

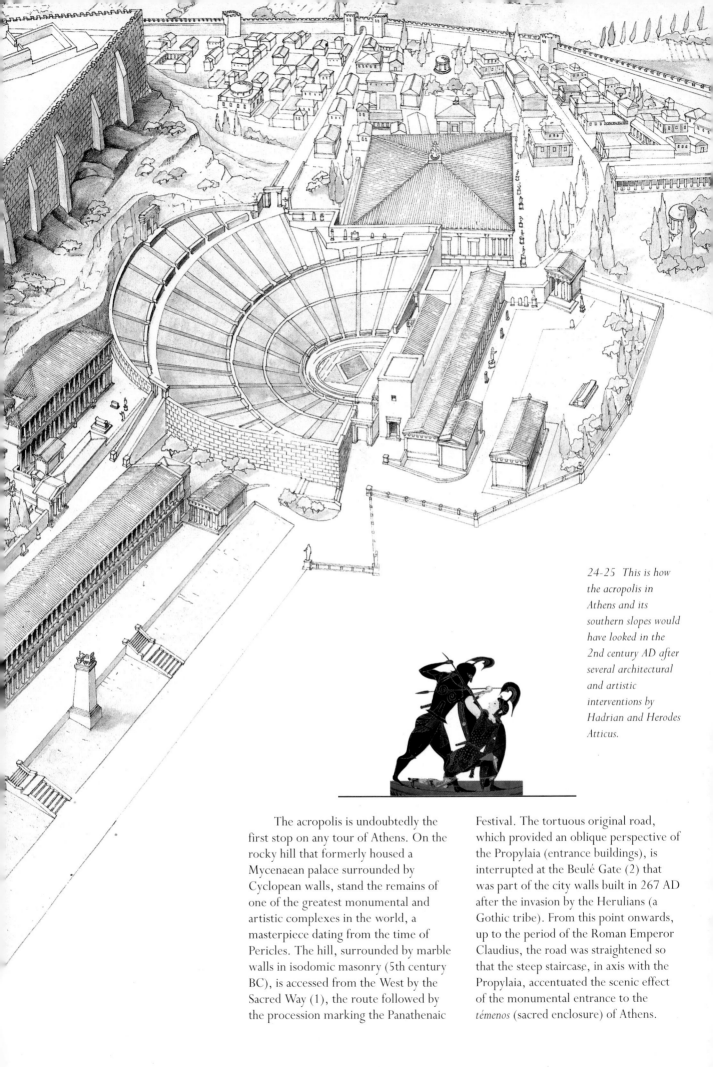

24-25 *This is how the acropolis in Athens and its southern slopes would have looked in the 2nd century AD after several architectural and artistic interventions by Hadrian and Herodes Atticus.*

The acropolis is undoubtedly the first stop on any tour of Athens. On the rocky hill that formerly housed a Mycenaean palace surrounded by Cyclopean walls, stand the remains of one of the greatest monumental and artistic complexes in the world, a masterpiece dating from the time of Pericles. The hill, surrounded by marble walls in isodomic masonry (5th century BC), is accessed from the West by the Sacred Way (1), the route followed by the procession marking the Panathenaic Festival. The tortuous original road, which provided an oblique perspective of the Propylaia (entrance buildings), is interrupted at the Beulé Gate (2) that was part of the city walls built in 267 AD after the invasion by the Herulians (a Gothic tribe). From this point onwards, up to the period of the Roman Emperor Claudius, the road was straightened so that the steep staircase, in axis with the Propylaia, accentuated the scenic effect of the monumental entrance to the *témenos* (sacred enclosure) of Athens.

26 bottom Beulé Gate precedes the entrance to the Propylaia in the defensive wall built to protect the acropolis from the invasion of the Herulians in 267 AD; it was excavated in 1852 by a French architect.

To the left lies the large base of the Monument of Agrippa (3), an admiral and son-in-law of Augustus Caesar, who reused an anàthema commemorating a horse race victory by Eumenes II of Pergamon at the Panathenaic Games in 178 BC. The Propylaia (4), designed by Mnesikles between 437 and 432 BC, stand more or less on the location of a modest previous entrance structure.

The Propylaia are well preserved in

their structure, with the stylobate in blue Eleusinian marble and the superstructure in Pentelic marble. The design and construction work focused on proportionally and aesthetically harmonizing the Propylaia with the temple dedicated to the goddess Athena. Perched on top of a wedge-shaped rock, the jaggedness of which is cleverly hidden, the Propylaia are proportioned to highlight their position and function. The design is a tribute to Mnesikles' architectural genius. A Doric hexastyle front opened onto a long entrance passage, divided into three parts by two rows of slender Ionic columns, with an end wall featuring five doors preceded by five stair-cases, that were also separated in the center by a level path for vehicular traffic. Magnificent painted coffers created a lacunar ceiling effect. On the eastern side, a second Doric hexastyle front, symmetrical to the first, opened onto a huge bronze statue of Athena Pròmachos (Athena the warrior) by

Phidias and, above to the right, a view of the Parthenon. The structure has two porticoed side wings. The south wing was ornamental, although it also connected with the south-western bastion (*pyrgos*). The north wing, designed as a banquet hall, was later trans-formed into a museum-sanctuary area, the *Pinakothéke* (5), that housed votive paintings offered to the goddess. One can only try to imagine, today, the huge series of works of art dedicated to Athena on show for ancient visitors from the Propylaia up to the open space in front of it. Further works of art were buried by the Athenians in the so-called "Persian Expiation" to purify the acropolis after the sack and sacrilege of the hill in 480 BC. On the southwestern *pyrgos* stands the small Ionic temple tetrastyle amphiprostyle dedicated to Athena Nike (Athena as god-dess of Victory) (6). Designed between 460 and 450 BC by Callicrates, the architect of the Parthenon, to celebrate the victories

against the Persians, the structure was com-menced in 449 BC but was completed in 425 or 421 BC, after a series of suspensions. The temple, in Pentelic marble, housed a cult statue that depicted Athena as "wingless victory" or Nike Aptera, in the vain hope that victory would never fly away from Athens. The structur also commemorated the Athenians who fell in the first phase of the Peloponnesian War. The temple is soon to be re-assembled using ana-stylosis, a technique that involves reconstruct-ing architectural debris, with the help of new materials, if necessary. The structure features proportional harmony, despite the loss of the pediments, the acroteria (sculpted pediment decorations) and part of the Ionic frieze. The temple's grace and beauty are amply expresse in the refined columns and the surviving slabs o the frieze. Sculpted in the workshop of Agoràkritos, the frieze depicts on its front the assembly of the Olympian gods, while its north and south sides reproduce battle scenes between

Greeks and Persians. Other battle scenes between Athenians and Persian-allied Greeks adorn the west side. The small *témenos* is surrounded by a marble parapet set up to protect the faithful. The parapet is decorated with relief sculptures depicting a procession of personifications of Victory going towards Athena Nike while the goddess looks over a sacrifice. Some scholars date the work to 410 BC and attribute it at least to the workshop of Kallìmachos, the refined post-Phidian sculptor, if not to the master himself. To the east of the *pyrgos* lie the foundations of the Classical sanctuary of Artemis Brauronia (7) and the *Chalkothéke* (8) a large room intended to house the bronze statues donated in offering to the goddess (circa 450 BC). A trapezoid piazza, oriented along the diagonal axis between the Parthenon and the Propylaia, stood in front of the staircase that led to the western side of the temple of Athena Parthènos. This piazza was surrounded, as Pausanias reports in his *Guide to Greece* (2nd century AD), by magnificent works of art.

27 top The small Ionic temple of Athena Nike is exquisitely elegant. It was built from a design by Callicrates, one of the architects of the Parthenon, during the first phase of the Peloponnesian War.

27 bottom The eastern view of the Propylaia is certainly more intact than the western view; the proportions of the structure designed by Mnesikles to solemnize access to the acropolis are clean and essential.

26-27 The steep flight of steps that still leads to the ancient entrance to the acropolis is dominated by the view to the west of the Propylaia and the nearby Pinakothéke, the work of the Athenian architect Mnesikles (437-433 BC).

The Parthenon (9), by far the greatest masterpiece of Greek architecture, was built entirely in marble. The marble used for the structure was Pentelic, while the sculptures were in Parian marble. The structure was built at the site of an earlier temple, the Archaic *hekatómpedon* ("the 100 ft (roughly 31 meters) long temple"). A first attempt at reconstruction was interrupted by the Persian sack of the acropolis, and some scholars feel that a second project under Cimon preceded the Periclean structure that symbolized the political, civil and religious identity of Athens. Built between 448 and 438 BC, from designs by the architects Callicrates and Ictinus, it still stands in all its splendor, despite its travailed past: it was sacked by the Christians after the Edict of Theodosios I, and transformed into a church in the 6th century, into a mosque in the 15th, and a powder magazine in the 17th, when a canonball ignited the warehoused gunpowder, which exploded and blasted the building's south side. Lastly, it was stripped of all its surviving sculptures by an English art dealer, Lord Bruce of Elgin who sold them to the British Museum in London. The Parthenon is an imposing (about 70 x 31 m) Doric peripteral octastyle temple, based on refined mathematical calculations in all its structural and decorative components. The architects fully achieved their goal of expressing harmony as an essential ingredient of absolute Beauty. Callicrates and Ictinus, in fact, applied the constant measurement module of 10 Attic inches (19.24 cm) to all components. This measurement module is present in multiples regulated by proportional criteria. They used the proportional ratio 4:9 between length and width and between height and width. The same ratio is applied to the base diameter of columns and the inter-axis of inter-columniate intervals. They created chiaroscuro effects in the colonnade, with columns that were thickened and closer than usual to the cella wall. All possible

28 top left The proportions, balance and compositional eurythmics of the peristasis on the Parthenon are still clearly apparent.

28 bottom left One of the best-preserved metopes in the battle between the Greeks and centaurs is to be found in the left corner of the southern side of the Parthenon.

28-29 The chiaroscuro of the Doric colonnade of the Parthenon is the result of the skilful use of proportions and almost imperceptible optical corrections.

29 top right This close-up shows the northwest corner of the Parthenon, where part of the original sculptural decoration by Phidias still remains.

corrections were used (curvature of the stylobate, *éntasis* and eccentric leaning of the columns, resolution of the angular conflict in the Doric frieze of the peristasis). The architects matched the lines of the mature Doric order with the grace of the Ionic, harmonizing them by exploiting the chromatic qualities of Pentelic marble. The peristasis (8 x 17 columns) surrounds a cella divided into two non-communicating parts, opening onto a pronaos and opisthodomos, both hexastyle. In the larger cella, facing east, a double row of Doric columns surrounded on three sides the marble base that once held the 12-meter tall chryselephantine (gold and ivory) cult statue of Athena Parthénos (the Virgin), a masterpiece by Phidias (438 BC). The smaller cella facing west, was the actual *Parthénon* or "Hall of the Virgins," so named perhaps because young Athenian maidens served the goddess here or because it was the site of the ceremony in which the *peplos* was draped over the wooden statue of the goddess. This cella is adorned by four Ionic columns.

29 bottom right This Roman copy known as the *Atena del Varvakìon* is a pallid reflection of the statue of Athena Parthénos made by Phidias for the chamber of the temple.

30 top This splendid horse head from the right corner of the east pediment of the Parthenon was based on the quadriga of the Moon, whose setting announced the birth of Athena (London, British Museum).

30-31 top This personification of the Ilyssòs and Kephisòs rivers in Attica from the west pediment of the Parthenon are equally famous examples of Phidias' work (London, British Museum).

30-31 bottom The sculptural group from the east pediment of the Parthenon shows the goddesses Hestia, Dione and Aphrodite, and is a splendid example of the "wet" drapery technique typical of Phidias (London, British Museum).

The decoration of the temple (438-432 BC), including the floral acroteria, the eaves shaped like lion protomes, the pediments, the Doric frieze on the peristasis and the Ionic frieze on the outer walls of the cella, was designed and in part sculpted by Phidias, who employed some of the best talents of Attic art to transfer onto stone the high political, religious and cultural content ordered by Pericles. The east pediment represents the birth of Athena from the head of Zeus while the Olympian gods look on. The west pediment depicts the mythical dispute between Athena and Poseidon over the possession of Attica, at the time of king Kèkrops. The 92 metopes of the Doric frieze depict four versions of the conflict between Good and Evil, justice and injustice, and civilization and barbarism, using the usual epic and mythological metaphors. On the eastern side of the temple, the frieze depicts a battle between gods and giants (*gigantomachy*), to the south, a battle between Lapiths (humans) and Centaurs (*centauromachy*) as well as other Attic myths, to the west, a

battle between Amazons (*amazonomachy*) and to the north, the destruction of Troy. The Ionic frieze of the cella, a novelty in Greek art, depicted various phases (sports competitions and parades) of the Panathenaic Festival in honor of Athena, a symbol of the ties between the people of Athens and the deity.

31 center These carriers of hydríai *(water jars) in the Panathenaic procession of citizens were from the north side of the Ionic frieze on the chamber of the Parthenon (Athens, Acropolis Museum).*

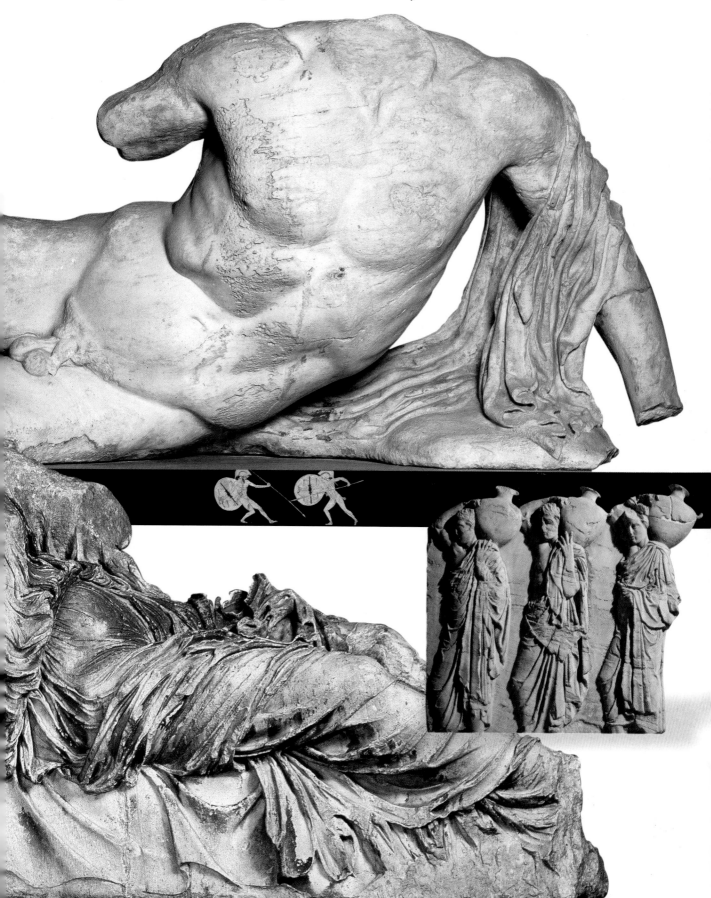

In line with the eastern side of the temple lie the remains of a small circular monopteral (that is, made up of columns only without an inner chamber or cella) temple dedicated to the goddess Roma (patron of Rome) and Augustus Caesar.

The last building on the tour of the acropolis is the Erectheion (11), as the temple of Athena Poliás ("patron of the city"), has been called for centuries. The name derives from Erectheùs, the name of a mythical Attic king as well as one of the names of Poseidon ("the shaker"). The temple was built between 421 and 407 or 405 BC, to replace the old temple of the patron goddess (6th century BC). The Erectheion, that was designed by Mnesikles, has an unusual plan in order to accommodate the requirements of many cults, some of which date back to ancient times. The elegance of its Ionic contours (columns with echinus and volutes as well as beautifully preserved lacunar ceilings) are among the highest expressions of Classical art. The eastern pronaos hexastyle provided access to one of the two cellae (the other was accessible from the northern pronaos). The precise position of the large number of cults in these two cellae is not known. The wooden cult statue of Athena Poliás, the altars of Poseidon Erectheùs, Zeus Hypatos, Hephaistos, of the hero, the tombs

32 top left A view of the north section of the acropolis: the marble mass of the Erectheion, dedicated to Poseidon and Athena Poliás (5th century BC) stands next to the few remaining traces of the Archaic temple.

of Erectheùs and Kèkrops, to name but the most important, all had to be accommodated. A hole in the roof of the pronaos tetrastyle to the north indicated the point where Zeus' lightning killed Erectheùs, while the marks left by Poseidon's trident and the salt water well created by the god in his mythical dispute with Athena over the possession of Attica, were venerated in the western cella. Along the entire edifice, against a background in blue Eleusinian marble, ran a Ionic frieze in Pentelic marble featuring several Attic myths in high relief and in an expressive style. A wide enclosed area, the *Pandróseion*, built in honor of an Attic heroine to the west of the Erectheion, protected the sacred olive tree

given by Athena who was victorious in her dispute with Poseidon (the tree visible today stands at the site of the ancient tree). The Porch of the Caryatids that housed the tomb of Kèkrops is noteworthy. The six statues of young women in Ionic costume are copies (an original is at the British Museum and the others are at the museum of the acropolis, which also houses an exceptional collection of artistic objects, ranging from the statues taken from the pediments of the Archaic temples to a splendid series of *kòrai, koùroi* and other votive offerings from the Persian Expiation to masterpieces by Phidias and his school, mostly taken from the buildings on the acropolis).

32 bottom left The lovely hexastyle Ionic pronaos of the Erectheion, recently rebuilt using the original materials, has superbly made capitals with elegant volutes and a delicate collar of palm leaves and ovals.

32 right According to Vitruvius, the Caryatids represented the gentlewomen of Karyès in Arcadia who were

made to wear elegant clothes by other Greeks despite having been made slaves for the support their city had offered to the Persians.

32-33 The elegant Ionic semi-colonnade on the west side of the Erectheion immediately shows the architectural complexity of the structure which was rightly defined by Pausanias as a "double building."

Going down the Sacred Way, it is well worth your while taking the *Perìpatos*, the path that went around the acropolis hill at midpoint, to visit the slopes of the acropolis. The first stop on the slope will be the *Odeíon* of Herodes Atticus (12), a scenic theater complex donated to the city of Athens in 161 by the wealthy orator in memory of his wife Annia Regilla. In ancient times, the grandiose concert hall was covered with a roof

dramatic arts, venerated in the sanctuary (15) in front of the theater. The surviving structures date to the renovation in 330 BC and to later embellishments added during the Hellenistic and Roman periods. Very little remains, however, of the famous *Odeíon* of Pericles (16) built in 445 BC, a large concert hall measuring over 4000 square meters. It is similar to the *Telestérion* at Eleusis, destroyed by Silla (in 86 BC) and rebuilt shortly thereafter.

34 top The green and archaeologically interesting hills of Pnyka, Mouseìon and Philopappos lie in the background of the view of the Herodes Atticus concert hall that stands at the foot of the acropolis.

supported by beams of Lebanese cedar, the most prized timber in antiquity. The semi-circular cavea (86 m in diameter) is in excellent condition. It is paneled in Hymettus marble and it is horizontally divided into two sectors with five cunei below and ten above the diazoma (horizontal passageway intersecting with the vertical steps). The orchèstra with its marble flooring and the frame of the three-story Roman *skenè*, is also well preserved. The rather unimpressive remains of the long Stoà of Eumenes II (13) featuring a 163-meter long Doric-Ionic-Pergamenian colonnade, lead to the most famous theater of the ancient world, the Theater of Dionysus (14). The stoà was apparently built in the 2nd century BC, to provide shelter to spectators in the case of bad weather. The theater itself was built in the 5th century BC to host the drama competitions during the Great Dionysian festivals in honor of the patron deity of the

34 bottom left The ruins of the Stoà of Eumenes II, though mostly stripped of materials used to build the walls of Valerian (350-360 AD), leave the size and magnificence of the original structure to the imagination.

34 bottom right The Dionysiac reliefs that decorated the marble proscenium of the theater building were carved during the reign of Emperor Hadrian in the classical style that was typical of the time.

34-35 The Theater of Dionysus Eleuthereùs took on its current appearance around 330 BC; its architectural characteristics formed the basis of design standards for theaters that were being renovated as well as for new ones.

35 bottom left A bearded Silenus, a mythological figure in the court of Dionysus, clearly expends great effort in his role as a telamon in the platform of the proscenium. The work was sculpted in the first half of the second century AD.

35 bottom right Everything artistic in the theater dedicated to Dionysus commemorates his role as tutelary deity; this is another example of reliefs from the age of Hadrian that were placed in the proscenium.

36 top The first modern Olympic games were held in the faithful reconstruction of the Stadium of Herodes Atticus (140-144 AD) which was

built over the one constructed by Lycurgus (330 BC) for the Pan-Athenian races.

36-37 The temple of Zeus Olympios was only

completed in the 2nd century AD; it was one of the last examples of architectural gigantism in the classical age and was clearly inspired by eastern Hellenistic models.

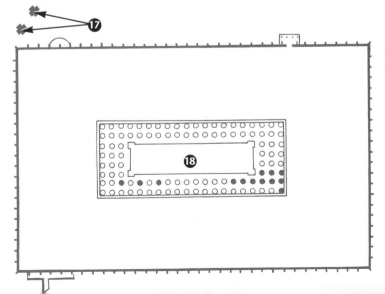

THE OLYMPIEION

17 HADRIAN'S ARCH
18 TEMPLE OF ...ZEUS OLYMPIOS

36 bottom This pseudo-monopteral building, today in the heart of the Plàka, was built to commemorate the wealthy Lysicrates who financed the theatrical spectacles in honor of Dionysus in 335 BC.

37 top The fragments of colossal capitals from the Olympieíon lie around the temple. The temple's sacred enclosure was originally adorned with dozens of works of art offered by various Greek cities.

37 bottom An unusual view of the south and east bastions of the acropolis: in the foreground stands Hadrian's Arch, the physical and symbolic boundary between the city of Pericles and the city that flourished under the philo-Hellenic emperor.

work to the Roman architect Marcus Cossutius (175-164 BC). Hadrian's unknown architect faithfully elaborated on this design to build the largest Corinthian temple in the ancient world (110 x 44 m).

Only about 15 columns on the south and east side now remain of what was once a forest of towering columns, but even these few provide a good idea of the dimensions and elegance of the building, in which Hadrian wanted to associate the Imperial cult with that of Zeus, who was venerated with a statue of gold and ivory in the temple.

The temple lies at the heart of the *neápolis*, the "new city" that boasted several famous monumental religious complexes and prestigious residences. At this point it is well worthwhile to pay a short visit to the Stadium of Herodes

Along the Dionisíou Areopaghìtou road, to the southeast of the acropolis lies the archaeological area of the *Olympieíon*. It starts at the large two-story arch (17) built by the Roman Emperor Hadrian to physically mark the border between the ancient "city of Theseus" and the "city of Hadrian," as indicated in the inscription above the barrel vault. Between 125 and 138 AD, Athens, the city that the successor of Trajan loved more than any other in the world, was subjected to a series of town planning reforms as well as large-scale embellishment projects. The year 132 AD, especially, saw the completion and inauguration of one of the

city's most ancient religious buildings, the colossal temple of Zeus Olympios (18), part of which still stands in the wide *témenos* accessible through a *pròpylon* hexastyle in the northeastern sector. Already of grandiose proportions at the beginning of the 6th century BC, it was re-founded a few decades later by the Pisistratids who decided on a macrotectonic structure along Asian lines to highlight the ideology and sumptuousness of their oriental-leaning ideology. The temple was re-designed in the Corinthian style with a dipteral plan and dimensions even more imposing under Antiochos IV of Syria, who entrusted the

Atticus (19) built in 140-144 AD and faithfully reproduced on the Ardittòs hill in 1896 to host the first modern Olympic games. The complex, in Pentelic marble, could seat 50,000 spectators.

Towards the east side of the acropolis, at the edges of the district of Plàka, lies the splendid Choregic monument of Lysicrates (20) built in 335 BC. This is an elegant pseudo-monopteral Corinthian structure on a high plinth, with walls and decoration alternately in Pentelic and Hymettus marble and low-relief ornaments depicting Dionysian motifs, including the famous myth of a god changing pirates into dolphins.

*38 top left A view of
the Roman* agorà *from
the east: remains of the
elegant internal
colonnades stand mixed
among remains from the
Byzantine and Turkish
eras; in the background
is the internal view of
the west propylaeum.*

*38 bottom left Slightly
lower than the
surrounding streets,
even in ancient times,
the* agorà, *seen here
from the east, was built
with* pòros
*foundations and paved
with Pentelic and
Hymettus marble slabs.*

*38 top right What
remains of the immense
and monumental
Library of Hadrian is
not enough, in all
probability, to give a
true idea of its overall
scenographic design
and its rich
decoration.*

The narrow streets of Plàka lead to the excavations of the Roman *agorà* that is approached from the Márkou Avrilìou street. The area features a large (roughly 170 sq. meters) Roman High Imperial public latrine for the convenience of the vendors in the nearby market square. The structure features a large hall with marble flooring and a central atrium tetrastyle to allow air and sunlight in. The building had marble seats along the walls and a drain running along the same side. The "Tower of the Winds," a jewel of Late Hellenistic architecture, is an octogonal building with two entrance porches in prothyron distyle, one to the northwest, the other to the northeast. The structure was built in the first century BC by Andronikos of Kyrrha and served as a hydraulic clock and wind indicator. The building, decorated and crowned by a dome, housed a mechanism that marked the hours by measuring the level of water as it dripped from a small circular tank to the south. The outer shell of the structure, with an octagonal roof and eaves in the shape of lion protomes, bore a bronze weather vane that showed wind direction, indicated by low-relief sculptures on the slabs that crowned the eight walls. The winds, depicted as clothed figures when cold and half-naked figures when warm, are indicated by epigraphs. In front of the meager remains of the *agoranómion*, a sort of trade supervision office, stands the eastern Doric *própylon* tetrastyle (similar to the impressive entrance gate to the west) that opens onto the porticoed Roman *agorà*. The western, northern and eastern sides of the square were occupied by shops, covering an area of 9500 square meters. The large number of precious marble works and monuments are part of the town embellishment program

*39 bottom left This is
the impressive and severe
elegance of the Doric
west propylaeum of the
Roman* agorà, *made
from Pentelic marble and
decorated with a
classical frieze of
metopes and triglyphs.*

*39 bottom right The
personification of the
Libeccio wind on the
southwest side of the
"Tower of the Winds" is
charming though a little
coldly classical in the
style chosen by the
unknown neo-Attic artist.*

38-39 The "Tower of
the Winds," the
astronomic clock and
    indicator of the
winds during the
first century BC that
    was turned into a
Koranic school under
the Turks, stands out
    among the remains of
the porticoes in the
vast Roman agorà.

ordered by the Emperor Hadrian.

The Library of Hadrian, to the north of the Roman *agorà*, is, as its name suggests, another complex dating from the reign of Hadrian. It lies at the very heart of the "city of Theseus." Built in 132 AD, the magnificent Corinthian façade, preceded by a *própylon* tetrastyle, faces the Arèos Way. It is difficult today, visiting the ruins, to imagine the sumptuous marble and profusion of artwork that embellished this large forum-like structure that, with its four porticoes, is reminiscent of the Templus Pacis, built under the Emperor Flavius in Rome. The peristyle courtyard with a long *natatio* (pool) at the center, was surrounded by 100 columns. To the east, in the center, was the library hall, featuring niches intended to hold papyrus rolls and bound parchment

tomes (the central niches were perhaps intended to hold statues of divinities and emperors). The rooms to the sides were used for philosophical discussions, rhetorical exercises and study.

Across Monastirakìou square, the Ermoù, a major shopping street, leads to thè evocative archaeological area of the

Dípylon-Kerameikós, the only ancient cemetery visible in Athens. It lies just outside the famous "double doors" (*dípylon*) of the Themistoclean wall, where the old potters' (*Kerameís*) district used to be. The cemetery was used from the 12th century BC up to Imperial Roman times.

The Archaic, Classical and Hellensitic *agorà*, on the north slope of Areopagus Hill was the ancient seat of the city's courts that tried offenders accused of violent crimes. To the west of the entrance to the *Thissío* (19), at a higher level lies the *Kolonós Agoréos*, an ancient gathering place for day laborers seeking employment, with a concentration of copper and bronze workshops. Here, intact mainly because it was transformed into a Christian church, lies the Doric peripteral temple hexastyle of Hephaistos, generally known as the *Theseíon* (20). Designed during the first half of the 5th century BC, perhaps under Cimon, but built at the same time as the Parthenon, the structure, in Pentelic marble, has a plan of about 32 x 14 meters, with a peristasis of 6 x 13 columns. Both in plan and in structure, it incorporates a combination of Early Classical architectural elements together with features borrowed from the Parthenon. For instance, while the pronaos and opisthodomos are deep, the cella is very similar to that of the Parthenon. Only meager fragments of the pediment and acroteria, generally attributed to Alkamenes, remain.

40-41 The remains of the Roman Odeíon, built by Agrippa, and the Altar of Zeus Agoraíos can be seen at the foot of the temple of Hephaistos on the west side of Athens' Archaic, Classical and Hellenistic agorà.

40 bottom left This fragment of a male statue found in the area of the Odeíon of Agrippa on the west side of the agorà, bears a classicist stamp.

40 bottom right Reconstructed in 1953-56, the Stoà of Attalus II fully restores the spectacular effect of Hellenistic architecture. The building houses the Agorà Museum.

41 top right Some scholars consider the temple of Hephaistos (440 BC) the work of the same architect who designed the Parthenon.

41 bottom Philopappos hill takes its name from the ruin seen in the foreground; thi was the funerary monument of the consul Gaius Giuliu Antiochos Philopappos, the benefactor of Athens under Trajan and Hadrian.

THE AGORÀ

19 ENTRANCE TO THE THISSIO
20 TEMPLE OF HEPHAISTOS (THESEION)
21 THOLOS
22 BOULEUTÉRION
23 METROON
24 STOÀ OF ZEUS ELEUTHERIOS
25 STOÀ
26 TEMPLE OF ARES
27 BASE OF THE STATUE OF HADRIAN
28 BASE OF THE EPONYMOUS ATTIC HEROES
29 GYMNASIUM AND ODEION OF AGRIPPA
30 STOÀ OF ATTALUS II

N

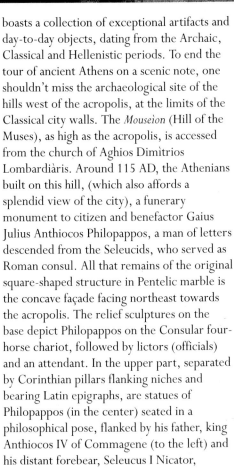

boasts a collection of exceptional artifacts and day-to-day objects, dating from the Archaic, Classical and Hellenistic periods. To end the tour of ancient Athens on a scenic note, one shouldn't miss the archaeological site of the hills west of the acropolis, at the limits of the Classical city walls. The *Mouseìon* (Hill of the Muses), as high as the acropolis, is accessed from the church of Aghios Dimìtrios Lombardiàris. Around 115 AD, the Athenians built on this hill, (which also affords a splendid view of the city), a funerary monument to citizen and benefactor Gaius Julius Anthiocos Philopappos, a man of letters descended from the Seleucids, who served as Roman consul. All that remains of the original square-shaped structure in Pentelic marble is the concave façade facing northeast towards the acropolis. The relief sculptures on the base depict Philopappos on the Consular four-horse chariot, followed by lictors (officials) and an attendant. In the upper part, separated by Corinthian pillars flanking niches and bearing Latin epigraphs, are statues of Philopappos (in the center) seated in a philosophical pose, flanked by his father, king Anthiocos IV of Commagene (to the left) and his distant forebear, Seleucus I Nicator, founder of the Seleucid dynasty (on the right).

The 18 metopes on the eastern side and the ends of the long sides adjacent to it, are in Parian marble, like the rest of the sculptural decoration. They depict the heroic tasks of Heracles and Theseus and are certainly pre-Phidian in style. The Ionic frieze of the pronaos and opisthodomos, depicting Theseus and a centaur battle (*centauromachy*), is in the style of Phidias. Along the path leading south from the temple lie the ruins of the *Thòlos* (21), which served as the seat of the 50 prytanes of the city. Built in 465 BC but redesigned in Roman times, the building has a circular plan and a conic roof. Close by stand the remains of the *bouleutérion* (22), the "parliament" of Athens, a hemicycle contained in a rectangular structure, dating from the 5th century BC. In front of it lies the *Metròon* (23), built during refurbishment operations funded by the king of Pergamon in the second century BC. The building is made up of a long portico that opened into various rooms, including the archives of the *Boulé* or city council. The square is flanked to the west, south and north by the modest remains of a large number of famous Athenian Classical and Hellenistic buildings, including splendid *stoaí* (24-25), the temple of Ares (26) and several dozen votive and commemorative monuments (27-28) built by the greatest artists of the ancient world. Most note-

worthy among these are the remains of the most important of all Roman buildings in Athens, the gymnasium and the *Odeíon* of Agrippa (29). Built in 15 BC, the *odeíon* is a large concert hall with a semicircular cavea, linked to a 4th-century AD gymnasium that served as a school of philosophy.

On the eastern side of the square, lastly, stands the modern reconstruction – by the American Archaeological School of Athens – of the large stoà (30) built by Attalos II of Pergamon in the 2nd century BC. It now houses the Agorà Museum that

Returning to the small church, the tour continues with a visit to the Pnyka (Pnyx in antiquity), that for a thousand years was the seat of the *ekklesía*, the people's assembly of democratic Athens. The site, rather than the ruins, inspires great historical reminiscences for it was here, with the crowd assembled in the huge semicircular cavea fanning out from an artificial embankment and converging towards the *bèma* or speaker's tribune, that the greatest politicians of Athens, including Themistocles, Aristides, Cimon, Pericles and Demosthenes, addressed their fellow Athenians. The orientation and structures visible today date from the reorganization/renovation work carried out in two phases (in 404 and in 330 BC). The two *stoaí* to the south perhaps served to provide shelter for the gathered citizenry in the case of bad weather.

Visits to the National Museum and Museum of the acropolis are absolutely essential but do not neglect – if you have the time – to enjoy the Museum of Cycladic Art and Ancient Greece, the Benàki Museum, the Byzantine Museum and the Kanellòpoulos Museum. It is impossible to describe all the masterpieces of the National and acropolis museums here but it is at least possible to give the reader some indication of the treasures they hold.

In the first of the two museums, the following are of particular importance. First is the large funerary amphora of the Painter of the Dìpylon (760-750 BC), an unquestioned masterpiece of Attic geometric art, whose surface has dense series of bands finely decorated with lines and geometric figures interrupted by two bands bearing the stylized outlines of feeding or squatting antelopes. There is a large rectangular metope painted between the handles of the vase with a scene showing the deceased laid out and the rite of the funeral laments celebrated by 14 women portrayed in lengthened and geometrized profile. Second, there is the splendid funerary koùros of Anàvyssos (530 BC) showing the young Kroìsos of the noble Alkmeonìdai family who was killed in battle against the supporters of the tyrannical Peisistratus. Third is the large bronze statue of Zeus or Poseidon, found off Cape Artemìsso in Euboea, that has been dated to 470-460 BC and is one of the first representations of the dynamic weighting of a body; it shows the god as he prepares to let fly at his target, with his left arm outstretched to counterbalance the momentum of the action. Fourth is the magnificent Diadoumènos by Polykleitos in which the sense of mathematical-proportional balance typical of this artist is combined with an absolute and virile gracefulness of movement. Fifth, the poignant funerary stelae from the second half of the 5th, and first half of the 4th century BC with moving scenes of farewell (as in the famous stele of Hegesò) or tragic

42   The famous statue of Zeus or Poseidon found off Cape Artemìsso is one of the unquestioned masterpieces of proto-Classical Greek bronzes; it was made around 470-460 BC (Athens, National Museum).

43 left One of the oldest sculptures found in the Persian Expiation is the Moschophòros (570-560 BC), which represents Rhòmbos as he carries a calf as a sacrifice (Athens, Acropolis Museum).

43 right This lovely Attic koùros of Anàvyssos (circa 530 BC) represents the noble Kroìsos, a member of the Alkmeonìdai family, who was killed in battle during the reign of the tyrant Peisistratus (Athens, National Museum).

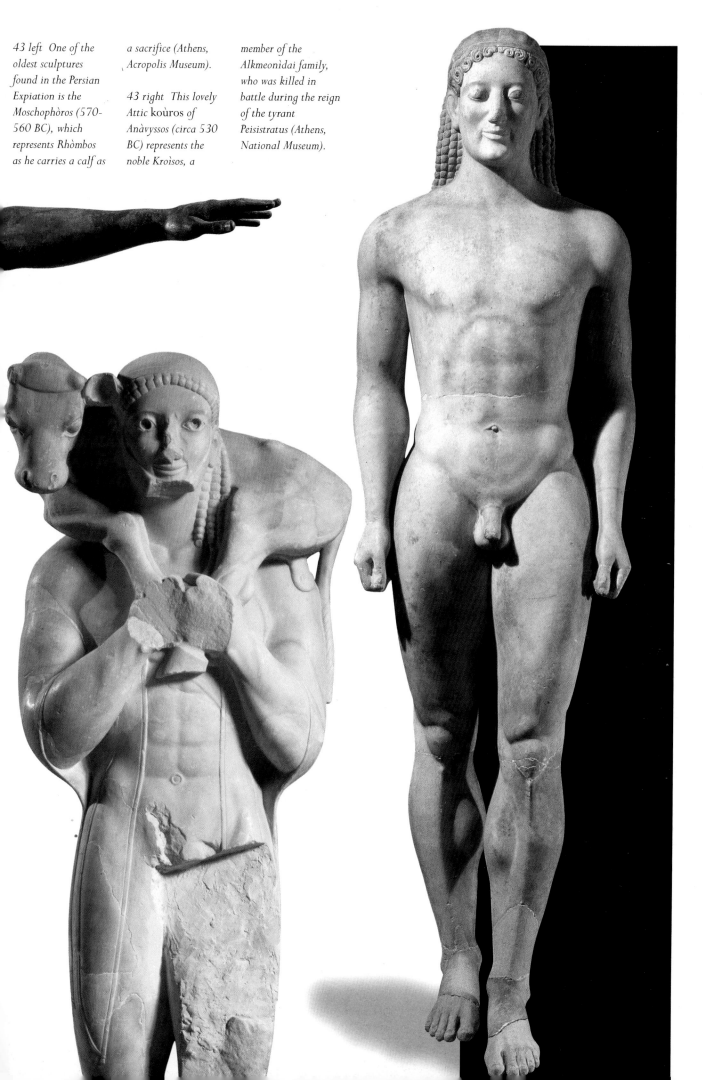

44 bottom right The enormous collection of figured vases in the National Museum in Athens includes rare funerary lekythoi with white backgrounds from the second half of the 5th century BC.

45 The head known as Hygieia of Tegea (circa 370 BC) in the National Museum in Athens is an excellent example of the delicate sculptural language of Praxiteles.

celebrations of warlike fervor (as in that of Dexìleos). Sixth, the superb sculptures of Skòpas and Timòtheas from Tegèa and Epidaurus. Seventh, the masterpieces of Hellenistic bronze sculpture: the Jockey from Cape Artemìsso, the Ephebus of Antikythira, and the portrait of a boxer by Sylànion. Upstairs, you will find the famous item known as Agamemnon's Mask and other items of goldwork from Mycenae; the cycle of Minoan frescoes from Akrotìri (Thìra), and an endless collection of Greek pottery from all ages. Displayed in the Museum of the Acropolis are Archaic kòrai, including the one "with peplos" and the superb creations of Antènor; there are also the Moschophòros and the "Rampin" Rider (the head is a copy of the one in the Louvre), and the superb slabs of Ionic frieze taken from the Parthenon in which one can admire the lovely script of Phidias in his handling of forms and drapery.

44 top left Also from the Persian Expiation, this beautiful head of the "blond Ephebus" (circa 480 BC) is a fine example of early proto-Classical statuary (Athens, Acropolis Museum).

44 bottom left Another lost bronze masterpiece (420-410 BC) by the sculptor Polykleitos is known to us from this Roman marble copy; this is the Diadoumènos, the athlete tying back his hair (Athens, National Museum).

EPIRUS AND CORFU

70 top right The
church in the
monastery of Aghios
Ioànnis Pròdromos (St.
John the Baptist) looks
down on the ruins of

the Nekromanteìon;
the photograph shows
the ruins of the service
rooms (11) used by the
clergy during the
ceremonies.

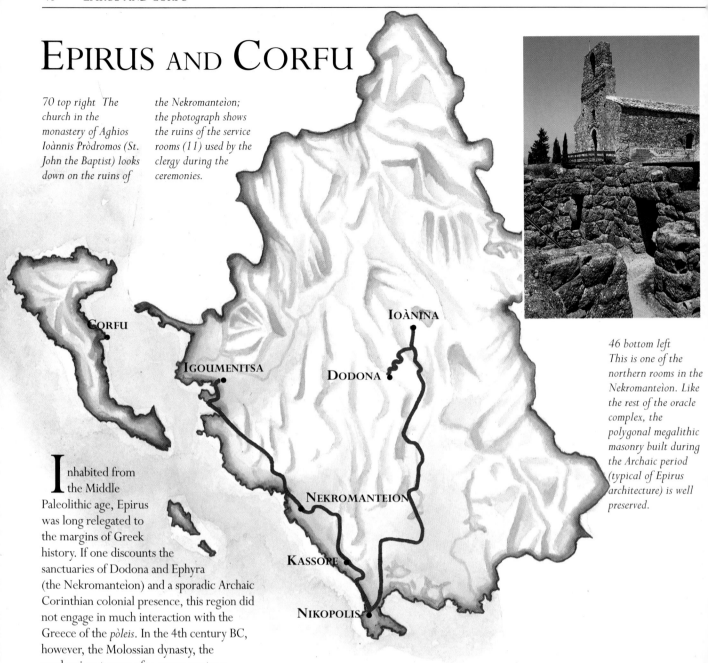

46 bottom left
This is one of the
northern rooms in the
Nekromanteìon. Like
the rest of the oracle
complex, the
polygonal megalithic
masonry built during
the Archaic period
(typical of Epirus
architecture) is well
preserved.

I nhabited from
the Middle
Paleolithic age, Epirus
was long relegated to
the margins of Greek
history. If one discounts the
sanctuaries of Dodona and Ephyra
(the Nekromanteìon) and a sporadic Archaic
Corinthian colonial presence, this region did
not engage in much interaction with the
Greece of the pòleis. In the 4th century BC,
however, the Molossian dynasty, the
predominant power for over a century,

albeit with alternating ups and downs,
projected Epirus into the political and
cultural orbit of the Hellenic world. After a
period when it was a republic federated to
the kingdom of Macedonia, the region was
conquered by the Romans in 167 BC and
became the province of Achaia in 27 BC.

Epirus has a fascinating landscape. The
coastal plains to the north of Igoumenítsa
contrast with the southern rugged and
rocky profile, notable for its cliffs and unin-
habited islands. Further inland, the high
peaks of the Pìndos mountains unfold to
give way to lower, gentler slopes that are in
places lush and green, overgrown with
Mediterranean scrub and pines. Unexpected
forests of latifogliae abound thanks to the
plentiful streams and springs, while in other
areas the land is bare and pebbly, disfigured
by millennia of grazing cattle and
deforestation. It takes just under an hour to

reach the blue expanse of the Ioànina lake,
fish. Ioànina is the picturesque regional capi
still reverberating with Byzantine and Otto
echoes.

From Igoumenítsa, after Pàrga and hav
reached the bay of Ammoudià, one should c
on by following the last leg of the Acheron,
infernal river of Greek mythology, now der
wooded or covered by agricultural cultivati
after the land was reclaimed from the mars
formed because of the river.

A little ahead, along the E55 highway,
to the village of Messopòtamos, lie the evoc
ruins of the **NEKROMANTEION**, the sanctuar
dedicated to the oracle of the dead, founde
ancient times on a hill overlooking the Ach
at the point where it meets two equally my
rivers, the Cocitos and the Phlegetontes, ne
from the city of Ephyra under the jurisdicti
which the sanctuary fell. The ruins of Ephy
on the hill of Kastri, close by. Mythology te

that here, at the Western limits of the world, in the vestibule of the infernal palace of Hades and Persephone, mortals could interrogate the souls of the dead and know the future. Partially spilling over into the convent of Aghios Ioànnis Pròdromos (St. John the Baptist or the Precursor), the remains of the cultural complex, dating back to the monumental renovation carried out between the end of the 4th and during the 3rd century BC, are open to visitors. The Archaic appearance created by the imposing structures built using polygonal Cyclopean masonry, was deliberately intended by the architects, with the complicity of the priests, to emphasis the aura of the ancient sacredness of the place.

The sanctuary is built on two levels

around a large central core which held the oracle. The current visitor's route is the same as that followed by pilgrims in ancient times. Pilgrims first entered the large central courtyard (1) and after going through two short corridors (2-3), reached the three chambers (4-6) to the north, where they went through a purification rite, which included a special diet based on beans and perhaps, hallucinogenic drugs (the Ephyreans were famous throughout the ancient world as experts in poisons and medicines). After the rite, the pilgrim would pass through a narrow door and throw a stone into the nearby chamber to the north (7), where a pile of stones in the chamber still bears witness to the practice to ward off evil. The pilgrim would then pass through a long corridor to the east (8), offer a libation to the gods of the underworld and enter the sanctuary itself. Access to the sanctuary is through a short, dark and tortuous labyrinth (9), designed to create the disorientation necessary for total mystical involvement. The rectangular central hall (10) was flanked on either side by areas reserved for the priests (11-12) where offerings were kept (the large clay jars holding the offerings have survived to

NEKROMANTEION

1	CENTRAL COURTYARD	8	CORRIDOR
2-3	CORRIDORS	9	LABYRINTH
4-6	PURIFICATION RITE ROOMS	10	CENTRAL ROOM
7	EXORCISM STONE CHAMBER	11-12	SERVICE AREAS

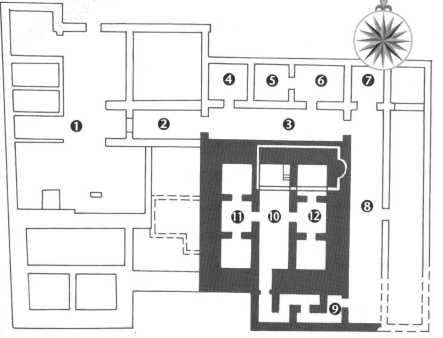

47 left The atmosphere of the vast underground room of the Nekromanteìon was supposed to inspire mystery and terror; here the priests performed the culminating phases of the rite of evocation of the spirits of the Dead.

47 right Near the northeast corner of the Acherontic sanctuary stands the room (on the left in the photograph) in which the pilgrims used to throw a stone to ward off evil before meeting the spirits (7).

this day). In the hall, obviously unbeknownst to devotees, steeped in an atmosphere of holy terror, a magic-religious farce was played out. Under the knowing direction of the priests and using ingenious primitive special effects devices, including a crane to make the pale ghosts of the dead appear, as well as secret passages running through the cavity walls that were more than three meters thick, the dead – after substantial offerings were piously collected by the priests – revealed the future, explained mysteries, and meted out advice to all those who consulted them. Completing the farce, under the central hall, was an artificial crypt with its ceiling supported by 15 long pòros arches, that served as the hall of Hades.

Besides its complex ground plan, the most interesting aspects of the manteìon, include the widespread use of arches – even with very wide spans – as support structures, borrowed from Macedon, the deliberate use of Archaic-style polygonal megalithic and pseudo-isodomic masonry, as well as the engineering tricks to produce the religious "show," all of which confirm the tendency of Hellenistic architecture to accentuate variations of Classical models and layouts. This was done with the clear intention of inducing emotions in the pilgrims visiting the building.

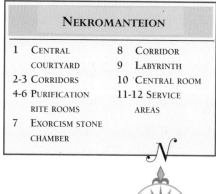

48 left This detail of one of the minor roads at Kassòpe shows the accuracy of the paving and the technique used to prevent puddles from forming.

From Messopòtamos, one ought to continue inland, and after Kanalàki, take the right towards Zàlongo, sadly famous for the massacre by the Turks in 1822 under Ali Pasha. The road continues towards Archèa Kassòpi, from where a short road leads to the ruins of ancient **KASSOPE**, founded at the beginning of the 4th century BC, possibly as a consolidation of smaller rural villages (that is to say, by synergism). It became the political, administrative and economic focal point of the region, enhancing its status after it became a protectorate of the Molossian dynasty.

Kassòpe is a splendid, although largely ignored, example of a city based on the Hippodamian grid plan with borrowings from the western Greek colonies and a few concessions to the

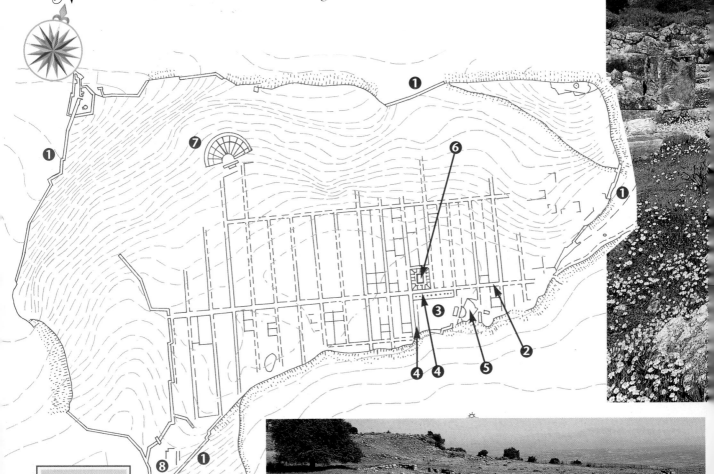

N

KASSOPE

1 WALLS
2 PLATEIA S
3 AGORÀ
4 STOAI
5 BOULEUTÉRION
6 KATAGOGION
7 THEATER
8 "MACEDON" TOMB

48 right The katagògion at Kassòpe, a sort of public inn used to accommodate important guests of the city, had 17 rooms arranged around a large courtyard.

48-49 The agorà at Kassòpe lay on the southern edge of the plateau on which the city stood. It was surrounded by a series of hills and rocky crests which provided a natural defense.

49 bottom left Kassòpe also used the Archaic polygonal construction technique: the photograph shows the northwest corner of the katagògion in the heart of the ancient city.

49 bottom right A number of stone seats with supports in the shape of lions' feet still stand in their original position near the agorà. The design was common in Hellenistic times.

monumental spectacularity typical of the period, as can be seen in the very location of the city on a vast natural terrace overlooking the Bay of Nikòpolis and the Amvrakikòs Gulf.

The city walls (1) (which generally follow the contours of the plateau) enclose a grid plan of city blocks. Each block was a standard 100 feet along the sides and was served by two large paved arteries on an east-west axis, intersected at right angles by 20 minor streets, following the increasing gradient of the slope. The paved roads, often featuring drains for rainwater, were built in steps, just as the individual houses seem to be built on terraces within city blocks.

A little after the entrance to the archaeological site, along the southern *plateìa* (2), lies a vast *agorà* (100 x 80 m) (3), originally bordered by the northern and western porticoes. To the east lie the ruins of the *bouleutérion* (5), a small semicircular covered "theater" that housed the city council and also served as a concert hall (*odeìon*) seating an

audience of about 2000.

Behind the double *stoà* to the north are the very interesting remains of the *katagògion* (360-350 BC) (6), a large, rather square building (33 X 30 meters), which served mainly as a *prytaneion* and public inn, to house local magistrates and official guests of the city. The building has 17 rooms that do not communicate with each other, arranged around a peristyle with Doric columns. Wooden staircases led from the corner rooms facing west, north and east, to the floor above. Quite like the Nekromanteìon, the *katagògion*

was built using the megalithic polygonal construction technique. The use of brick in the construction of the upper floor is decidedly ahead of its time when compared to the structures of most of the Greek world.

The theater (300-250 BC) was intelligently located in a spectacular position away from the main town. Served by two roads, it had a seating capacity of 7,000. It is not very easy to access the "Macedonian"-type chamber tomb, known as the Vassilòspitos ("royal house") at the southwestern end.

50 left A famous view of the excavations at Nikòpolis; this is Basilica B, whose marble portal is outlined against the sky and indicates the passage from the narthex to the cult building proper.

The highlight of this area is the archaeological site of the **NIKOPOLIS** or Aktia Nikòpolis founded by Caesar Octavian, the future Emperor Augustus, in 30 BC to celebrate his victory over Mark Antony and Cleopatra VI of Egypt, assigning the surrounding verdant countryside to his war veterans and to the inhabitants of the main cities of Acarnania and Epirus (including Kassòpe) to reward them for their war effort. The city reached the height of its prosperity between the first and third centuries AD and underwent a slight boom in Justinian's time.

The visit should start at the southern slopes of the Michalítsi hill (1) on which Augustus built his victory monument, within the sanctuary of Apollo, located outside the walls and including a forest dedicated to the

god. The victory monument is made up of an artificial terrace surrounded by a wall. Rams of the ships in Mark Antony's navy were hung on the southern face of this wall and dedicated to Neptune and Mars. Lower down the hill, close to the road, lie the theater (2) (first century BC – second century AD) and the stadium (3) (first century BC). The theater has a frame built using bricks and mortar, which has disintegrated in places and lies crumbling amongst the high undergrowth. The stadium is of the amphitheater type (with two curves), just about recognizable under the undergrowth. The temple and the stadium were part of the sanctuary and served to host the *Aktia*, the four-yearly games held to celebrate the victory in 31 BC. The meager remains of the *thermae* (hot baths) (4) may be skipped to carry on south towards Parga to reach the North Gate of Justinian's walls (5). At this point, following the lightly beaten paths close to the walls, one can get an interesting idea of the Byzantine defense system as well as the much larger Augustan defenses to compare techniques and admire the high coarse brick walls, the towers, and the city

NIKOPOLIS

1 HILL OF MICHALITSI AND SANCTUARY OF APOLLO
2 THEATER
3 STADIUM
4 NORTH BATHS
5 NORTH GATE
6 WALLS OF JUSTINIAN (BYZANTINE)
7 WALLS OF AUGUSTUS
8 BASILICA OF ALKYSON
9 BASILICA OF AGHIOS DIMITRIOS
10 ODEION
11 ARCHAEOLOGICAL MUSEUM

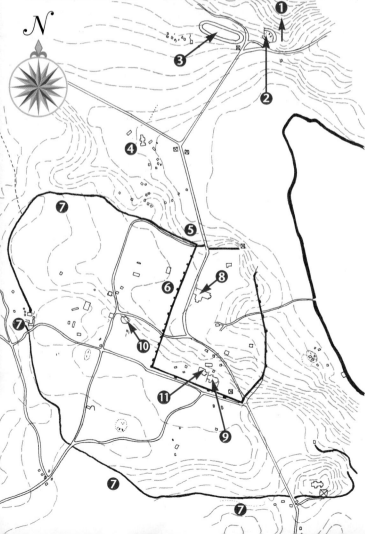

gates. Otherwise, one can visit the largest of the Early Christian basilicas of Byzantine Nikòpolis, known as Basilica B or the Basilica of Bishop Alkyson (550-600 AD) (8). The basilica features five aisles, a transept, narthex, and portico, as well as fountains for holy water. Visitors should then proceed to Basilica A (9) dedicated to St. Demetrios (525-550 BC), with mosaic floors in the central nave depicting the earth surrounded by the ocean. Visitors should take a last shortcut along the path that leads beyond the western side of Justinian's walls to the well-restored *odeíon* (10), a Late Imperial concert hall, and the small archaeological museum (11), where one can still see a circular early Christian altar with mosaics in gold and glass paste (5th century AD).

50 right The Roman odeíon at Nikòpolis is one of the most interesting examples of this sort of concert hall (originally covered) in all Greece. Restoration now allows the hall to be used.

50-51 *The dramatic cavea of the large theater in Dodona looks over woods of oak trees and the Pìndos mountain chain; it is a sight not to be missed.*

51 bottom *The heavy-handed changes that were made during the mid-Imperial age are clearly recognizable in the shape of the orchèstra and the skenè of Dodona theater; the transformation was made so that fights with gladiators and wild animals could be staged.*

After Nikòpolis, proceed up the valley of the Loùros towards Ioànina. Before reaching Ioànina, however, it is well worthwhile to veer to the left to reach the pearl of Epirot archaeology, the religious center of **DODONA**, the location of a very important sanctuary that held the oracle of Zeus. The sanctuary dates as far back as the Mycenaean period (16th century BC) and reached the height of its splendor between the 4th and 3rd centuries BC, maintaining its status until it was destroyed by the Romans in 167 BC. The cult of Zeus supplanted a previous cult to Ghè, or mother earth, venerated for her oracular power. The oracle spoke through a sacred oak, the leaves of which would rustle in the wind, making sounds that were interpreted by the *Selloí*, the priests of the sanctuary. The *Selloí* were mystics descended from a small number of ancient families that observed

DODONA

1 TEMPLE OF ZEUS
2 THEATER
3 SOUTH WALLS OF THE ACROPOLIS
4 STADIUM
5 REMAINS OF THE STADIUM TIERS
6 BOULEUTÉRION
7 TEMPLE OF APHRODITE
8 TEMPLE OF GHE-TEMIS
9 TEMPLE OF DIONE
10 LATE TEMPLE OF DIONE
11 TEMPLE OF HERACLES

ancestral rituals such as sleeping on the bare ground and never washing their feet. To answer those who interrogated the oracle, they also interpreted the song and the flight of the sacred doves that nested in the oak as well as the sound made first by a series of bronze tripods placed in a crown at the foot of the tree and then by a sort of bronze gong built at Corfu in the 4th century BC.

There are 5 documented phases of construction of the temple (1) from the 7th century BC to the first century AD. These

18,000 spectators. Massive stone walls extending over 20 meters in height still survive today. These walls were built in local limestone using the isodomic technique on ashlar. Little remains of the stage area, which was destroyed and modified several times, up to the Roman period during which the orchèstra and the proscenium were restructured to become a circular arena used for hunting games and gladiator contests. The stadium (4) was built at the end of the 3rd century BC and leans partially against the

phases are consistent in form, dimensions and orientation. The ruins that remain today mostly date to the complex as it was in 219 BC with a *témenos* opened by a Ionic pròpylon hexastyle, facing on the other side a small temple that was a sort of Ionic *oikos* prostyle tetrastyle with an *àdyton*. The Ionic portico on the north, west and south sides dates back to the time of Pyrrhus (early third century BC) and was aimed at honoring the ancient oracle. Evocatively, an oak still stands at the spot where the sacred tree gave divine advice to the faithful.

Dodona owes its current renown, however, to its splendid theater (2). Built by Pyrrhus at the beginning of the third century BC, it was renovated by Philip V just a few decades later and further restructured towards the middle of the second century BC. The huge semicircular cavea (auditorium) is built against the hill, a little below the crumbling walls of the vast area perched at the top of the acropolis, left bereft of all permanent structures. Divided horizontally by three diazomata or corridors and served vertically by ten staircases, the cavea could accommodate

western anàlemma of the theater. It is surrounded by 20 rows of stepped seats. Opposite the theater lies the *bouleutérion* (6), the Epirot parliament, made up of an imposing hypostyle Ionic hall preceded by a Doric portico. The structure was built between the third and second centuries BC. Less attractive to the visitor are the remains of a large number of small sacred buildings around the temple of Zeus, dedicated to Aphrodite (7) (with renovations during the Roman period), Ghè-Temis (8), Dione (9) and Heracles (11), covered by part of a small Roman Christian basilica built later.

The archaeological museum at **IOÀNINA** is well worth a visit, since it provides quite an accurate overview of the ancient history of the region, from prehistoric times to the Byzantine period. The museum houses a varied collection of interesting religious and votive objects from the sanctuaries of Dodona and the Nekromanteìon, including very rare lead sheets containing the questions posed to the oracle of Zeus up to the 7th century BC.

52 Dodona stadium was used for horse races and athletic competitions. Twenty rows of seats at the bottom of the solid western analémma *have been well preserved.*

52-53 One of the holy oak trees next to the temple of the oracle of Zeus at Dodona still murmurs, but in vain. The place of worship has no remarkable ruins but it is still fascinating.

53 bottom left The foundations of the prytaneìon, *seat of the important magistrates in the city and sanctuary, have been unearthed. The building dated from the early 3rd century BC.*

53 bottom right The bouleutérion *(parliament) of the Epirots stood near the eastern section of the theater. A pillar of the Doric portico can be seen in the foreground.*

According to legend, beautiful CORFU is the mythical island of Schería, home of the Phaeacians whose king Alcinous sheltered and entertained the shipwrecked Ulysses, on his way back to Ithaca. Chersikrates, of the powerful Corinthian aristocratic Bacchiadai family, founded the trading colony of Kèrkyra on the island in 734 BC. It soon gained independence from Corinth and flourished during the 7th and 6th centuries BC. After a series of bloody civil wars between the 5th and

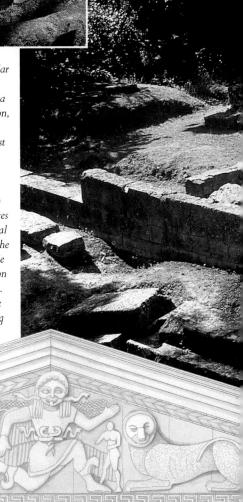

54 top With its circular structure and mound originally crowned by a statue of a funerary lion, the cenotaph of Menekràtes is the oldest cenotaph in the Greek world (circa 600 BC).

54 center and bottom One of the oldest leaves in Hellenic pedimental sculpture comes from the west side of the temple dedicated to Artemis on Corfù (590-580 BC). The frightening mask of Medusa has a strong emotional impact.

6th centuries BC, it flourished in peace and prosperity following the Roman conquest in 219 BC.

Highlights of the archaeological sites in the historical town center include the circular base of the cenotaph of Menekràtes (600 BC), the remains of the early Christian Basilica of the Paleòpolis ("Ancient City") built in the 5th century AD over the ancient *agorà*, using materials recovered from classical buildings (see the marble roof gutter

with lion protoma or water-spouts) and the foundations of the Artemìsion (590-580 BC). This last structure, a milestone in archaic Greek architecture, is a pseudo-dipteral octastyle temple featuring austere yet harmonious proportions, with a long three-aisled cella as well as a pronaos and opisthodomos, both distyle *in antis*.

The Artemìsion featured one of the most ancient and rare examples of pedimental sculptural decoration. The

relief-sculptured slabs of the west pediment, now at the local archaeologica museum, depict the terrifying Gorgon, Medusa, in flight (in the "kneeling-running" position commonly found in Archaic art) flanked by two crouched panthers from whose claws rise Pegasus and the monster Chrysaor, children of Medusa. The sculptures near the corners depict the death of Priam at the hand of Neoptolemus to the left and Zeus striking a rebellious giant with lightning, to the

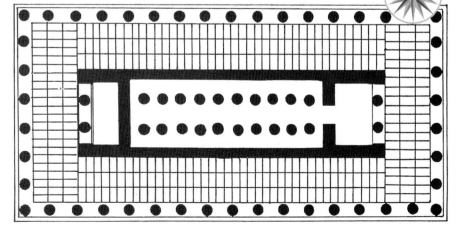

54-55 The hexastyle peripteral Doric temple in the archaeological park at Paleòpolis dates from the 6th-5th centuries BC and can almost certainly be attributed to the cult of Hèra Akraía ("protectress of the hill").

55 bottom The ground plan of the temple of Artemis shows that the unknown architect was attempting to create a feeling of grandeur and stateliness, especially in the dense colonnade, twice the normal distance from the walls.

N

right. Little remains today of the far-corner sculptures of fallen giants. The lack of compositional and proportional balance as well as narrative correlation does nothing to diminish the expressive force of these sculptures, taken from one of the earliest pages of Greek pedimental decoration. Lastly, the stone lion that adorned the base of the cenotaph of Menekràtes is the most ancient example of Greek funerary sculpture uncovered so far.

THESSALY

From Ioànina, in Epirus, the E92 highway climbs towards the northern Pìndos mountains and the massive Làkmos , leaving the beautiful mountain region of Zagòria-Vìkos to the north. Beyond Mètsovo, at the Katàra pass (1,705 m), one enters Thessaly to cross the region of Meteore, with its monasteries perched on almost inaccessible cliffs.

The tour of the region starts at TRIKALA, ancient Trikke: the area between the main square and the church of Aghios Nikòlaos (St. Nicholas) houses the remains of a famous sanctuary of Asklepios, built in the 3rd century BC and restored during the Middle Roman Imperial period. The sanctuary has a beautiful mosaic.

Continuing along the road to Volos, one reaches FARSALA. This was probably the ancient Phthìa of Homer's Achilles. It was also the backdrop to the battle between Pompei and Julius Caesar in 48 BC. Not far away lies Kynòs Kephalaí (Cynoscephalae) scene of a Roman victory

56 left The park of Nea Ankhialos contains the remains of eight cult buildings and an Episcopal palace dating from between the 4th and 6th centuries AD.

56-57 In the agorà at Pyrasos (Nea Ankhialos), remains have been found of a Roman bath house built during the mid-imperial age; the photo shows the pottery supports that held up the floor of a calidarium.

57 left This mid-imperial age Roman sarcophagus is decorated with festoons and pàtere.

57 right The photo shows a Ionic column topped by a typical Byzantine dosseret from the ruins of the early Christian basilica in Constantinople.

over the Macedonians in 197 BC.

After the crossroads with the E75, nea Mikrothíves, it is well worth your time stopping for a brief visit to the excavations at PHTHIOTIDES THEBAI, a city of the Classical and Hellenistic periods, destroyed by Philip V of Macedonia in 217 BC. Surprisingly intact, the walls of the city, with 40 towers, descend from the acropolis to the plain, enclosing ruins of houses and public buildings.

One shouldn't miss a visit to the archaeological park of NEA ANKHIALOS, only four kilometers down the coast and including the ruins of the Archaic and Classical city of Pyrasos, known in Roman times by the name of nearby Phthiotìdes Thèbai. Pyrasos was a flourishing center even in the early centuries of Christianity. was created as a Bishopric and as a result was subjected to large-scale monumental-ization: the remains today make Nea Ankhialos the most important Early Christian site in Greece. After taking a quick look at the almost circular ancient natural port from which the rather low hill of the acropolis of Pyrasos is clearly visible one should proceed to the excavations of

during or just before the Emperor Justinian, are especially noteworthy. About 250 meters to the southwest, after the remains of a paved road flanked by porticoes with workshops, one reaches the ruins of Basilica A. Dating back to the second half of the 5th century AD, with three aisles and featuring a propylon, narthex and atrium, the Basilica also has a baptistery with a mosaic inscription that mentions the name of Aghios Dimìtrios (St. Demetrios), indicating that it may have been dedicated to this saint. Linked to the basilica are the ruins of an imposing building of baths, perhaps originally related to a 5th-century villa close by. The meager remains of what used to be the bishop's palace are of little interest. One-hundred meters west lies Basilica C, an early Christian cathedral of Phthiotìdes Thèbai. This cathedral actually includes the ruins of three successive and partially adjacent churches built between about 350 and 532, with remains of mosaics on the floor and ruins of the baptistery. Outside the city walls, to the southwest, one can conclude the tour by visiting the park of Basilica F, built in 431 AD, by order of the bishop Martyrios (as recorded in the mosaic inscription in front of the altar).

The ruins of **DEMETRIAS**, the city founded in 294 BC by the Antigonid Demetrios Poliorketes lies after Volos. Demetriás, the last of a series of centers that from the Mycenaean age dominated the Gulf of Pagásai, was the scene of often dramatic battles, especially during the

Roman conquest of Greece and the Mithridatic wars. It remained a lively port city until the 4th century AD. The city was protected by a 13-kilometer-long double fortifying wall. Large tracts of the wall still survive, and 76 of the 175 rectangular towers along the wall are still clearly visible. From the northern tract of the wall, visitors should take the road that leads to the ancient port and climb up to the low hill of Pefkàkia, a *magoùla* inhabited from the Neolithic period up to the Mycenaean age (as seen from the ruins of houses). From here, visitors should proceed toward the flat plain on which Poliorketes built his city. The western sector was dominated by the royal palace, built on terraces to adapt

Basilica B. The basilica was built at the end of the 5th century and rebuilt during the first half of the 6th century by the architect Stephanos, under the bishop Elipdios (as recorded in the inscription on the atrium). The basilica has a narthex and a baptistery with seats for the priests in the *synthronon* on both sides of the bishop's throne. A little towards the west, at the foot of the acropolis, lie the extended ruins, in several layers, of a complex of public buildings standing face to face. Some of these buildings were built over the ancient *agorà*. The unusual thermal baths, with their circular plan and 18 bathtubs arranged in rows, as well as an imposing square building surrounded by arches built to the uneven ground. Rectangular in shape with square towers at its corners, the palace overlooked the *agorà*. Visitors can walk along the city's grid-plan streets that created regular city blocks of about 100 x 50 meters. On the way back to the modern road, visitors should not miss the theater (3rd century BC – 4th century AD), the surviving arches of the Roman aqueduct and above all, the remains of the mausoleum, probably in the shape of a ship, in which Demetrios Poliorketes wished to be buried.

The archaeological museum at VOLOS houses a large collection of

important material on the Helladic-Mycenaean civilization (funerary objects) as well as Late Classical and Hellenistic jewelery. The museum is famous for its unique series of painted grave stelae, scavenged from the cemetery of Demetriás in 87 BC to consolidate the city wall. These stelae were spared destruction only because they were used as building materials.

The tour continues towards Làrissa, but just a few kilometers from Volos, to the left, is the famous Neolithic archaeological site of DIMINI (3900-3000 BC). The site was later occupied by modest Helladic and Mycenaean settlements (a large late-Mycenaean *thòlos* tomb on the northern slope of the mound and another about 300 meters to the south are open to visitors). Traces of up to six concentric fortress walls can be identified. The walls were interrupted by four narrow passages leading to the central area. There are ruins of a few

modest Neolithic houses, in groups of three or four around a common courtyard, in a layout widespread throughout the Mediterranean. The most interesting building, however, is the Helladic *mègaron* that was built by unifying several late Neolithic structures into a single rectangular residence, with a central chamber featuring a wall hearth framed by two columns, an entrance distyle porch and a small back room. It is the most ancient example of a *mègaron* in Greek architecture.

A little after the turn for Dimini, again to the left, lies the turnoff for SESKLO, the most ancient Greek Neolithic settlement, inhabited since 7000 BC. In the 5th millennium BC, Sèsklo was a true Neolithic city, with over 500 houses, well defended by walls and terraces. A fire destroyed the city in 4400 BC and the ruins provide valuable information about this particularly prosperous period. Visitors shouldn't miss the small *mègaron*, with three rooms at right angles, the large *mègaron*, a clear indication of re-settlement after the fire (3900 BC), very similar to *mègaron* A at Dimini, the

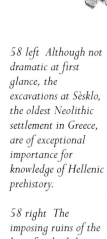

58 left Although not dramatic at first glance, the excavations at Sèsklo, the oldest Neolithic settlement in Greece, are of exceptional importance for knowledge of Hellenic prehistory.

58 right The imposing ruins of the huge fort built by Demetrios Poliorketes at the start of the 3rd century BC on Gòritsa hill near Volos could accommodate more than 2000 men-at-arms.

58-59 This oak and
laurel leaf crown made
from gold leaf was
found in a 4th-3rd
century BC princely
tomb in the
archaeological area of
Demetriás-Pagásai
(Volos, Archaeological
Museum).

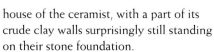

59 top The uniform
town planning of the
residential quarters of
Demetriás can be seen
on the slopes of the
small Pefkàkia hill.

59 bottom The more
recent of the two
ancient theaters at
Làrissa, dated to the
2nd century BC,
requires serious
restoration work, like
many other Hellenic
complexes.

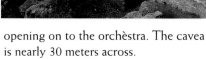

house of the ceramist, with a part of its crude clay walls surprisingly still standing on their stone foundation.

Continuing towards Làrissa, at Velestìnon one can visit the walls of PHERAI, a powerful Mycenaean and Archaic city, that re-flourished in the 4th century BC. The walls were built at about this time, using the isodomic technique, with rectangular towers. Other fascinating city walls can be admired in Petra, close to the small village of Stefanovíkio, along the old road for Làrissa. These Mycenaean walls in megalithic polygonal masonry, similar in thickness to the walls of Tirinto, stretch for over 4 kilometers. The identity of the site is still under debate.

LÀRISSA was the dominant pòlis of Thessaly between the 7th and 4th centuries BC. The town's small archaeological museum is squashed between a former mosque and the two ancient theaters. The first theater, on the southern slopes of the acropolis, has an interesting skene, with Doric semi-columns. The second temple, dating from the 2nd century BC, has a skenè with paraskenia and a wide cavea opening on to the orchèstra. The cavea is nearly 30 meters across.

The tour may continue towards Macedonia and the shady, lush Valley of TEMPE (Tèmbi). The valley so enthralled the Roman Emperor Hadrian that he had it artificially reproduced at his sprawling villa at Tivoli, a jewel of town planning. The E75 highway running through the valley leads to the foot of Mount Olympos, the home of the Gods of ancient Greece, eternally shrouded in thick clouds that add to its mystery and charm.

MACEDONIA

EDESSA

PELLA

LEFKÀDIA

SALONIKI

VERIA

VERGHINA

OLYNTHOS

DION

Macedonia is the largest Greek province and is a mountainous and hilly region (with the northern Pìndos mountains including Mts. Vèrno, Vèrmio, Olympos, Rodopi) and a few plains. The abundance of water makes it a lush and prosperous region. Except for the coastline along the Chalcidic peninsula however, the Macedonian coast does not feature many natural harbors and is generally made up of long sandy beaches.

Macedonia, the ancestral home of Philip II and Alexander the Great, and the cradle of the first universal empire in history, is rich in archaeological treasures.

Approaching Mt. Olympos from the Valley of Tempe, along the E75 highway, at Limàni Litochòrou, lie the vast ruins of the city of **DION**, founded around 300 BC. Even before that, it was an important sanctuary of Zeus and the Muses, who, according to myth, chose this region, Pieria, as their home. Dion was continuously beautified and monumentalized by all its rulers from the Macedonian kings through to the Middle Roman Empire, right up to its destruction by the Goths in 346 AD.

The tour route is well organized, and visitors can go up in some of the towers to enjoy a splendid view of the main public buildings and the well-preserved grid of roads surrounded by a fascinating green square, looking lusher than ever against the backdrop of the nearby marshland. Visitors enter by passing through the southeastern gate (1) of the quadrilateral city walls that run for 2600 meters, with rectangular towers placed at intervals of 33 meters. The paved floor, dating back to the Augustan era, of the wide *cardo maximus* (2) can still be seen today. Immediately to the left, a narrow stairway, between a public latrine and the *tabernae* (3), overlooking the street, leads to a courtyard (4) that houses to the right, the remains of a small covered concert hall, the *odeíon* (5), with a cavea supported by radial walls. Opposite, there is a complex of Roman Imperial baths (1st to 3rd centuries AD). On both sides of the entrance, one can see traces of the changing rooms (*apodytèria*). The northern wing (6) was dedicated to the cult of the gods of health (the remains of a large number of marble statues from this site are housed at the local archaeological museum). The hall to the west was used for cold baths (*frigidarium*) (7), and features a large marble-paneled bathing pool. From the *frigidarium*, the users of the baths could pass on to the *tepidaria* (warm water) (8) and to the *calidarium*, the hall for hot baths (9). The supports of the floor of the *calidarium* are still in place. Hot air, produced in furnace chambers (*praefurnia*), was circulated under the floor of the calidarium as well as through clay pipes built into the walls, to reach the chimney nozzles (now lost) on the roof.

A long base made up of regular rows of stone and decorated with shields and armor in relief runs along the main street (10). This base now bears copies of the votive statues commissioned by Alexander the Great in memory of his 25 aristocratic companions (*hetaìroi*) who fell during the

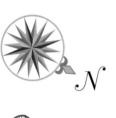

DION

1	SOUTHEAST GATE	11	AGORÀ-FORUM AREA
2	CARDUS MAXIMUS	12	PALEO-CHRISTIAN BASILICA
3	TABERNAE		
4	BATHS' SQUARE	13	VILLA OF DIONYSUS
5	ODEION		
6	SHRINES	14	SANCTUARY OF ISIS
7	FRIGIDARIUM		
8	TEPIDARIA	15	HELLENISTIC THEATER
9	CALIDARIUM		
10	"DONARIO DEL GRÀNIKOS"	16	ROMAN THEATER

60 top left A copy of the Aphrodite Hypolimpìdia, (the original was produced in the 2nd century BC) stands in the niche in the sanctuary dedicated to Egyptian goddesses at Dion.

60 bottom left A modern copy has been substituted for the statue of Isis in the porticoed court in front of the chambers reserved for the worship of Egyptian deities.

60 right The remains of Dion lie among thick vegetation and stretches of marsh; the photo shows a section of the presumed sanctuary of Zeus that lay outside the city walls.

61 top left The sanctuary of Isis had a standard ground plan for this type of Roman cult complex during the reign of Severius (3rd century AD).

61 bottom left The supports (suspensurae) of the suspended floor (now lost) in a calidarium at the Dion baths are well preserved. Hot air supplied by the praefurnia (boilers) would circulate below the floor.

61 top right This is another view of the heated rooms at the baths at Dion, made

entirely of a Roman type of cement that was the forerunner of concrete, and lined with bricks and stones.

61 bottom right The polychrome floor mosaics of the Roman baths depicted figures in geometric and optical patterns; note the fine bull's head that has been dated to the start of the 3rd century BC.

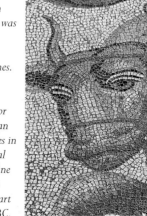

62 top left The huge Villa of Dionysus (2nd-3rd c. AD) perhaps belonged to a family or to a group of followers of Epicurus; sculptures and mosaics of a Dionysiac and Epicurean nature have been found there.

62 center right A statue of the god of wine was found in the apsidal area shown in the photograph to the southeast of the atrium of the Villa of Dionysus; a mosaic in the vestibule depicts an enthroned Dionysus crowned with ivy.

62 bottom left The pavement on the cardo maximus has stood the test of time. This was the main north-south road at Dion, built by the Romans over a Hellenistic road, and lined with houses and shops.

62 bottom right This is a detail of the decoration of the Monument of the Swords on the cardo maximus, which was actually decorated with alternating Macedonian style, round shields and pieces of body armor.

battle of Grànikos (334 BC). The original statues sculpted by the great Lysippus, which were housed in the sanctuary of Zeus and the Muses, were transferred to Rome in 149 BC.

Where the street meets the *decumanus maximus* (11), the site of the Hellenistic *agorà* and later, the Roman forum, lies a large marble block with six hemispheric hollows arranged from largest to smallest. This is a rare intact *mensa ponderaria*, a table of official measures (the table bears the name of the magistrate of the colony of Iulia Augusta Diensis, the Augustan name of the city).

After a quick visit to the excavations to the west, with the meager remains of Roman houses and an Early Christian basilica (12),

one should head for Dionysus' Villa (13), a wonderful example of a prestigious residence during the Middle Roman Empire, with its private baths. It was probably an Epicurean club and was decorated by mosaics showing Dionysiac themes, large portions of which remain today.

To the east, beyond the ancient river port and an embankment, lie the ruins of a sanctuary outside the walls dedicated to Isis (14). Because of the dense vegetation and marshy ground, it is not easy to explore this complex in depth. The sanctuary is made up of four buildings overlooking a courtyard surrounded by arches. The main Ionic temple prostyle tetrastyle on a high podium was dedicated to Isis and perhaps also to Serapis and Anubis. Immediately to the right is a small cella with a copy of a cult statue of Aphrodite (2nd century BC), overlooking an oval basin.

Southwest of the sanctuary lie the remains of a Hellenistic theater (200 BC),

precariously strewn over the slope of the artificial embankment (15) that used to support the structure where the theatrical festival in honor of the Muses, was held. A little further south are the ruins of a Roman theater (16) and its proscenium (2nd century AD).

Continuing along the old road that runs parallel to the E75 highway, just past the village of Eghìnio, one enters the province of Emathìa, at the heart of historical Macedonia.

Close to the village of **Verghina**, archaeological excavations commenced a few decades ago have revealed the remains of the ancient Macedonian capital, Aìgai, with its royal palace and cemetery, dating from the 4th to the 3rd centuries BC. It is best to start the tour at Palatìtsia, one kilometer before Verghìna. The ground plan of the palace is easily identifiable, despite heavy erosion. Exceptionally huge (about 104 x 89 m), the royal palace was probably built by Cassander at the end of the 4th century BC. It lies at the edge of a plateau overlooking the vast valley of the Haliákmon river. Higher up the plateau lay the walled acropolis with its temples, while the city itself extended a little away, at the same level as the palace. Around a large square courtyard (1) with 16 Doric columns to each side, there was a structure

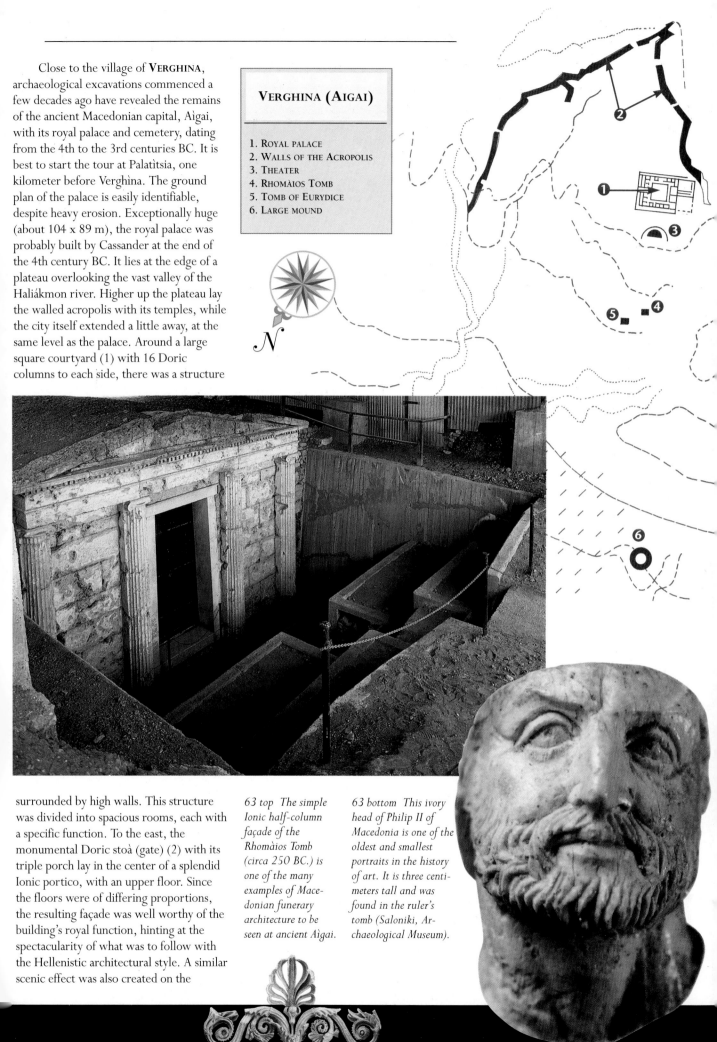

VERGHINA (AIGAI)

1. ROYAL PALACE
2. WALLS OF THE ACROPOLIS
3. THEATER
4. RHOMÀIOS TOMB
5. TOMB OF EURYDICE
6. LARGE MOUND

N

surrounded by high walls. This structure was divided into spacious rooms, each with a specific function. To the east, the monumental Doric stoà (gate) (2) with its triple porch lay in the center of a splendid Ionic portico, with an upper floor. Since the floors were of differing proportions, the resulting façade was well worthy of the building's royal function, hinting at the spectacularity of what was to follow with the Hellenistic architectural style. A similar scenic effect was also created on the

63 top The simple Ionic half-column façade of the Rhomàios Tomb (circa 250 BC.) is one of the many examples of Macedonian funerary architecture to be seen at ancient Aìgai.

63 bottom This ivory head of Philip II of Macedonia is one of the oldest and smallest portraits in the history of art. It is three centimeters tall and was found in the ruler's tomb (Saloniki, Archaeological Museum).

building's northern side, featuring a long porticoed panoramic balcony overlooking the plane below, almost providing a preview of the covered walkways that would later grace the most sumptuous Roman residences.

Inside the courtyard, on the left was a circular building, most probably a temple to Heracles, the mythical ancestor of the Ageads, the Macedonian royal family. This building may also have served as the throne room (there is the base of a large chair against the wall). The central buildings to the south, divided by the tristylar hall, were probably used as halls for audiences: in room 5 there is a beautiful polychrome mosaic made with pebbles, featuring elegant entwined floral and plant motifs, with female figures at the corners. To the west are three large banquet halls.

A little below the palace are the remains of the theater (3), with a single row of marble seats (the rest of the structure was made of wood). The theater was built in the same period as the palace over a previous wooden theater dating from the 5th century BC, where Philip II of Macedonia was assassinated in 335 BC.

Along the road towards Verghìna lie the first Macedonian *thòlos* tombs with corbel-vaulted circular chambers, masterpieces of ancient funerary architecture. The Rhomàios Tomb (4) (named after the archaeologist who excavated it) was built around 250 BC. The façade features a pediment and four Ionic half columns with a frieze bearing floral motifs. The burial chamber, preceded by a *dròmos* or short entrance passage, still contains a marble throne and a brick bed against the wall. Nearby is the tomb of Eurydice (5), the mother of Philip II. This tomb was built about a century earlier and has the largest vaulted ceiling found in structures of this type. The burial chamber is very interesting with a false architectural façade featuring Ionic half-columns on the

back wall and a splendid inlay and painted throne.

Further ahead lies the Great Tumulus (110 m in diameter), that was built around 272 BC, on top of a pre-existing burial site containing the tombs of Philip II and other 4th-century BC royals of the Argead dynasty, so as to protect the site against pillaging and theft. These tombs were unearthed in the autumn of 1977 during particularly fruitful excavations by M. Andornikos. Tomb I, known as the Persephone Tomb, is not open to visitors. It is the only tomb that was pillaged, probably in ancient times. It is a cist tomb and is still

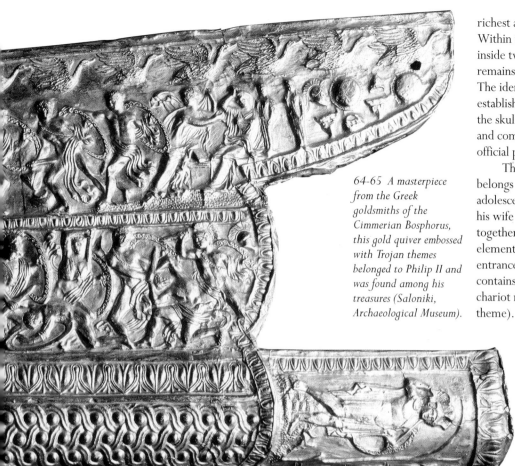

64-65 A masterpiece from the Greek goldsmiths of the Cimmerian Bosphorus, this gold quiver embossed with Trojan themes belonged to Philip II and was found among his treasures (Saloniki, Archaeological Museum).

richest archaeological treasures ever found. Within two splendid gold larnakes placed inside two stone cases, were the cremated remains of Philip II and his wife Cleopatra. The identification of the cremated bodies was established beyond doubt by reconstructing the skull and the facial features of the male and comparing the result with surviving official portraits of the king.

The smaller Tomb of the Prince perhaps belongs to Alexander IV, the unfortunate adolescent son of Alexander the Great and his wife Roxane, who was murdered together with his mother in 310 BC. More elementary both in façade and structure, the entrance passage (dròmos) to this tomb contains the remains of frescoes (showing a chariot race, a typically aristocratic funerary theme).

65 bottom Philip II's parade crown was made from iron but with studs and decorations in gold. It is one of the most impressive items found in the tomb of Philip and his wife (Saloniki, Archaeological Museum).

adorned by an exquisite wall fresco showing the Rape of Persephone by Pluto, painted in a style very close to that of Nikias, one of the greatest artists of ancient Greece.

The Tomb of Philip II is, however, miraculously intact, even in its structure. It is an excellent example of a double-chambered Macedonian tomb with an oval plan. The façade is a mock portico. The entrance is through a marble double door with mock knobs in relief, framed by elegant Doric columns with a colored Doric epistyle and a frieze showing a hunting scene in a wooded setting, with mountains in the background. The hunters are both on foot and on horseback. Some have identified the figure of Alexander at the center and the horseman fighting with a lion as Philip II. The exceptional artistic level and the unusual theme indicate that the work was specifically designed for this tomb. The vigorous figures are arranged in a realistic perspective, with shadows in proper perspective. The figures assume a variety of postures aimed at reproducing the excited atmosphere of a hunt. Even the colors and nuance tend toward the dramatic realism of the great painting tradition of the 4th century BC, so highly praised by ancient authors. Inside the chamber, the walls are in large blocks of pòros stone, carefully coated with plaster and covered by a corbel-vaulted ceiling. The two chambers held one of the

64 top The ruins of the magnificent royal palace at Aìgai (Palatìtsia) near Verghìna still preserve rooms around the central courtyard that are decorated with high quality polychrome mosaics made using pebbles from a river bed.

64 bottom left This reconstruction of the tomb of Philip II at Verghìna shows the layout of the rooms and burial treasures in the chamber and ante-chamber.

64 bottom right The zoophorous frieze painted on the façade of Philip II's tomb raises problems of preservation. It is a rare example of late-Classical Greek wall painting that has survived intact.

presenting the dead warrior to the gods Hades, Aeacus and Rhadamanthys.

The lower and upper floors are separated by an entablature made up of a painted Doric frieze with alternating triglyphs and metopes, topped by a continuous Ionic frieze in painted plaster. The upper floor features seven false paired windows with knobs, separated by Ionic half-columns. The Doric frieze on the entablature features eleven metopes with scenes of battles between Lapiths (humans) and Centaurs. The continuous Ionic frieze depicts a violent and dramatic battle between Macedonians and Persians. The theme is reminiscent of the battle scenes between Greeks and Persians or between Acheans and Trojans that commonly appear on architectural decorations of sacred buildings as a metaphor for the eternal conflict between Good and Evil. In this case, however, the motif is also an allusion to the aristocratic and therefore "heroic" state of the deceased and the melancholic memento of the brutality of Death. The Great Tomb was built during the reign of Alexander the Great (336-323 BC). Other important tombs nearby include the "Kinch" tomb named after the Danish researcher who first studied it in 1880 (the tomb dates back to around 300 BC) and the tomb of Lyson and Kallikles, that bears the names of its dead occupants, inscribed on the architrave of the door. This tomb, which looks like a sort of aristocratic

chapel with a very simple plan, dates back to the middle of the 3rd century BC.

When in **EDESSA**, a beautiful thermal resort of the province of Pèla (famous for its waterfalls), it is well worth you taking the time to visit the part of the ancient lower city uncovered during excavations. The walls are especially noteworthy, with remains of towers and a city gate (4th century BC) that opens onto a long stretch of paved road flanked by Ionic arches (there are numerous Late Classical inscriptions on the columns). Well-preserved Hellenistic residential districts overlook the road.

There is an archaeological museum in the nearby city of **VERIA**, ancient **BEROIA**. Not far from the village of Kopanòs, on the road to Edessa, near Isvòria, lies the archaeological site of **MIEZA**. Philip II sent his son Alexander to study under Aristotle here, at the sanctuary of the Nymphs, made up of three caves transformed into a school. The school has porticoes and balconies tastefully inserted to blend into the scenic landscape.

To get a complete idea of Macedonian funerary architecture, however, one must also visit **LEFKÀDIA**, nestled in the midst of lush vineyards and orchards. The Great Tomb, featuring a rectangular antechamber (*dròmos*) that is wider than the burial chamber proper (*thàlamos*), seems to be in keeping with the widespread Macedonian style, with a corbel-vaulted ceiling, walls in soft limestone and a façade built along the lines of a two-story temple tetrastyle *in antis*, crowned by a richly decorated tympanum. The façade is especially interesting because of its architectural and pictorial decoration. Four Doric half-columns divide the lower storey into five panels, the largest of which is the door (*stomìon*) to the burial chamber. The upper halves of the side panels are decorated by four well-preserved frescoes portraying scenes never found elsewhere in the entire history of Greek art, apart from a few poor-quality vases. The scene shows Hermes Psychopompos (that is to say, in his role as guide to the souls in the Underworld),

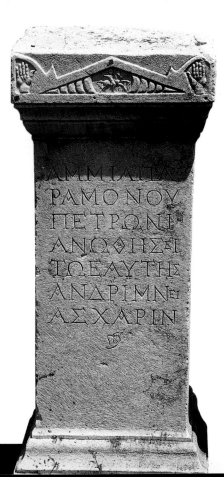

66 top left The collection of funerary stelae, sarcophagi and architectural fragments in the town of Vèria came from ancient Bèroia and has been laid out in the garden of the local archaeological museum.

66 bottom left Engraved in Greek but dedicated during the mid-imperial Roman age by a lady of Bèroia

to herself and her husband, this marble funerary stele is kept in the garden of Vèria archaeological museum.

66 top right A beautiful but disturbing head of the Gorgon Medusa — here portrayed in the tranquil Hellenistic-Roman version — watches from the ornaments of a marble piece in the Vèria museum.

66 center right This lovely view is of the long portico at Edessa, one of the attractions in the large archaeological zone in the Macedonian town. Many of the Ionic columns are still standing.

66 bottom right Long stretches of the solid walls of Edessa are still in good condition and are worthy of admiration before entering the gate that leads to the areas of the town excavated thus far.

67 top A famous view of one of the banquet rooms in the House of Dionysus that looks onto the Ionic peristyle. The room has a mosaic floor with diamond patterns in black and white made from river pebbles.

67 bottom Miraculously still intact, two huge terracotta píthoi (jars) stand in the western section of Pèlla agorà where numerous workshops and commercial shops used to stand.

A compulsory stop along the E86 highway towards Saloniki is the very large archaeological area of **PELLA**, which became the capital of the kingdom of Macedonia in the 4th century BC. The city flourished for over two centuries and is a splendid example of a grid-planned city.

It is advisable to start the visit from the large *agorà* (1). The city square, one of the largest in the Greek world (238 x 262 m), was entirely surrounded by arches that led to a large number of craftsmen's workshops. Researchers were

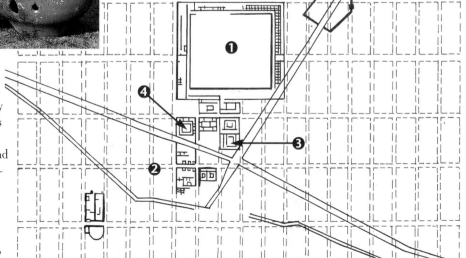

PELLA

1 AGORÀ
2 SOUTH QUARTER
3 HOUSE OF DIONYSUS
4 HOUSE OF THE RAPE
   OF HELEN
5 ROYAL PALACE
6 WALLS
7 SANCTUARY OF THE
   MEGÀLE METER

able to determine the use of these premises from the large number of clues found. On the east side, the shops mainly sold ceramic objects (vases and statuettes to meet the insatiable demand for votive objects used as offerings at sanctuaries and to satisfy the growing popularity of mass-produced souvenirs). The south side featured shops selling food products as well as blacksmiths' workshops. To the west were perfume boutiques and hardware shops. Some of the premises to

68-69 This masterpiece of Macedonian mosaic art can be seen in the House of Dionysus: it shows Alexander hunting a lion (Pèlla, Archaeological Museum).

68 bottom Another fine mosaic provides the name for the House of the Rape of Helen; while Theseus is squeezing his victim between his arms, the trustworthy Phorbas is ready to set the chariot in flight.

the north, on the other hand, were used as administrative offices (especially the semicircular building). The tour continues with a visit to the large aristocratic residential district (2) that, according to some experts, once housed the luxurious homes of the *hetaìroi* (royal peers) of Alexander the Great (325-300 BC). The House of Dionysus (3) is cut by the E86 running though its smaller courtyard, with a Ionic peristyle (A), partly restored using anastylosis (that is to say, by reconstructing scattered parts, often with the addition of new materials). The most prestigious rooms on the west and north sides of the courtyard with a Doric peristyle (B) are clearly recognizable: the mosaic floor of the banquet hall (C) with its geometric motif is well-preserved. The mosaics of the following rooms (D-E), now very famous, depict Dionysus on a panther, a deer caught in the grips of a griffon, and Alexander hunting a lion. These precious mosaics are now housed in the museum.

69 right "Made by Gnósis!" — this is the signature proudly added by an artist on the mosaic showing a deer hunt in the House of the Rape of Helen (Pèlla, Archaeological Museum).

The original rhomboid-shaped checkered mosaic in the entrance hall to the north, is however, still intact. Two blocks to the west lies the interesting House of the Rape of Helen (4), a good example of a Hellenistic residence with a Doric peristyle, and at least two splendid floor mosaics, from among the many that once adorned the rooms overlooking the peristyle. The large banquet hall (G) on the north side has a partly preserved mosaic depicting the little-known story of the abduction of

Helen by Theseus, who unwittingly preceded Paris. The adjacent room (H) is adorned by the famous mosaic depicting a brutal deer hunt, a masterpiece by Gnósis, whose signature appears on the top (Gnósis epoíesen).

The main attraction of the archaeological museum is the mosaic showing Alexander hunting a lion, a masterpiece of proto-Hellenistic mosaic art. The scene depicts an actual hunt that took place near the Persian city of Susa (during a particularly vicious hunt, the king's life was saved by the *hetaìros* (royal peer) Krateros. The piece is a splendid example of the "stone carpets," aimed at translating and recording in stone the paintings by the great Macedonian court artists, that once adorned the homes of the aristocrats of the capital. Some experts believe that the work was created by one of the greatest painters of the time, either Melantios or Apelles, inspired by a work by the great sculptor Lysippus.

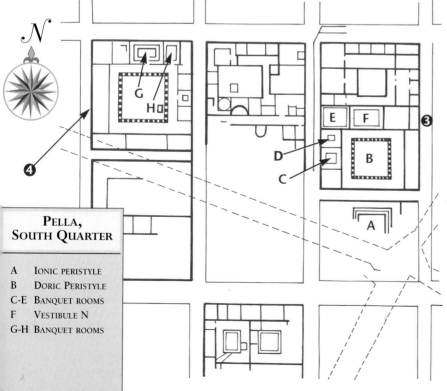

PELLA, SOUTH QUARTER

A	IONIC PERISTYLE
B	DORIC PERISTYLE
C-E	BANQUET ROOMS
F	VESTIBULE N
G-H	BANQUET ROOMS

SALONIKI

1 ARCH OF GALERIUS	5 ODEION
2 IMPERIAL PALACE	6 WALLS OF
3 MAUSOLEUM OF	THEODOSIUS
GALERIUS (AGHIOS	7 AGHIOS DIMITRIOS
GHEORGHIOS)	8 ACROPOLIS
4 AREA OF THE AGORÀ	

The last stop on the tour of Macedonia ought to be the regional capital, **SALONIKI**, ancient Thessalonìke, founded by Cassander in 316 BC. The city was further enhanced after the Roman conquest and the construction of the via Egnatia that linked the Adriatic port of Dyrràchion (now Durres in Albania) with Byzàntion (Istanbul in Turkey). It later became the Imperial Tetrarchic capital under Galerius, and an important center for the spread of Christianity.

The splendid archaeological museum houses a well organized collection of objects providing a historical overview of the city and region, from prehistoric times up to the period when the Archaic center of Thèrme was at its peak. A collection of sumptuous Archaic and Classical gold work from the cemetery at Sìndos, as well as items dating back to the foundation and blossoming of Thessalonìke, is on show in a separate wing. The prominent role of Cassander's city in the region is clearly highlighted by archaeological findings from the Macedonian and Roman periods. These articles were created as a direct result of the largesse of imperial patronage (see the interesting portrait gallery). Even the most hurried visitor cannot but be astounded by the jewels from the royal tombs at Verghìna, especially objects recovered from the tomb of Philip II. One of the most prized exhibits is surely the Krater of Dervèni (330 BC), a masterpiece of Macedonian metal work. This piece is a large bronze volute krater, found in a tomb of a Thessalian aristocrat, close to Saloniki.

The body of the krater depicts the wedding scene of Dionysus and Ariadne. The god is seated naked on a rock next to a panther. Ariadne, in a translucent *peplos* (robe) brushes aside the nuptial veil, offering herself symbolically to the groom. Around them unfolds a dizzying feast with Maenads (or Bacchantes, women devoted to the god of wine, Dionysus) in the throes of ecstasy as they dance, and Satyrs excited in their frenetic undulations. Especially noteworthy is the splendid plastic figure of a Maenad seated on the shoulder of the vase, in a tender slumber – her face seems just slightly veiled by the melancholy of the end of the feast or out of sheer tiredness. Equally

70 bottom left Damaged by man and worn by time, the Arch of Galerius (297-303 AD) is still impressive, with its descriptions of the epic deeds of the Roman army in the East.

70 bottom right The walk along the Theodosian walls of Saloniki (late 4th-century AD) can be very interesting even

for a tourist in a hurry. They are an excellent example of a late-Ancient defensive system.

71 Important Roman historical moments illustrated on the Arch of Galerius at Saloniki: from top to bottom, the emperor lecturing to his troops, the surrender of barbarian chiefs, and a sacrifice.

72 top This bronze "drum" lamp from the mid-4th century BC was found in Philip II of Macedonia's grave treasures (Saloniki, Archaeological Museum).

72 bottom Of great historical importance is the collection of "Attic" sarcophaguses from the 2nd and 3rd century AD kept in the archaeological museum in Saloniki; this example is decorated with reliefs of an epic nature.

72-73 One of the jewels of Macedonian art is the Krater of Dervèni (circa 330 BC). The photograph shows a detail of the gilded bronze reliefs depicting the wedding of Dionysus and Arianna (Saloniki, Archaeological Museum).

73 top right This is the Krater of Dervèni, with large volute handles, elegant reliefs, well-defined figures, and Dionysiac decorations (Saloniki, Archaeological Museum).

73 bottom This gold stud shows the face of Medusa, the monster whose look turned her victim to stone; it is displayed in the Archaeological Museum in Saloniki.

...rilliant are the terrible heads of Heracles inserted like masks in the olutes of the handles, bordered by limy snakes.

The Arch of Galerius (1) was built in 97-303 AD to celebrate the Roman imperial victories in Armenia, Persia and Mesopotamia. This cube-shaped structure was part of a monumental system that connected, on a single axis at right angles to he via Egnatia, the imperial palace (2) to the mausoleum-temple of the deified emperor, he so-called "Rotunda," now the church of ghios Gheòrghios (St. George). The church ill bears mosaics featuring gilded backdrops om the Theodosian period, depicting gures of saints and images of the New erusalem. The arch is the greatest sculptured onument of the Tetrarchic period.

Originally covered by a dome, two of its four huge pillars with high sculptures in relief, depicting Galerius' victories, are still preserved. The relief sculptures, divided by heavy moldings featuring plant motifs, are easily decipherable. They are crowded with figures sculpted in high relief, in rather stereotyped poses, placed without regard to spatial definition or perspective and without any specific order. The battle scenes seem to reproduce models codified for decades in the Middle Hellenistic

Imperial school of decorating sarcophagi with historical motifs. In this particular case however, there is also the rigid hierarchical placement of the Romans above and the Barbarians below, to enhance the ethical and celebrative functions of the decoration. The foreshortenings of exotic landscapes as well as the attempts at reproducing views of the Imperial Tetrarchic palaces are very original. Scholars are still debating the attribution of the arch that seems to have been designed by a single sculptor, yet executed by artists from various schools.

The Hellenistic and Roman *agòra* (4) bears recognizable traces of the 2nd century concert hall or *odeíon* (5) and the porticoes overlooking the square. The Walls of Theodosius (6) are well preserved to the east and north, and were restructured in Medieval times. Early Byzantine art treasures can be seen in the splendid churches of Aghios Dimìtrios (7) and the Panaghìa Ahiropiìtos.

From Saloniki it is possible to reach **OLYNTHOS**. The site takes its name from a town-planning project implemented in the second half of the 5th century BC, in keeping with the grid plan devised by Hippodamus of Miletus. The ancient city, located on the Chalcidic peninsula, was prosperous and independent until its destruction by Philip II of Macedonia in 348 BC. The town is designed on a grid plan, centered around large arteries running from north to south, intersected by straight narrower streets that framed long city blocks (86 by 35 meters). The blocks were divided along the longer axis by a lane for passage, ventilation and drainage, into two rows of five houses with a standardized ground plan. While the layout of the public areas (*agorà, bouleutérion*, etc.), is rather discreet, strictly in keeping with conventional town planning regarding urban traffic, the city's houses present a new design. Residential houses had a more or less standardized ground plan, with rooms around a partly porticoed courtyard.

Each house had a living room,

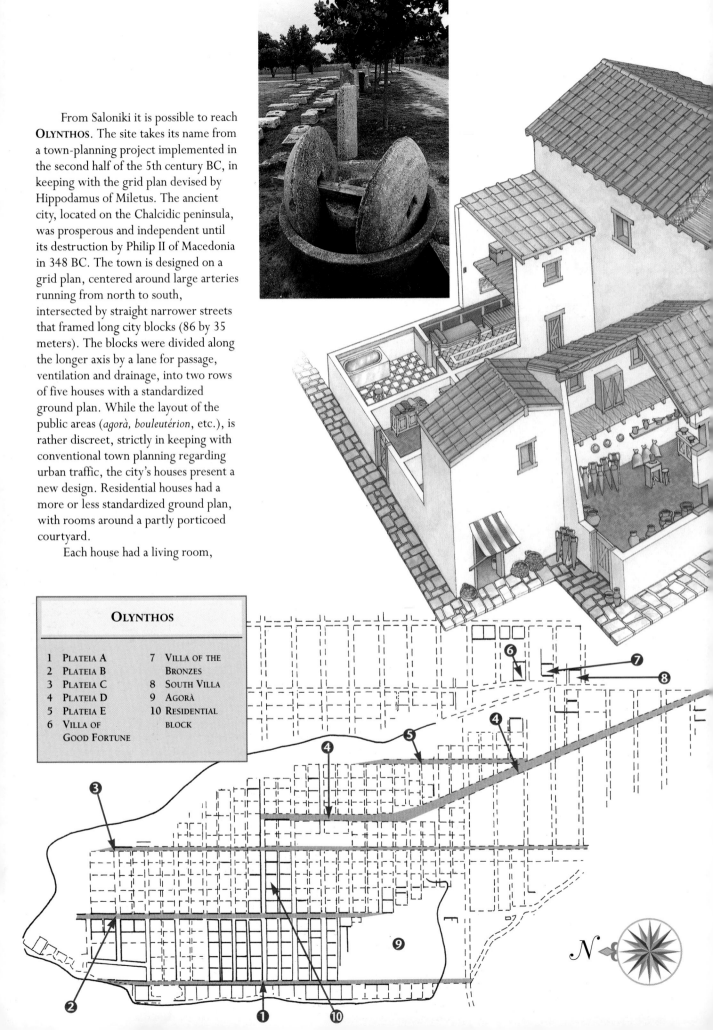

OLYNTHOS

1 PLATEIA A
2 PLATEIA B
3 PLATEIA C
4 PLATEIA D
5 PLATEIA E
6 VILLA OF GOOD FORTUNE
7 VILLA OF THE BRONZES
8 SOUTH VILLA
9 AGORÀ
10 RESIDENTIAL BLOCK

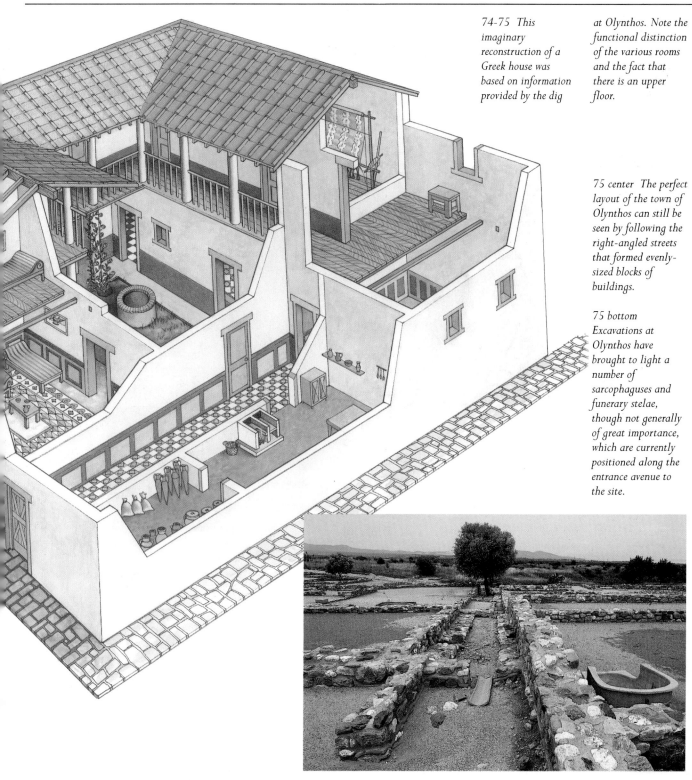

74-75 This imaginary reconstruction of a Greek house was based on information provided by the dig at Olynthos. Note the functional distinction of the various rooms and the fact that there is an upper floor.

75 center The perfect layout of the town of Olynthos can still be seen by following the right-angled streets that formed evenly-sized blocks of buildings.

75 bottom Excavations at Olynthos have brought to light a number of sarcophaguses and funerary stelae, though not generally of great importance, which are currently positioned along the entrance avenue to the site.

74 top This millstone in excellent condition is to be found along the avenue that enters the excavation zone at Olynthos. The millstone came from a 4th-century BC house.

kitchen and a small bathroom. Several houses also had an upper floor, at least covering part of the lower floor.

The luxurious villas to the east of the city, forerunners of future Hellenistic and Roman residential architecture with peristyles, often feature floors decorated with mosaics made from river pebbles, depicting mythological scenes. The best mosaics can be seen in the famous "Villa of Good Fortune" (circa 400 BC).

THRACE

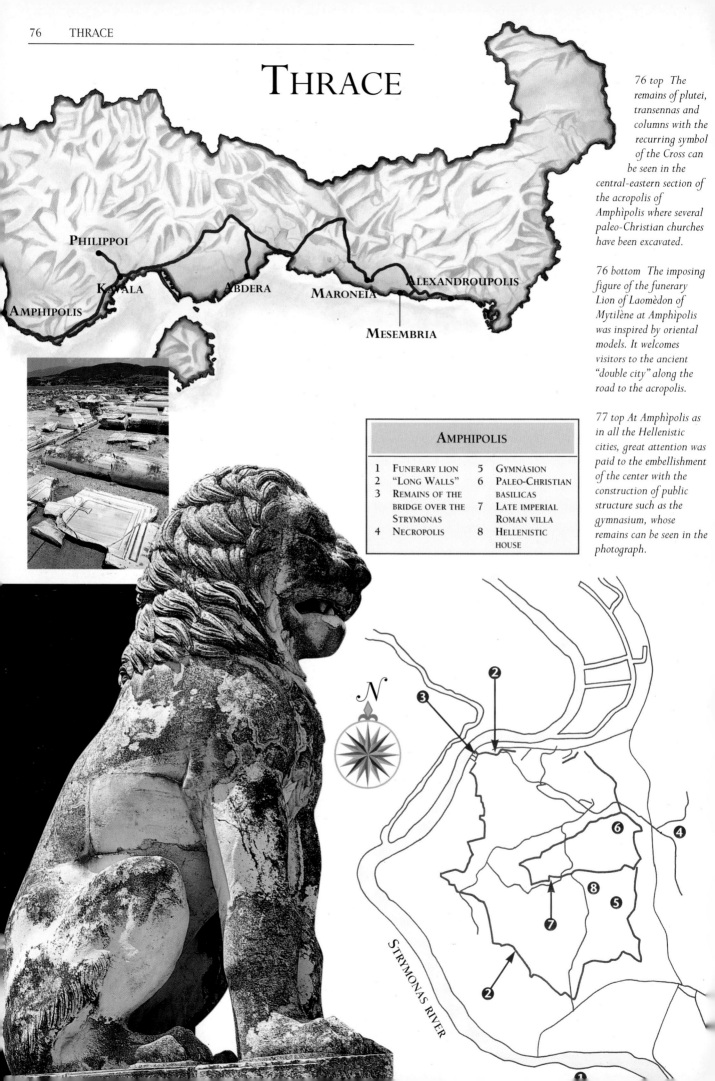

PHILIPPOI

KAVALA

ABDERA

MARONEIA

ALEXANDROUPOLIS

MESEMBRIA

AMPHIPOLIS

76 top The remains of plutei, transennas and columns with the recurring symbol of the Cross can be seen in the central-eastern section of the acropolis of Amphìpolis where several paleo-Christian churches have been excavated.

76 bottom The imposing figure of the funerary Lion of Laomèdon of Mytilène at Amphìpolis was inspired by oriental models. It welcomes visitors to the ancient "double city" along the road to the acropolis.

77 top At Amphìpolis as in all the Hellenistic cities, great attention was paid to the embellishment of the center with the construction of public structure such as the gymnasium, whose remains can be seen in the photograph.

AMPHIPOLIS

1	FUNERARY LION	5	GYMNÀSION
2	"LONG WALLS"	6	PALEO-CHRISTIAN BASILICAS
3	REMAINS OF THE BRIDGE OVER THE STRYMONAS	7	LATE IMPERIAL ROMAN VILLA
4	NECROPOLIS	8	HELLENISTIC HOUSE

STRYMONAS RIVER

Ancient Thrace covered a much wider area than the modern Greek region that bears its name. The western part of what was ancient Thrace now falls in the neighboring region of Macedonia, while all of ancient Thrace to the east of Evros is part of modern Turkey, and the northern part now belongs to Bulgaria. This chapter however only deals with the Thrace that falls into modern Greece. The landscape of Thrace is very varied, dominated by the rugged chain of the Rodòpi mountains to the north. The coast alternates between mountainous cliffs, charming lagoons, woody hills and extensive pastureland. It is easy to imagine Orfeus enchanting wild beasts and moving boulders with his sublime voice.

The region was occupied by the Thracians from the 2nd millennium BC. Their flourishing civilization (8th to 4th centuries BC) was politically structured like an Archaic pyramid with a monarch at its summit, supported by a warrior aristocratic class. Their economy was based on the mineral resources of the main mountain chains. Since Thrace links the Aegean to the Black Sea, the region had to strenuously defend itself against Greek and Macedonian expansionist ambitions. Macedonia managed to conquer the region in the 4th century BC, to be succeeded by the Romans in the 2nd century BC. Created as a province under the Emperor Claudius and repeatedly attacked by Barbarians in the 4th century AD, it regained some of its previous glory under the Eastern Emperor Justinian.

The first stop in Thrace should be **AMPHIPOLIS**, the "dual city" on the banks of the Strymònas, an ancient crossroads. Founded by the Athenians in 437 BC and immediately taken by Sparta (424 BC) and then by the Macedonians (356 BC), it

became the capital of one of the four administrative regions of the Roman province of Macedonia (2nd century BC). It flourished throughout the Roman Imperial period, until the 6th century AD. The tour starts at the Lion of Amphìpolis (1), a grandiose funerary monument built around 300 BC in memory of Laomèdon of Mytilène, admiral of the fleet of Alexander the Great. Although supported by a base less imposing than the ancient plinth, the monument still preserves all the charm of the vigorously expressive stone lion, seated with its jaws apart. On the other side of the river lies the southern stretch of the Long Walls (2) that ran 7.5 kilometers around the hill. The walls featured towers and turreted city gates, large parts of which still stand today. Most of the city walls, in isodomic masonry, seen today date from the renovation of the fortifications,

commenced in the 5th century BC. The walls were completed using the pseudo-isodomic technique between the end of the 3rd and the mid-2nd centuries BC. The most spectacular stretch is in the northwest sector, where exceptional remains of the timber starling of the Classical bridge (3) can still be seen today. The bridge is famous as the scene of the counterattack unleashed here by the Spartan Brasidas during the Peloponnesian War.

To the north, on the east side of the Long Walls, after a section of the Classical and Hellenistic cemeteries, lies the excavation area of the *gymnàsion* (5), that dates from the 3rd to 2nd centuries BC. A staircase, over 15 meters wide and facing east served as the main entrance to the gymnasium, to which a two-columned Ionic *propylon* (entrance gate) was added in the Augustan era. Around the large courtyards, counter-clockwise, lie the athletes' changing and washing rooms (*loùtron*), with marble floors and basins, the shrine (*sacellum*) dedicated to Hermes, the caretaker's office, the wrestling hall with an oval sandpit built into the floor, and the training areas. The courtyard used for religious ceremonies and sacrifices in honor of Heracles lies to the north, and beyond the connecting staircase is the *xystos*, the covered track for races along the single and

77 bottom left The lovely mosaics in the paleo-Christian basilicas at Amphìpolis belong stylistically to a sort of thematic and formal koinè that spread from Macedonia towards Constantinople in the 4th and 5th centuries.

77 bottom right The overturned early Christian sarcophagus from the second half of the 5th century AD decorated with a cross catches the eye among the ruins of the basilica of Amphìpolis.

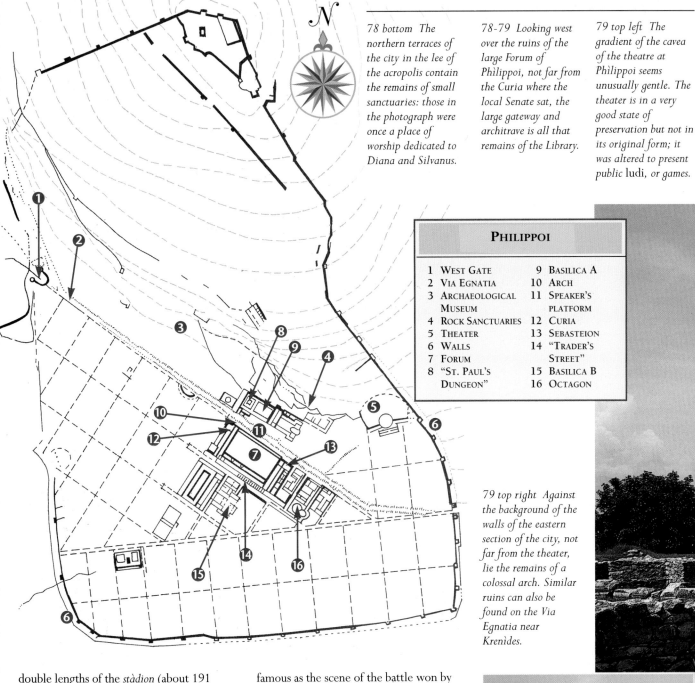

N

78 bottom The northern terraces of the city in the lee of the acropolis contain the remains of small sanctuaries: those in the photograph were once a place of worship dedicated to Diana and Silvanus.

78-79 Looking west over the ruins of the large Forum of Philippoi, not far from the Curia where the local Senate sat, the large gateway and architrave is all that remains of the Library.

79 top left The gradient of the cavea of the theatre at Philippoi seems unusually gentle. The theater is in a very good state of preservation but not in its original form; it was altered to present public ludi, or games.

PHILIPPOI

1	WEST GATE	9	BASILICA A
2	VIA EGNATIA	10	ARCH
3	ARCHAEOLOGICAL MUSEUM	11	SPEAKER'S PLATFORM
4	ROCK SANCTUARIES	12	CURIA
5	THEATER	13	SEBASTEION
6	WALLS	14	"TRADER'S STREET"
7	FORUM	15	BASILICA B
8	"ST. PAUL'S DUNGEON"	16	OCTAGON

79 top right Against the background of the walls of the eastern section of the city, not far from the theater, lie the remains of a colossal arch. Similar ruins can also be found on the Via Egnatia near Krenìdes.

double lengths of the *stàdion* (about 191 meters).

The remains of a few early Christian basilicas (6) dating from the 5th and 6th centuries AD can be seen within the walls of the acropolis. The tour continues with a visit to the ruins of a large Late Imperial Roman villa (7), with mosaic flooring, featuring mythological motifs. Nearby lie the remains of a Hellenistic dwelling (8) featuring rare preserved pieces of painted wall plaster, showing imitations of the paintings that adorned the now lost Hellenistic dynastic palaces. The paintings here are among the oldest in existence. There is a small archaeological museum in the modern village.

The next stop is the archaeological park of **PHILIPPOI**, founded in 360 BC as a colony of Thàsos on the road leading to nearby gold mines. The city was re-founded under its current name by Philip II of Macedonia (356 BC). It was a transit point on the via Egnatia,

famous as the scene of the battle won by Mark Antony and Octavian against the assassins of Julius Caesar (42 BC). A Roman colony since 41 BC, it was assigned a vast centuriation (piece of land divided into more or less equal lots), populated by veterans of the civil wars. It reached the height of its architectural and artistic glory between the 2nd and 3rd centuries AD, and most of the ruins surviving today date from that period. The eastern emperors built splendid Christian buildings here: Philippoi was in fact evangelized by St. Paul, who set up Europe's first Christian community in the city. It is perhaps not mere coincidence that the first martyr in the history of the Western church, St. Lydia, was born here.

The road to Kavàla runs through the turreted Byzantine walls at the ancient West Gate (1), with its circular, three-passage entrance way, flanked by two circular columns. The road runs parallel to the

ancient via Egnatia, the paved surface of which is still well preserved (2). The path leading from the archaeological museum (3) to the theater (5) built into the rocks of the southeastern slope of the acropolis provides a splendid panorama of the vast archaeological area. The path runs through the rocky sanctuaries (2nd and 3rd centuries AD) dedicated to Diana, Cybele, Minerva, Jupiter and the Thracian Knight, a local divinity absorbed into the Roman religion since the time of Augustus (4). On the top of the acropolis hill, one can admire the remains of the Hellenistic walls, in isodomic ashlar (6).

Ruins of the walls of the corridors (pàrodoi) leading to the orchèstra and vestiges of the cavea cut into the rock, are all that remain of the theater that was built at the same time as the city. The crumbling proscenium was built in the Antonine period. In Severan times, the orchèstra was transformed into a circular arena with underground corridors for gladiator competitions, as indicated by votive relief sculptures at the site.

The center of the ancient city is dominated by the square of the Roman Forum (7), one of the largest in the ancient world (about 100 X 50 meters), built under the Emperor Marcus Aurelius. The upper terrace that marked the northern end of the Forum housed the city's Capitolium. There is no trace of the Roman temples and buildings that once adorned this scenic architectural "step." All that remains today is an underground chamber (8) in the courtyard that precedes, to the west, the atrium of Basilica A (9). There is no clear indication of what the chamber was used for, but it has traditionally been called "St. Paul's Dungeon" despite the lack of any evidence to support this. Basilica A is an imposing 5th-century Christian religious complex. The entrance is through a porticoed atrium with a lively architectural sequence on the west side featuring exedrae between niches. Past the narthex, an area reserved for the faithful who were as yet not baptized and directly communicating with a small baptistery to the north, lies the church, with its basilical plan in the shape of a Latin commissa cross, three naves and a central apse bordered by the *synthronon* where the priests used to sit. The presbytery was surrounded by transennae, and a staircase in the central nave led to the crypt below.

The staircase in front of the courtyard of "St. Paul's Dungeon" used to lead towards the podium of the temple built over the underground chamber. The staircase is now interrupted by the via Egnatia (2) and leads to the square of the Forum through an arch (10). The wide paved open area was surrounded by porticoes to the east, south and west, while the north side housed, to deliberately create a spectacular effect, the tribune used by orators (11), quite similar to the *Rostra* of the Forum in Rome, a grand podium decorated by the prows of enemy vessels captured in battle. Two large fountains were placed symmetrically on the

sides. At one corner stood the Curia (12), a Corinthian temple distyle in antis that housed the Senate and administrative offices of the city. At the other corner was the *Sebasteíon* (13), identical in all respects except for the fact that it actually served as a temple, dedicated to the cult of the Emperor under Marcus Aurelius, but built over an earlier chapel dedicated to the gens Julia-Claudia (the Julio-Claudian family). Adjacent to the temple is a long base that once held the

statues of the priests of the cult of Livia Augusta, modified in Antonine times. The large square was flanked to the south by a street, the "Trader's street" (14) featuring porticoes under which a number of shops are still recognizable today. The shops were originally modular, with a top floor. The remains of a luxurious Augustan residence with a mosaic floor also lie on this road.

Basilica B (15), with a narthex preceding the central body, is incomplete. The structure, featuring heavy central columns, was designed around 560 AD based on architectural experiments in Constantinople during the time of the Emperor Justinian (St. Sophia), but the large dome (about 30 m high) collapsed. The baptistery and the elongated, apsed *diakonikón* lie to the sides of the apse of the basilica. Basilica B was built over the meat market (*macellum*) of the Roman city. Several features of the market are still recognizable (such as the curious remains of the public latrine on the south side).

80-81 The design of Basilica B was supposed to be awe-inspiring, as is indicated by the massive pillars that have survived, but an error in the calculation of the proportions was responsible for the collapse of the dome.

81 top This is Basilica A: note the remains of the unfinished marble flooring and the architectural structure. The classical-influenced building was constructed at the end of the 5th century AD.

81 bottom Another view of Basilica B shows the superb marble flooring of the portico or "Trader's Street," one of the main thoroughfares in the Roman city.

The city blocks to the east of the Forum, on the other hand, feature precious remains of the Octagon (16), a basilica with a central plan, linked to the via Egnatia by a columned road preceded by propylaia (entrance gates). The building, which probably sported a dome, was built at the end of the 4th century to replace the earlier Basilica of St. Paul (circa 350 AD). Remains of the earlier structure can be seen in the mosaic flooring with Christian motifs. The basilica was rebuilt in the 6th century.

KAVÀLA, the beautiful coastal city of art, has an interesting archaeological museum that houses rare finds from the

80 top As in the coeval churches of Aghía Sophía in Constantinople and San Vitale in Ravenna, a double order of arches on Corinthian capitals with dosseret regulated the space between the pillars in Basilica B.

80 bottom The photograph shows an example of a "leather leaf" Corinthian capital lying on the ground near Basilica B at Phìlippoi; the design was influenced by models used in Constantinople.

82 In accordance with a practice that was common in the design of Greek theaters, the small theater of Maroneia was set against the slope of the hill looking out over the sea.

82-83 Ancient Mesembrìa, a colony of Samothrace, was easily reached from Alexandroùpoli; the photograph shows part of a 6th-5th century BC building in the town with amphora drainage below the flooring.

83 bottom left The sporadic and modest ruins of Abdera can be seen in the heart of an area of great naturalistic interest and historical importance; this was the homeland of atomist philosophy.

83 bottom right This is another view of the ongoing excavations at Mesembrìa. The site was particularly important during the 7th-5th centuries BC but the Hellenistic era and Roman domination marked its decline.

main cities of Thrace. The collection includes a large number of funerary stelae in relief from the cemeteries at Amphìpolis, famous for the acclaimed painted double tomb. Other interesting pieces include Classical and Hellenistic gold work and remarkable decorated architectural elements from the early Christian basilicas and churches of the region.

At Vafèika, a little beyond Xánthi, capital of the Thracian province of the same name, one can find the excavations at **ABDERA**, a colony of the Ionic Klazomènai (654 BC), which was re-founded by Téos in 543 BC. The city flourished between the 6th and 4th centuries BC (it was home to the great philosophers Leucippos and Democritos, the father of the atomic theory of matter, as well as Protagoras, the greatest of the Sophists). It maintained a certain degree of prosperity even under Macedonian and Ptolemaic domination, but became insignificant in the Roman period. The excavations are along the sea front, south of

the modern village of Avdira. Highlights include the remains of the turreted West Gate (4th cent. BC), the grid plan road network that has been excavated in several places, and the foundations of Hellenistic and Roman houses.

The E90 highway cuts through the memorable landscape of the Vistonída lagoon, and after Komotiní, turns south towards the coast. The archaeological museum at Komotiní houses a rare gold-plated bronze bust of the Roman Emperor Marcus Aurelius and a polychrome mosaic floor featuring vine branches, excavated at Maroneia. The ruins of ancient Maroneia stand among the olive trees that cover the low hills around the village of Aghios Charàlambos and the nearby beach. The remains of the Cyclopean walls of the Thracian city of Ismaros (13th-12th century BC) are not very easy to get to. The same applies to the walls, in polygonal masonry, of the Archaic colony of **MARONEIA**, founded by Chìos in the first half of the 7th

century BC on the hill of Aghios Gheòrghios (St. George). The Classical and Hellenistic city is famous for its Dionysiac sanctuary, some foundational remains of which can still be seen today. The theater, built in the 3rd century BC but completely redesigned during the Roman Imperial period, is especially noteworthy. Rather small (about 25 meters across), and seating "only" 2500 spectators, it still has three rows of seats, the *skenè* and the *orchèstra*, later enclosed by a high protective balustrade to transform it into an arena for gladiator battles and games using wild beasts.

ACARNANIA, AETOLIA AND PHOCIS

84 top The remains of an interesting group of houses from the late Bronze Age (13th-12th centuries BC) can be seen near the temple of Apollo at Thermos. Worthy of note are several examples of apsidal ground plans.

84 bottom left The theater at Stratos has been recently excavated and is dated by some to the 4th century BC. During the Middle Ages and more recently it was stripped of materials to build houses in the nearby village, since abandoned.

This interesting itinerary running across central Greece lets one reach the famous sanctuary of Apollo Pythios at Delphi, one of the greatest archaeological sites in the world. From Aktion – whose vast enchanting lake saw in 31 BC the fleets of Octavian battling those of Mark Antony and Cleopatra VII of Egypt – one goes towards Amphilochìa, a gracious coastal town on the Amvrakikós Gulf. From here one reaches **STRATOS** 30 km southeast, on the right bank of the mythical river

by buildings but served to provide food and a point of refuge for the rural population and cattle in the case of war or siege.

The temple, built against the walls, dates from the 4th century BC. The peripteral temple hexastyle (6 x 11 columns), was never completed as indicated by the lack of finishing detail. The structure is interesting because of the strong presence of Archaicisms such as the proportional ratio (1:2) and its length (100 feet), side by side with much later concepts

The archaeological museum at Agrìnio houses materials found at various excavation sites around the region. To the east lies the road that follows the northern shore of the crystalline Lake Trichonìda, leading to the ruins of **THERMOS**, where the Aetolian League, in the federal sanctuary of Apollo Thèrmios, founded its prestigious administrative center.

The *témenos* is surrounded on three sides by walls in raw brick dating from the end of the 3rd century BC. The walls feature

Acheloòs.

The large archaeological site features ruins dating from the 5th to the 2nd centuries BC, when the ancient capital of Acarnania was at the peak of its glory. Along the road leading from the modern village to the famous temple of Zeus Stràtios, one can easily recognize the remains of imposing city walls, which cover three hills. The walls were built in the 5th century BC but were later extended to run for 4 km, when several smaller Acarnanian settlements joined together to form a single city (a process known technically as synoecism), in 314 BC. The walls, in pseudo-isodomic masonry, have over 50 rectangular towers and about 20 gateways and smaller emergency exits. As at Dodona in Epirus, even in Stratos, it is reasonable to think that most of the space within the walls was not taken up

including a combination of Doric and Ionic architectural elements (such as the Doric peristasis, pronaos and opisthodomos both distyle *in antis* and the Ionic tripartite architrave as well as the Ionic colonnade on three sides of the cella).

Passing through the southern gate, preceded by and locked between stout towers, one reaches the early Hellenistic *agorà*, partly lying on a scenic artificial terrace and bordered by a portico. The terrace provides a panoramic view of the structure of the theater still under excavation and perhaps dating from the 4th century BC. Also clearly visible is the contour of the thick wall, the *diateíchisma*, that ran north-south, dividing the city in half. This wall was intended to reduce the area to be defended so as to concentrate resources in case of attack.

rectangular towers and two scee gates, one of which is flanked by circular towers. The most interesting structure inside the *témenos* is the temple of Apollo Thèrmios. The foundations dating from about 625 BC are all that remain of the temple today. The temple has a very Archaic elongated rectangular plan (the ratio between length and width is more than 1:3). The cella with its two entrances is enclosed by a peribolos of five by 15 columns, originally built in timber on stone bases and later (in about 450 BC) done completely in stone. The cella does not have a pronaos but features a deep opisthodomos on its north side. It is divided into two aisles by a row of ten pillars that helped support the hip roof, ending in a triangular tympanum to the south and a pavilion tympanum to the north. The size of the building, nearly 40 meters long, gives an idea of the technical possibilities available to Early Archaic builders, who combined the resistance and durability of stone with the flexibility of a timber frame and also adopted the low-cost solution of using wood and raw brick for non-supporting structures. One can still admire the lightness of the roof in clay tiles and the architectural paneling in painted terracotta, among the oldest of its kind and certainly attributable to Corinthian craftsmen.

The remains of the foundations of the so-called *Mègaron* B, the small temple building (21 x 7 m) that pre-dated the Archaic building described above, are hardly recognizable. The small temple consisted of a pronaos, cella and *àdyton* with the back walls slightly apsed, and was built during the 9th century BC. In the next century, it seems to have been fitted with an elliptical peristasis made of timber poles that enclosed its west, north and east sides, one of the first examples of outer perimetral support. The

85 top The ruins of the port buildings at Oiniàdai exist beside those of the marsh at Melíte. A series of paths provide a short and attractive route around the ancient city.

remains of the even older (13th-12th century BC) *Mègaron* A are clearly recognisable close to the north-western corner of the Archaic temple. Similar in size to the other *mègaron*, this structure features an apsed *àdyton*, included in a group of houses from the same period. Little remains of the monumental *stoaí*. The *stoaí* dating from the 3rd century BC housed works of art sacked by the Macedonians when they destroyed the sanctuary in 218 BC.

The museum is very interesting for its collection of Archaic polychrome architectural terracotta elements, masterpieces of Corinthian work.

The E55 highway leads from Lake Trichonìda up to Kefalòvrisso where the road turns towards Aetolikò, passing through the splendid landscape of the delta

of the Achelòos and the Messolónghi lagoon, to reach Katochì, from where a secondary road leads to the archaeological site of **OINIÀDAI**, about 10 km away. The site lies on a low hill overlooking the marshy area of Melíte, which in ancient times was a lagoon linked to a branch of the Achelòos delta by a canal. The city flourished especially under Philip V of Macedonia, who conquered it in 219 BC. The turreted city walls are about 7 km long and are built using the polygonal (6th century BC) and isodomic techniques with arched gates (3rd century BC). The city had a well-equipped port and remains of hauling ramps and a jetty that were perhaps once part of the naval port, are still well-preserved today. The small 3rd-century BC theater features 20 rows of cavea seats still in good condition.

84 bottom right This graceful Hellenistic fountain stands at the opposite end of the area of the temple dedicated to Apollo Thèrmios. It is still fed by a spring unusually consecrated to the brother of Artemis.

85 bottom The cavea in the theater of Oiniàdai, seen here from the topmost row, is well preserved. Note the many flights of steps that divide the hemicycle into evenly sized sections.

On the E55 towards Messolónghi, it is well worth you taking the rather tiresome detour to visit the ruins of **NEA PLEURON**, on the lowest western slopes of the Arákynthos. The city, built on a natural terrace with a view of the sea, has spectacular pseudo-isodomic and trapezoidal walls, with seven gates (230 BC) and at least 30 towers served by stairways. Apart from the extraordinary walls, the portico and gymnasium close to the wide *agorà* are also worthy of note, together with a large communal cistern to the west. City districts were arranged according to function, the residential district lying to the south and the sacred area to the north of the *agorà*, making Nea Pleuron a good example of Hellenistic town planning. The small theater features a few structural curiosities such as its placement in a rectangular structure and the fact that the proscenium is built against the inner face of the city walls that date from the same period.

A little past Messolónghi, badly sign-posted roads make it difficult to find, to the left of the E55, the dirt road leading to the large archaeological site of **KALYDON**. This Aetolian city is associated with the feats of the hero Meleager and the famous myth of the hunt of the Kalydonian boar. It is also the site of a very sacred shrine to Artemis Làphria (8th-3rd centuries BC). The turreted city walls in sandstone and gravel are partly open to visitors. The remains of the so-called *heròon* and the *Artemìsion* bear ample witness to the glory of the city. The *heròon*, long thought to have been a sanctuary consecrated to a hero, is now clearly identified from its ground plan as a gymnasium. It was built by the inhabitants of the city in honor of

the citizen Lèon and his wife Kráteia for their contributions to the city (110-100 BC). Around a peristyle courtyard reserved for gymnastics and accessible from the north, were a meeting room and banquet halls, as well as recreational and educational game rooms. There was also a chapel with an altar in honor of Lèon depicted in a heroic pose with his family, to indicate the hero buried in the underground chamber below the chapel. The chamber can only be accessed from outside the building. It features two sarcophagi in the shape of funerary beds in which were found urns containing ashes. The walls were painted with plant motifs, a common grave decoration. The path leads to the remains of the southwestern gate that opens on to the straight sacred road that linked the city to the sanctuary.

86 bottom The temple of Apollo Làphrios can be easily reached from the end of the sacred area at Kalydòn. As with the larger temple of Artemis, only the foundations survive.

86-87 Another interesting example of a theatrical building deserving of a visit is at Nea Pleuron. Its position is especially dramatic, in sight of the marshy plain of the river Achelòos.

87 top With a little effort, but rewarded with great satisfaction, visitors can complete the circle of the defensive walls at Nea Pleuron, a section of which can be seen in the photograph.

87 bottom It seems as though extreme care was taken — as often occurred in the ancient world — in the construction of the large tank at Nea Pleuron which supplied water to the inhabitants during its centuries of existence.

Past the foundations of a few Archaic and Classical *thesauroì* lies a wide artificial terrace, where the *Làphria* (nocturnal rites in honor of Artemis) were celebrated. Overlooking the terrace are the remains of a large Hellenistic stoà with a central colonnade. The large temple of Artemis, rebuilt several times between the 7th and 4th centuries BC, lies beyond a small propylon (entrance building) once sumptuously decorated by marble eaves. The temple itself was covered by terracotta decorations as important as those found at the temple of Apollo at Thèrmos. The foundations (4th century BC) visible today once supported a Classical Doric peripteral temple hexastyle. Nearby lie the foundations of the small temple of Apollo Làphrios (575-550 BC).

DELPHI

DELPHI is the last thrilling stop on this tour of Acarnania, and is reached by following the coast of Aetolia and Phocis, from Náfpaktos to Itéa, to climb towards Mt. Parnassòs, so dear to Apollo and the Muses. Large tracts of the area are immersed in the so-called "sea of olives." The rust-colored twin limestone peaks of the Phaidriades seem to materialize suddenly out of nowhere, rising steeply above the ruins of the sacred city of Apollo. The famous sanctuary of Apollo Pythios was built around the end of the 9th century BC on the site of a previous Mycenaean settlement (15th-12th centuries BC) that, it seems, was already an important cult center. According to the myth, Apollo killed Python the dragon-snake son of Ghè (or Gaia, the Great Mother Earth), who was also the guardian of the rocky chasm from which Ghè released vapors that induced a trance-like state, during which the subject acquired prophetic powers. Once again at Delphi, therefore, an Olympian deity stole, not entirely with impunity, the place of an ancient divinity. This generally indicates the arrival of the latest Indo-European wave in Greece, and is almost inevitably followed by the further development and expansion of Hellenic civilization.

In any case, Apollo usurped the site and the prophetic powers of the mysterious, primordial natural force that was released from the chasm, delegating to a priestess, the Pythia, the task of expressing and divulging his wishes through ambiguous oracles, interpreted by a special board of priests.

These religious prerogatives and well-advised relationships that the priests of the sanctuary maintained with the *pòleis*, made Delphi, the mythical "navel of the world," one

88 top This large òmphalos *ringed by a wool mesh is a copy from the Roman era of the symbol of Delphi, the "navel of the world"; it was originally in the* àdyton *of the temple of Apollo (Delphi, Archaeological Museum).*

of the greatest political epicenters of antiquity. The exceptional wealth of the sanctuary – in terms of both economic resources and donated art treasures – is clear from the 7th century BC. Inside the *témenos*, at the temple of Apollo, the god himself, through prophecy and answers, authorized or vetoed all the proposed actions of the Greek people and (at least from the 6th century BC) of a large number of non-Greeks who consulted the Pythia, from the founding of the earliest colonies up to the wars. It is solely for this reason that, between the 6th and 4th century BC, "sacred" wars were fought and strong tensions built up around the city of Apollo's oracle.

The large ruins of several imposing buildings dedicated to shows and games (the stadium, the theater, the gymnasium and the *palaestra*) bear witness to the im-

portance of the Pythia, the Pythian Games, held every four years. In addition to sports competitions, these games also featured "championships" in the performing arts (music, singing, dance and theater, inspired by and in honor of Apollo, patron divinity of these arts). Over time, a large number of various types of buildings sprung up around the temple of the son of Zeus and Latona at Delphi. The most important of these are the *thesauroì*, or "treasures," small temple-like museums built to hold the precious votive offerings made to the divinity. The treasures also served as tools of political propaganda, boosting Delphi's prestige not only in a large number of Helladic city-states but also in the eyes of the Etruscans. The city abounded with all sorts of structures more beautiful than useful, altars and works of art. From the 6th century BC to the 4th century AD, successive governments, tyrants, and later, sovereigns and high-ranking magistrates, commissioned hundreds of buildings that have come to light thanks to the excavations that commenced at the end of the 19th century. Much of this archaeological evidence has confirmed information provided by Pausanias in his *Guide to Greece* written in the Antonine period.

88 bottom The Treasury of the Athenians was erected at an important point on the Sacred Way, at the "elbow" between the first and second ramps. The remains of votive monument bases can be seen in the foreground.

88-89 This view of the Treasury of the Athenians is taken from Hàlos, where Python was supposed to have lived before the advent of Apollo; the ruins of the Stoà of the Athenians can be seen on the right.

89 right A beautiful panorama can be admired during the climb along the Sacred Way, which looks over the "sea of olives," the valley in which tens of thousands of olive trees grow.

DELPHI
SANCTUARY OF APOLLO PYTHIOS

1 SOUTHEAST GATE
2 ROMAN AGORÀ
3 SACRED WAY
4 BASE OF THE BULL OF KERKYRA
5 MONUMENT TO THE ADMIRALS OF SPARTA
6 MONUMENT TO THE TRIUMPHS OVER THE PERSIANS AT ATHENS
7 OFFERING CONTAINER OF THE ARCADIANS
8 MONUMENT TO THE HEROES OF ARGOS
9 MONUMENT TO THE KINGS OF ARGOS
10 THESAUROS OF SIKYON
11 THESAUROS OF SIPHNOS

12 THESAUROS OF ATHENS
13 SACRED ROCKS AND SPRINGS
14 PILLAR OF THE NÀXIOI
15 STOÀ OF THE ATHENIANS
16 ALTAR OF THE TEMPLE OF APOLLO PYTHIOS
17 BASES OF THE GOLD TRIPODS OF SYRACUSE
18 BASE OF THE STATUE OF APOLLO SITÀLKAS
19 BASE OF THE PILLAR OF AEMILIUS PAULUS
20 PILLAR OF PRUSIAS
21 TEMPLE OF APOLLO PYTHIOS
22 THEATER
23 STADIUM

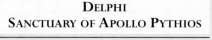

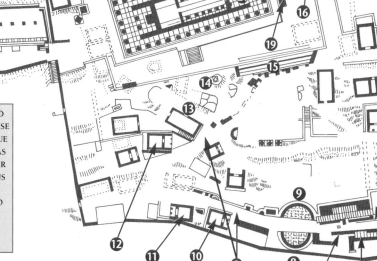

The entrance to the archaeological area of the sanctuary of Apollo Pythios is located at the southeastern corner of the *témenos*. The sacred walls, built between the 6th and 5th centuries BC using large blocks that are sometimes polygonal and sometimes parallelepiped in shape, have nine gates, the largest of which is precisely at this point (1), on the western side of the Roman *agorà* (2), a Roman Imperial rectangular forum-like plaza. The plaza is flanked to the north by a Ionic portico dating from the 5th-6th centuries AD. The portico is all that remains of a facelift given to Delphi when it was an archbishopric, before being destroyed during the Slavic invasion. To the north lie the ruins of shops that once sold votive objects and religious souvenirs.

The solemn processions along the tortuous Sacred Way (3) left from here. The Sacred Way is a paved road that houses, from its very beginning, an impressive number of bases of monuments built by major *pòleis* between the 5th and 4th

centuries BC, to commemorate important historical events. These monuments were clearly also used for propaganda purposes, featuring works by the most prestigious artists of the time, and bearing epigraphs that are still legible today. An exception to this general rule is the base to the right (4) on which the Corcyreans (the inhabitants of Kèrkyra or Corfu) built a huge bronze bull (in 480 BC) to thank Apollo for a miraculous catch of tuna. The votive monuments decorated with splendid bronze statues, now only identifiable by the bases on both sides of the Sacred Way, are clearly political, self-celebratory and polemic. These include the grandiose Monument of the Admirals (5), built by the Spartans, one year after their decisive victory over Athens in the naval battle of Aigospotamoì (405 BC), during the Peloponnesian War. Another is the monument celebrating the victories at Marathon and at the Eurimedòn (6), commissioned by the head of the Athenian government, Cimon, son of the

famous general Miltiades, to immortalize the victories his city and family scored against the Persians in 467 BC. Other such monuments include the Offering Container of the Arcadians (7), which celebrated the liberation of the Peloponnesians after the victories over Sparta (371 and 362 BC), the Monument to the Heroes of Argos (8) dated at 456 BC; and the Monument to the Kings of Argos dating back to 371 BC; both built to celebrate humiliating defeats inflicted on the hated Spartans. These two monuments stand face to face on two symmetrical exedrae.

A little further down the road are a series of *thesauroì*, small temple-like museums dedicated by *pòleis* all over the Mediterranean to the glory of Apollo. These structures were built to house the often precious offerings, amounting to 10% of all war booty or other forms of wealth attributed to the favor of the god. Only the foundations of many of these structures survive today and their builders remain uncertain. One of these is the *thesauròs* of

90-91 *The dating of the Treasury of the Athenians to 490 BC is based on a passage taken from the writings of Pausanias and the inscription on the triangular terrace of the Donary of Marathon (not visible in the photo).*

91 left *A good example of the island's Ionic Archaic sculpture is the Sphinx that decorated the top of* the column dedicated to Apollo by the inhabitants of Nàxos (Delphi, Archaeological Museum).

91 right *The "cyclopean" polygonal construction technique used in Mycenaean Greece was taken up by the architect that designed the Stoà of the Athenians in 478 BC in the lee of the terrace of the temple of Apollo.*

Sikyon (10), opening on a Doric distyle *in antis* built around 500 BC on foundations made from blocks scavenged from two previous buildings, one of which bore precious middle Archaic metopes (now in the museum).

The most beautiful Delphic *thesaurós* is certainly the treasure of Siphnos, a rich Cycladic island (11). Only the foundations are currently at the site, since the superstructure with its two Caryatids *in antis* and the precious sculptured decorations (530-525 BC) have been shifted to the museum.

The *thesaurós* of Athens (12), on the other hand, built soon after the battle of Marathon (490 BC) is nearly intact, thanks to efforts to restore it. A little larger than the treasure of Siphnos is another Doric structure distyle *in antis*: note the simple harmony of the proportions and the metope frieze alternating with triglyphs, depicting Theseus' victory over the Amazons and the heroic feats of Heracles, still expressed through the late Archaic figurative language. This has led some experts to believe that the foundations date from the end of the 6th century BC. In the midst of the desolate destruction that lies strewn around this stretch of the Sacred Way, it is difficult to imagine the splendid architectural spectacle, with hundreds of artworks, that greeted ancient pilgrims at the beginning of the second ramp. Halfway up the ramp, to the left, lie the rocks at which, according to myth, Sibyl, the first Pythia, spoke her prophecies and where Apollo killed Python.

The sacred springs, now dried up, are not open to visitors. They are probably the basis of the ancient origins of the cult. On the summit of the third rock lies the base of a pillar. This is all that remains of the very high 10 meters) Pillar of the Nàxioi (14) built by the inhabitants of the island of Nàxos at the same time as the temple they built in honor of Apollo on his native island, Delos (570-560 BC). A winged Sphinx was placed at the top of the Ionic capital (now at the museum).

A little ahead is another monument associated with the glory of democratic Athens, dating from 478 BC, the year in which the Delio-Attican League was founded. Built against the high wall containing and supporting the terrace on which the temple of Apollo Pythios was built, lie the remains of the long, elegant Stoà of the Athenians (15). The polygonal masonry of the wall against which the stoà was built bears hundreds of perfectly executed Hellenistic epigraphs, mostly decrees granting freedom to slaves. The stoà itself, a Ionic portico in Parian marble and

timber, was meant as a memorial and "museum" area for objects consecrated to Apollo. It also acts as a showpiece of Athens' might, bearing the prows of captured Persian vessels and the *gòmene* (flax cables) taken from the pontoon bridge that Xerxès threw over the Hellespont in 480 BC, using boats lashed together, as indicated in the inscription on the stylobate. The Sacred Way continues through the eastern wall of the terrace of Apollo, in the midst of monuments and *thesauroì*. The altar of the temple (16), a sumptuous gift from the inhabitants of Chìos (478 AD), is built in white and bluish marble, on a gray base. Other highlights include the twin bases (17) on which the tyrants Gelon and Hieron of Syracuse placed the golden tripods to commemorate Magna Grecian victories against the Carthaginians (in 480 BC) and

Etruscans (in 474 BC). The high base of the colossal statue of Apollo Sitàlkas (18) was built around 355 BC by the member cities of the Delphic Amphictyony. Almost at the southeastern corner of the temple, the base of the famous Pillar of Lucius Aemilius Paulus (19) is recognizable. The pillar was built to commemorate the Roman victory at Pidna in 167 AD that marked the end of the Macedonian Empire. A marble frieze illustrates the battle, in keeping with the typical Roman tendency towards "historiography," although the artistic expression is clearly of Greek inspiration. It is now in the garden of the museum. To erase all doubts as to who were then the new powers in the Mediterranean, however, the Roman Consul demanded the epigraph to be written in Latin, the language of the new conquerors, and the entire monument to be

92 top The open space in front of the entrance to the temple of Apollo was heavily decorated with works of art: in the foreground, note the bases of the gold tripods of Gelon and Hieron of Syracuse; further forward, the high Pillar of Prusias.

92 center Outside the west side of the sacred enclosure of Apollo stand the remains of the largest stoà in Delphi, erected by the cities in the Aetolic League after their defeat of the Galatian invaders.

92 bottom right The only elements still visible on the Doric colonnade in the temple of Apollo are on the east side of the building. The columns were made from tufa and lined with white plaster in an imitation of marble.

92-93 The cavea of the theater at Delphi inclines gently from the lee of Mount Helikòn, the mountain on which the Muses of Apollo lived and shared the institution and honors of the Pythian Games with the god.

93 bottom left Opposite the eastern façade of the temple of Apollo, to the left, remains of the altar are visible, placed as in all ancient buildings on the outside; the cella itself was the house of the god.

93 bottom right Here is a splendid image of the Stadium in which the sporting portion of the Pythian Games were held; the pillars in the foreground (with two niches for statues) supported a three-fornix arch.

situated in the location of one of the greatest sanctuaries of the ancient world. Near the northeastern corner, to the right of the Sacred Way lies, reconstructed in all its imposing glory, the Pillar of Prusias (20), dedicated by the Aetolians to Prusias II, king of Bithynia, to celebrate his victory over the Galatians in 182 BC. The remains of the temple of Apollo (21) date from its sixth reconstruction (373 BC)

and followed the shape and dimensions of the preceding structure (548-514 BC). The sixth reconstruction was commissioned by a powerful aristocratic family from Athens, the Alcmaeonids. It is a Classical Doric peripteral temple, hexastyle (6 x 15 columns in plastered tufa, like the walls), with a bluish limestone base (about 60 x 23 meters) built over a beehive

of artificial terraces. The cella, peristasis, pronaos and opisthodomos were decorated with works of art running along historical and religious lines, some of which can still be seen today. A staircase at the back of the cella led to the *àdyton* of the Pythia, at the center of which stood the *òmphalos*, the sacred navel of the world, preceded by the bronze tripod that covered the chasm in

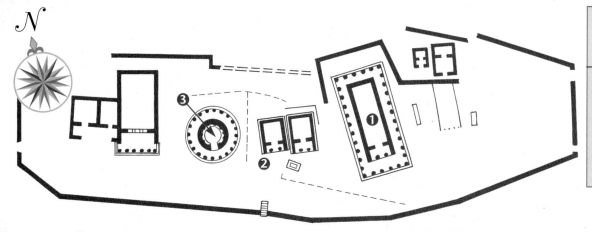

SANCTUARY OF
ATHENA PRONAIA

1. TEMPLE OF
ATHENA
2. THESAUROS OF
MASSALIA
3. THOLOS (HEROON
OF PHYLAKOS)

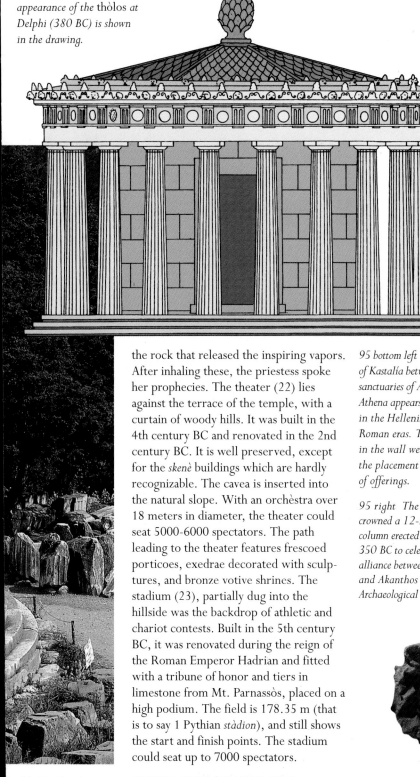

95 top left The original appearance of the thòlos at Delphi (380 BC) is shown in the drawing.

the rock that released the inspiring vapors. After inhaling these, the priestess spoke her prophecies. The theater (22) lies against the terrace of the temple, with a curtain of woody hills. It was built in the 4th century BC and renovated in the 2nd century BC. It is well preserved, except for the *skenè* buildings which are hardly recognizable. The cavea is inserted into the natural slope. With an orchèstra over 18 meters in diameter, the theater could seat 5000-6000 spectators. The path leading to the theater features frescoed porticoes, exedrae decorated with sculptures, and bronze votive shrines. The stadium (23), partially dug into the hillside was the backdrop of athletic and chariot contests. Built in the 5th century BC, it was renovated during the reign of the Roman Emperor Hadrian and fitted with a tribune of honor and tiers in limestone from Mt. Parnassòs, placed on a high podium. The field is 178.35 m (that is to say 1 Pythian *stàdion*), and still shows the start and finish points. The stadium could seat up to 7000 spectators.

95 bottom left The Spring of Kastalía between the sanctuaries of Apollo and Athena appears as it looked in the Hellenistic and Roman eras. The niches in the wall were used for the placement of offerings.

95 right The "Dancers" crowned a 12-meter high column erected in 375-350 BC to celebrate the alliance between Sparta and Akanthos (Delphi, Archaeological Museum).

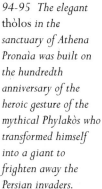

94-95 The elegant thòlos in the sanctuary of Athena Pronaìa was built on the hundredth anniversary of the heroic gesture of the mythical Phylakòs who transformed himself into a giant to frighten away the Persian invaders.

Outside the sanctuary of Apollo, along the road leading to the sanctuary of Athena Pronaìa lie, in a romantic setting, the remains of two fountains (one Archaic and the other Hellenistic in style) that collected the waters of the Sacred Spring of Kastalìa. The Pythia used to ritually wash her hair in the spring before any physical contact with Apollo. A little ahead lie the rather scanty remains of the *gymnàsion*. Smaller than the sanctuary of Pythian Apollo, the sanctuary of Athena Pronaìa stands on an artificial terrace partially enclosed by walls featuring polygonal masonry. Among the most interesting monuments is the Archaic temple of Athena (1), a Doric peripteros hexastyle dating from the end of the 6th century BC. The temple was heavily damaged during a landslide in 480 BC (restoration work led to the walling in of the spaces between columns to the north) and was long frequented by visitors. Another landslide in 1905 completed the demolition of the temple (boulders can be seen in the area today, amid the tumble of column debris). A little ahead lies the base of the Treasure of Massalia (2) (present-day Marseilles) built towards 535-530 BC. This small Ionic temple, distyle *in antis* (bearing a splendid molding on the base) once featured rare Aeolian capitals (now at the museum). The splendid *thòlos* (3) is a rare example of a temple with a circular ground plan, a masterpiece by the Phocian architect Theòdoros (380-370 BC). The structure, now identified as the *heròon* of Phylakòs, who defended the sanctuary against the Persian threat in 480 BC is clearly Attic in proportions and style, especially in the outer *peribolos* with 20

96 *This splendid male head, perhaps of a god, was made from gold and ivory (550-530 BC) and found* in a deposit of votive offerings along the Sacred Way in 1939 (Delphi, Archaeological Museum).

96-97 *The frieze from the treasure of Siphnos is a masterpiece of Ionic sculpture from the late Archaic era; the slab in the picture is decorated with a dramatic battle scene between Gods and Giants (Delphi, Archaeological Museum).*

97 bottom *The koùroi of the twins Klèobis and Byton were some of the first examples of large stone Archaic statuary; the religiousness of the twins was rewarded by the gods (Delphi, Archaeological Museum).*

Doric columns. Theòdoros' genius shines through, particularly in the way he dealt with the tricky spatial organization inside the rather cramped cella, which features 10 elegant Corinthian columns in white Pentelic marble, running tangent to the walls and placed on a high base in dark limestone from Mt. Eleusis. The Doric frieze with metopes in low relief, the lacunar ceiling with diamond-shaped coffers, and the eaves indicate a decorative intention that is no longer rigidly based on Classical aesthetic criteria.

A visit to the archaeological museum at Delphi is a must for a complete tour of the excavations. The museum's collection includes all the archaeological findings of Greek and French researchers since 1892. Even the most hurried visitor should not miss the masterpieces of the twin statues of the *koùroi* Klèobis and Byton, by Polymèdes of Argos (590-580 BC). Other highlights include the western pediment of the late Archaic temple of Apollo depicting the gods in Delphi from the land of the Hyperboreans on a four-horse chariot, a masterpiece by the Athenian Antenòr (515-510 BC); the famous Auriga, one of the highest expressions of early Classical plastic art (475 BC), from the monument of the tyrant Polyzelos of Gela, who commissioned the work to commemorate his victory in the chariot race; and the marble copies of the monument of the Thessalian tetrarch Dàochos II at Phàrsalus (now Farsala) (336-332 BC), a masterpiece by the great sculptor Lysippus.

BOEOTIA AND EUBOEA

The Boeotia of Oedipus, Eteocles and Polynices, of Antigone and Dirce, mythical characters immortalized by the tragic poets, the proud Boeotia celebrated by Hesiod, the wild Boeotia of Dionysus and the Muses, is a rolling sunny plain, only slightly interrupted by a few irregularities in the terrain. Surrounded by high mountains, the province is no longer broken by Lake Kopaís, drained of its water in the name of agriculture. From Thessaly, it can be reached by crossing the Phthiotida river and the

beginning of Macedonian hegemony over Greek cities. The monument is 5.5 meters high and depicts a lion sitting on a stepped plinth, in the center of a cemetery in which 254 hoplites of the Sacred Band of Thebans, lie buried. Towards the river, a few kilometers to the east, lies the large (70 meters across) Macedonian funerary Tumulus. On the north slope of the hill, to the south of the modern village is the well-preserved cavea of the 5th-century BC theater, hewn into the rock. The orchèstra

overlooking the Kopaís plain. The small theater (4th-3rd century BC), once the scene of feasts in honor of the Chàrites, the goddesses that inspired grace in artists, stands close to the ancient Byzantine church of Kìmissis tìs Theotókou (Convent of the Sleep of the Virgin). The church is built with materials stripped from earlier structures, over a Mycenaean construction. Next to the theater is the splendid *thòlos* (round chamber) tomb known as the "Treasury of Minyàs." Very similar in size and ground plan to the

Thermopyles mountains, where a modern monument commemorates the sacrifice of Leonidas and 300 Spartan hoplites during the First Persian war in 490 BC. .

It is best to start the tour at the birthplace of the biographer and moralist, Plutarch. The modern village of Cherònia lies close to the ancient city of **CHAIRONEIA**, scene of the battle (338 BC) between the invincible army of Philip II of Macedonia and the coalition of Thebans, Athenians, Megarians, Phocians and Corinthians brought together by the efforts of Demosthenes. The funerary monument of the Thebans bears solemn witness to this battle that marked the

was transformed in the first century AD to serve as an arena for gladiator battles. The archaeological museum close to the Lion of the Thebans, houses interesting Neolithic, Helladic, Mycenaean and Classical archaeological finds, including grave objects from the funerary tumulus dating from 338 BC.

The next stop is **ORCHOMENOS**, which bears the same name as the ancient Arcadian city. Ancient Orchomenòs was the largest city in Mycenaean Boeotia and was the rival of Thebes for hegemony over the region between the 8th and 4th centuries BC. The acropolis dominated the Kephissus river,

famous "Treasure of Atreus" at Mycenae, the *thòlos* tomb features a long, wide entrance passage or *dròmos*, a trilithon door of impressive height with an architrave fashioned from a six-meter-long stone block. The domed ceiling of the circular chamber has partly collapsed. The burial chamber or *thàlamos* was paneled with green tiles decorated with rosettes, spirals and floral motifs that can also be seen in the ceramics produced during the same period (14th to 13th century BC).

On a low island in the Kopaís plain stand the spectacular ruins of **GLÀ**, perhaps the ancient Mycenaean city of Arne, which flourished and was abandoned during the 13th century BC. The Cyclopean walls in polygonal masonry were over five meters thick (only about three meters of which have survived), run for almost three kilometers and are interrupted by four gates. After entering through the southeastern gate, one should head left to the Mycenaean "palace," an L-shaped structure with a large number of rooms spread over two floors around two *mègara*. The palace lies on the northern edge of the acropolis, a trapezoidal area enclosed by walls. A wall running east-west clearly demarcates the so-called *agorà*, a plaza bordered by warehouses and the homes of their administrators. Not far from Glà lie the ruins of the large sanctuary of Apollo Ptóios, on the hill of Ptóion, near the ancient spring of Perdiko Vrìssi. The complex prospered for centuries (7th to first centuries BC) at the site of the ancient cult and oracle of the local hero Ptòos. The sanctuary lies on three stepped terraces. The current layout probably dates from the end of the 4th century BC. The peripteral Doric temple octastyle, dedicated to the god, reflects the shape and proportions of the first temple (7th century BC), and lies on the lowest terrace. Northwest of the temple is the oracular spring, while the upper terraces contain a water system and porticoes. A few Archaic *koùroi* statues of Boeotian, Attic and Cycladic design were taken from here (they are now in the museums of Athens and Thebes).

98 top There are few Greek theaters in which the cavea is dug out of the rock rather than lined with blocks of stone or marble; one of the best preserved is that of Chairòneia (5th c. BC).

98 bottom A visit to the sanctuary of Apollo Ptóios on Ptóion hill is rather awkward as the extensive ruins are dispersed among, and in some cases hidden by, the thick vegetation.

99 top An attractive picture of the entrance to the large thòlos-*type* Mycenaean tomb with the striking gate and architrave known as the "Treasury of Minyàs" at Orchomenòs in Boeotia, and the remains of the funerary chamber.

99 center Proud and daunting, the magnificent funerary Lion of the Thebans still watches over the field of Chairòneia where those members of the city-state coalition against Philip II (338 BC) who died in battle were buried.

99 bottom Another Greek theater discovered in good condition is at Orchomenòs in Boeotia where the musical and literary competitions in honor of the Chàrites were held. The Chàrites were the goddesses of grace.

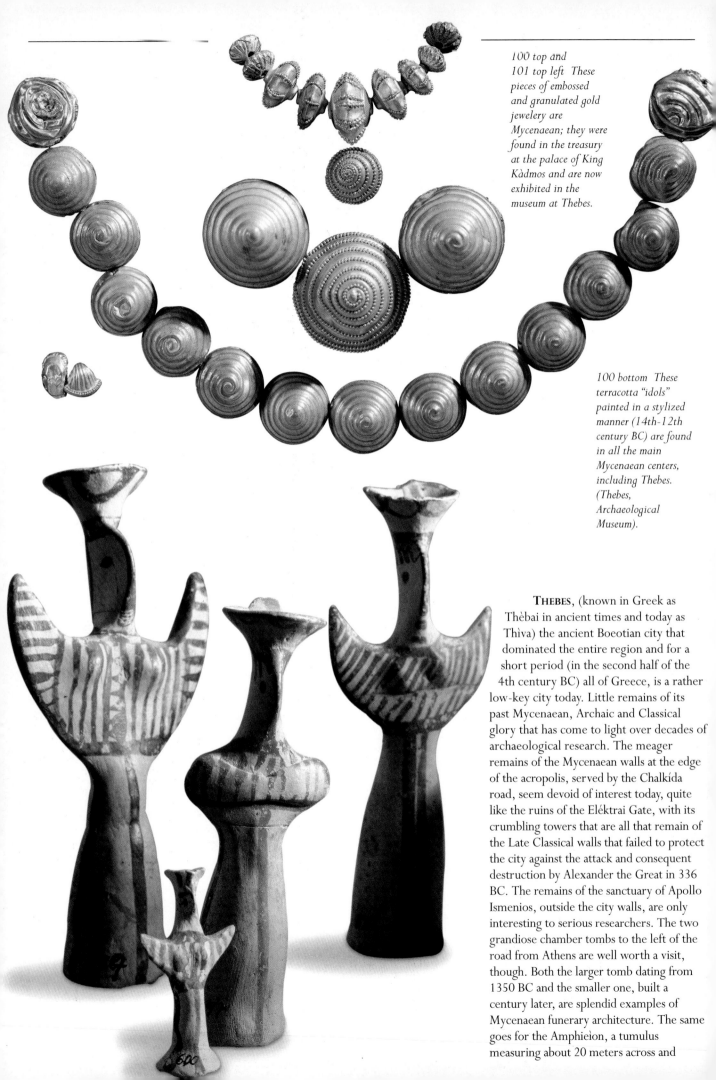

100 top and 101 top left These pieces of embossed and granulated gold jewelery are Mycenaean; they were found in the treasury at the palace of King Kàdmos and are now exhibited in the museum at Thebes.

100 bottom These terracotta "idols" painted in a stylized manner (14th-12th century BC) are found in all the main Mycenaean centers, including Thebes. (Thebes, Archaeological Museum).

THEBES, (known in Greek as Thèbai in ancient times and today as Thìva) the ancient Boeotian city that dominated the entire region and for a short period (in the second half of the 4th century BC) all of Greece, is a rather low-key city today. Little remains of its past Mycenaean, Archaic and Classical glory that has come to light over decades of archaeological research. The meager remains of the Mycenaean walls at the edge of the acropolis, served by the Chalkída road, seem devoid of interest today, quite like the ruins of the Eléktrai Gate, with its crumbling towers that are all that remain of the Late Classical walls that failed to protect the city against the attack and consequent destruction by Alexander the Great in 336 BC. The remains of the sanctuary of Apollo Ismenios, outside the city walls, are only interesting to serious researchers. The two grandiose chamber tombs to the left of the road from Athens are well worth a visit, though. Both the larger tomb dating from 1350 BC and the smaller one, built a century later, are splendid examples of Mycenaean funerary architecture. The same goes for the Amphieìon, a tumulus measuring about 20 meters across and

*101 top right
The remains of a
defensive tower that
was once part of the
city walls stands in*

*the garden of Thebes'
archaeological
museum; the walls
were built during the
late Classical age.*

placed on a stepped brick pyramid,
reminiscent of the 3rd-dynasty Pharaonic
pyramids at Saqqarah in Egypt. This is a
rare example of a monumental tomb
dating from 2200-2000 BC, already
considered in ancient times the tomb of
the hero Amphìon, and identified as the
cist grave covered by marble slabs at its tip.

The rich archaeological museum of
Thebes houses the splendid *koùroi* of
Ptóion, Helladic and Mycenaean ceramics
and gold work, several tablets inscribed in
a script now called "Linear B," from the
archives of the Mycenaean palace of the
mythical king Kàdmos, and a series of
beautiful painted terracotta sarcophagi
from nearby Tanàgra.

*101 bottom left
What remains of
Dirce's spring on the
west side of Thebes
marks the scene of the
nymph's death.*

*101 bottom right
An inscription in
"Linear B" adorns this
large Mycenaean
amphora found in the
palace of King
Kàdmos, which is
today part of the
collection of the
museum in Thebes.*

Continuing to Eretria, it is well worth stopping for a short visit to **Lefkandi**, on the promontory of Xeròpolis. It was an important center, dating as far back as protohistorical Eretria, from the end of the 3rd millenium BC up to the middle of the 8th century BC. It rose to prominence especially in the Mycenaean period (14th-13th centuries BC) and in the Geometric age. It was destroyed during the Lelantine War (circa 750 BC) between Chalkìs and Eretria over possession of the plain around the river Lèlas. The site features the remains of the grandoise *Heròon* (nearly 500 sq. meters), that was perhaps the royal residence later transformed into a tomb and the site of a heroic cult with a funerary tumulus built over it.

The last stop on this tour is therefore **Eretria**, which played a key role in Greek history between the 10th and the 8th centuries BC. It was later overshadowed by the power of Chalkìs and the expansionist ambitions of

Athens, only to flourish once again between the 4th and 3rd centuries BC, before falling victim to Roman vendetta during the unfortunate events that led to its inclusion as part of the senatorial province of Achaia. The northwest sector of the archaeological site shows part of the city walls that were rebuilt several times, close to the Western Gate (1). Five construction phases of the gate (between the 7th and 2nd centuries BC) are identifiable. Passing through the gate, one reaches the theater (2), dating from the end of the 4th century BC. The theater is structurally similar to the theater of Dionysus at the foot of the acropolis in Athens, and could seat over 6000 spectators. The nearby Doric peripteral temple hexastyle, dedicated to Dionysus, was built during the same period, and only the foundations (3) are visible today.

To the south of the Western Gate lie the remains of a monumental Eretrian complex, known as Palace I (4) dating from the fifth and last phase of reconstruction of what was an aristocratic residence built – with symbolic and cult-related intentions – over tombs of the Geometric period in which heroic aristocrats lie buried. These heroes were venerated in a chapel reserved for funerary sacrifices and banquets in honor of members of the *ghénos*. The rooms of the aristocratic residence seem to

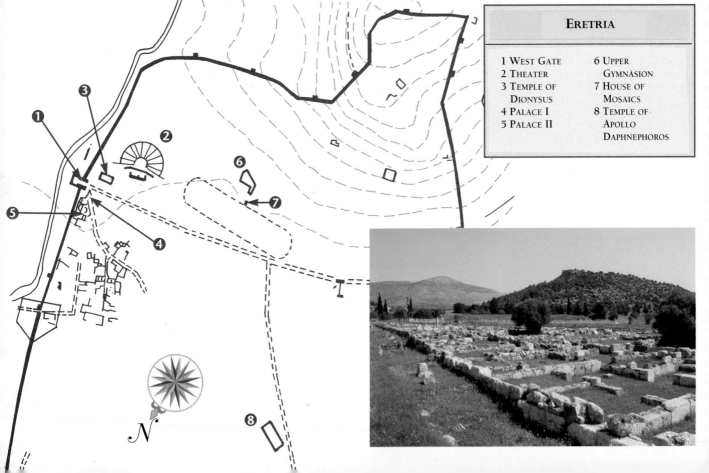

Eretria

1 West Gate	6 Upper
2 Theater	Gymnàsion
3 Temple of	7 House of
Dionysus	Mosaics
4 Palace I	8 Temple of
5 Palace II	Apollo
	Daphnephoros

102 top The 3rd-2nd century BC fragmentary statue of a lion, probably from a funerary monument, is exhibited in front of the entrance of the Archaeological Museum of Eretria.

102 bottom Archaeological excavations have uncovered part of the town of ancient Eretria; the photograph shows the remains of some houses and the acropolis in the background.

102-103 Although the shape and proportions of the theater at Erètria (320-300 BC) resemble those at the theater of Dionysus in Athens, its artificially raised cavea and orchèstra lowered by three meters are unusual.

103 The demonic image of the Gorgon, Medusa, survived centuries of antiquity without ever falling into oblivion; this clay example is from the Hellenistic age (Eretria, Archaeological Museum).

be arranged around peristyle courtyards, with large banquet halls (*andrón*) flanked by one or more bedrooms. Further south lie the remains of the so-called Palace II (5) which is also trapezoid in shape, with a large (almost 2000 sq. meters) peristylar courtyard, that was used as a residence between the 5th and 3rd centuries BC, before its destruction in 198 BC by the Romans. The functional layout of the complex is almost identical to that of Palace I.

Returning to the theater, one reaches the excavations of the upper *gymnàsion* (6), built in the 4th century BC and reconstructed in the 2nd century BC. The complex is built around a square peristyle courtyard measuring about 1000 sq. meters. It is fitted with a bathroom (with a hypocaust for heating) and a shrine. The mosaic remains in two of the rooms are exceptional. To the southeast of the depression that indicates the location of the stadium of Eretria lie the remains of the most interesting ancient building, the House of Mosaics (7) built in 370 BC. The building was inhabited for about one century, perhaps by the family of the famous Cynic philosopher Menedemos, renowned for his wise government of the city during the first quarter of the 3rd century BC. Around 100 BC, the building was transformed

into a sort of *heróon* that held two tombs solemnized by a monumental funerary structure. The tombs date from the first decades of the 3rd century BC. The palatial residence was almost square in plan (25 x 26 meters) and was made up of two sectors, one of which was clearly used for public audiences, while the other was a private residence. To the northwest and north of the peristylar courtyard (about 60 square metres) that once housed an altar dedicated to Zeus, patron of households, lie halls used for men's banquets. The banquet halls are decorated by splendid mosaics. The last structure of interest at this site is

the famous Doric peripteral temple hexastyle dedicated to Apollo Daphnephoros ("protector of the laurel") that stands close to the ancient *agorà*. It was rebuilt five times between the 9th and 5th centuries BC and decorated with splendid sculptures now on view together with other interesting finds at the museum. The late Archaic reconstruction (520-490 BC) depicts the Rape of Antiope by Theseus. Other interesting archaeological sites in green and pleasant Eubea include Dìstos, Kàrystos, Cape Artemìsso (Artemision), Loutrà Edipsoù and Kymi, where perhaps some of the founders of Cuma in Southern Italy set out (740 BC).

ATTICA AND AEGINA

The Attica of Pisistratos and Pericles, Plato and Demosthenes, with its flourishing *demes* (districts), its bustling harbors, the illustrious sanctuaries that dotted its pleasant country-side, covered with vines and olive trees and its sinuous coastline, is today an almost impossible dream, devoured by the expansion of the Athenian mega-city and its recent conurbations. The small and proud *Megara* that so staunchly resisted Athenian might is today a rather ugly suburban town, seemingly without historical memory, totally overcome by spreading industrialization. A little more to the east, towards Athens, it is almost grotesque to visit the famous ruins of the sanctuary of Eleusis – for thousands of years bathed in the sublime mists of the great religious mysticism – now drowned in the fumes of the nearby petrochemical plants and the roar of speeding traffic. Fortunately, the coastline and the mountain areas, further away from "Great Athens" still maintain all their charm and character.

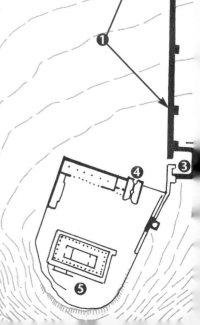

104 left Only the columns on the south and north sides of the peristasis and the pronaos of the temple of Poseidon at Cape Soùnion have survived the ravages of time and weather that have softened its rather stern appearance.

104-105 The temple of Poseidon seen from

the west: this stretch of the Aegean coast is dotted with bare rocky islets like the one in the photograph, known as the "rock of Patroclus."

105 bottom left Almost nothing remains of the cella, pronaos and opisthodomos among the columns of the temple of Poseidon at Cape Soùnion; the Doric

appearance of the columns was tempered with the proportional elegance of the Ionic order.

105 bottom right Cape Soùnion is a meeting place between the glories of nature and the genius of man; it also attracted Lord Byron, who carved his name on one of the temple columns.

CAPE SOUNION

1 WALLS
2 NORTHWEST GATE
3 BASTION
4 PROPYLAIA
5 PROPYLON
6 TEMPLE OF POSEIDON

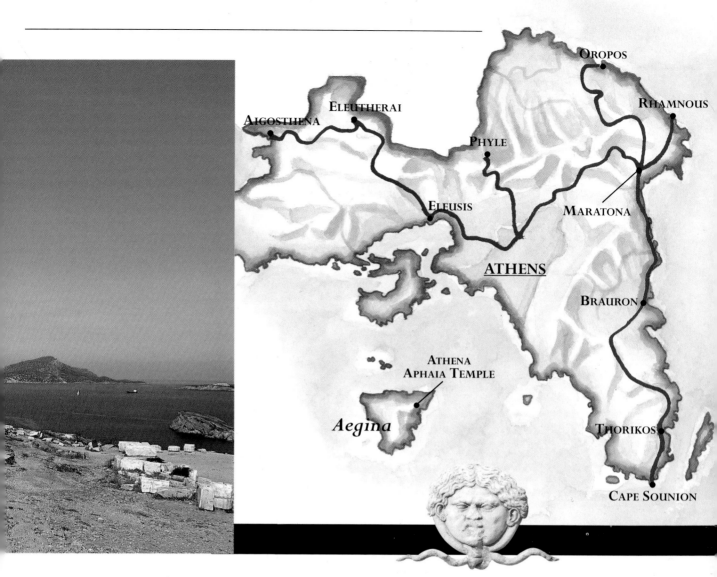

AIGOSTHENA · ELEUTHERAI · OROPOS · RHAMNOUS · PHYLE · ELEUSIS · MARATONA · ATHENS · BRAURON · ATHENA APHAIA TEMPLE · Aegina · THORIKOS · CAPE SOUNION

Attica is literally teeming with archaeologically significant ruins, but no lover of ancient Greek art and history would want to miss the sites that lie within the large area between **CAPE SOUNION** and ancient Aigòsthena.

Cape Soùnion, a natural acropolis that marks the southeastern border of Attica, is a favorite destination even for visitors who have little or no interest in ancient ruins. The open area that houses the spectacular remains of the temple of Poseidon also affords a breathtaking view that will not fail to move even the most insensitive of visitors, especially at sunrise and sunset.

The ancient Attic *deme* (district) of Soùnion rose around a protohistoric religious sanctuary devoted to the cult of the god of the sea. The *témenos* of the sanctuary was adorned by huge *koùroi* statues dating from the last quarter of the 7th century BC. These statues are now at the National Archaeological Museum in Athens. Enclosed by turreted walls (1) that were modified several times between the end of the 5th and the middle of the 3rd centuries BC, Soùnion was accessible through a scea gate to the northwest (3) and reinforced by a bastion (3) on the eastern side of the natural acropolis.

The sanctuary of Poseidon stood at the highest point, inside a sacred area demarcated by a hall for sacred banquets and a double stoà to the north. Another single portico ran along the western side. The entrance to the sanctuary consisted of a double *própylon* (4) built into the midpoint of the north side. The temple on the southern tip of the promontory appears even more touching against the backdrop of the meager ruins of the rest of the complex.

The Doric peripteral temple hexastyle in white-bluish marble from Mt. Agrilèza was built in 444-440 BC to replace an earlier structure, founded around 490 BC and perhaps destroyed by the Persians. It is widely believed that the temple was designed by the same architect and artists who worked on the temples dedicated to Hephaistos and Ares in the *agorà* of Athens as well as on the temple of Nemesis at Rhamnoùs. The measurements and layout of the peristasis, architrave and the continuous frieze in Parian marble that adorned the front and sides of the pronaos and opisthodomos, as well as the proportional ratios, obviously aimed at creating a streamlined effect of lightness, all point to an architect from the Ionic islands or at least someone well-versed in the Ionic order. The frieze depicts the common themes of Gigantomachy and Centauromachy (battles between Gods and Giants and between humans and centaurs), as well as the heroic feats undertaken by Theseus.

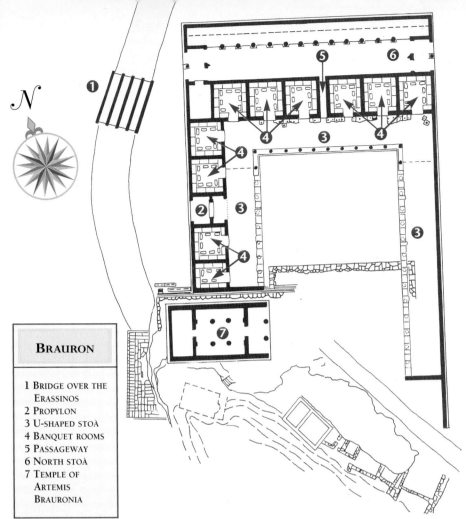

BRAURON

1 BRIDGE OVER THE ERASSINOS
2 PROPYLON
3 U-SHAPED STOÀ
4 BANQUET ROOMS
5 PASSAGEWAY
6 NORTH STOÀ
7 TEMPLE OF ARTEMIS BRAURONIA

106 top left The theater of Thorikòs was flanked by an altar dedicated to Dionysus.

106-107 The portico in the sanctuary of Artemis Brauronia.

106 bottom left The Tumulus of the Athenians at Marathon.

107 bottom left The theater of Oropòs has an earthen cavea and a well-preserved stage.

106 top right The unfinished croziers in the temple of Nèmesis at Rhamnoùs.

107 bottom right The postern to the south of Phylè is well-preserved.

A few kilometers from Soùnion, on the eastern Attic coastline lies the ancient *deme* of **THORIKOS**, a strategic point in Aegean maritime traffic. The nearby silver, zinc and iron mines of Laùrion (now Lávrion), were the lifeblood of Athenian prosperity in the 5th century BC. Plans are underway to transform the area into an archaeological and mineralogical reserve park. The coastal road leads to the theater. Construction on the structure commenced in the 6th, but was only completed in the 4th century BC. The unusual cavea, irregularly semi-elliptic is divided by a *diàzoma* (horizontal passageway) split into two sectors and three cunei. The construction phases are identifiable from the changes in technique (from pseudo-isodomic to isodomic masonry) and the introduction of separate entrances for the high portion. 200 meters to the northwest, excavations have uncovered a residential and a craftsmen's district dating from the Archaic and the Classical periods (6th – 4th centuries BC). Especially noteworthy are the structures of a plant with canals, decantation basins and drying tables for washing and pre-conditioning silver-bearing lead before it was conveyed to the fusion ovens. The remains of houses and roads around a circular tower as well as a stretch of the wall of the *deme*, dating from the Peloponnesian War, are of equal interest.

Another site of great interest is the famou sanctuary of Artemis Brauronia at **BRAURON** (n Vravróna). The excellent Retsìna wine, at Markópoulo on the way, is perhaps the best in Greece. Inside the sanctuary, where Athenian g used to go through the initiation rites of passage adulthood, one can still see five pylons and the plane of the bridge (1) built across the Erassinó river around 450 BC. The road crossing the bri led to the sacred enclosure. The surviving structures mostly date from the last quarter of 5th century BC.

Access to the sacred area is through the *própylon* (2) that opens onto the remains of the light colonnade of the U-shaped stoà (3) that enclosed the central courtyard. The elegant Do portico featuring three rows of columns, is preserved in parts on the north side. The colonnade stands on a stylobate in tufa while th columns and epistyles were in *pòros*, with meto and capitals in marble. Ten sacred banquet hall reserved for girls preparing for initiation (4) stood around the portico. Nine of these halls could hold up to 11 *klìnai* (beds for diners to recline) and seven tables (several table supports can still be seen). One of the halls is slightly smaller than the others. To the north, a narrow passage (5) leads to remains of the northern stoà intended to hold the votive offerings of the faithful. Very meager are the remains of the rather smallish temple

east, towards the village, lies the Tumulus of the Plataians that housed nine tombs of hoplites from the small Boeotian city allied with Athens.

Not far from Marathon, on the coast, lie the ruins of the sanctuary of Nemesis, goddess of vengeance, at **RHAMNOUS**. Built in polygonal masonry on an artificial terrace, the sanctuary consisted of two cult buildings. The small temple, astyle *in antis*,

Museum in Athens. The ruins of the larger structure dedicated to Nemesis in 436-432 BC indicate an unfinished Classical Doric peripteral temple hexastyle, almost certainly designed by the same architect who built the sanctuary at Cape Soùnion. Excavations at the temple have uncovered various fragments of the marble statue of the goddess, a masterpiece by Agoràkritos of Pàros.

The site of the *Amphiaraeíon* lies further north of Rhamnoùs, along the coastal road. This is basically a sanctuary to the Argive hero, poet and healer Amphiaraòs, at **OROPOS**, in a very evocative setting. The complex was built in the 4th century BC. The highlights of the site include remains of the Doric temple hexastyle *in antis*, dedicated to the hero. The temple features a cella divided into three parts by two rows of Ionic columns. The cella once housed a gigantic cult statue. Other high points of the site include the altar in front of the temple, still bathed by water from the sacred spring, the terrace supporting Hellenistic and Roman votive monuments, the long double portico used for the incubation of the sick who sought miraculous healing at the sanctuary, and the small theater built in 332 BC with a seating capacity of 3000. The proscenium with Doric half-columns and the skenè with Doric columns and three doorways, are especially noteworthy.

From Rhamnoùs or Oropòs the tour heads back towards Athens. At Archarnès one should go up the rugged valley that leads to the spectacular ruins of the Athenian fortress of **PHYLE** (now Filì), one of the best preserved bulwarks of Attica and an excellent example of Classical military architecture. Built between the end of the 5th and the beginning of the 4th centuries

of the goddess. The temple, distyle *in antis* with a cella featuring four columns and an *àdyton*, seems almost a copy of the very ancient *mègaron*-style Mycenaean cult temple. The archaeological museum at Brauron should be visited.

The road continues north along the coast toward the evocative site of **MARATONA** (Marathon), backdrop of the famous battle between the Athenians and Persians that was fought on the plain there in 490 BC. The main highlight at this site is the Tumulus of the Athenians, a 10-meter-high tomb in which 192 Athenian hoplites who fell in the battle lie buried. From here visitors proceed to the large 14th-century BC Mycenaean *thòlos* tomb near the locality of Vràna. This tomb contained a rich collection of funerary objects as well as the remains of two horses sacrificed and buried towards the beginning of the long (25-meter) entrance passage (*dròmos*). To the

in polygonal masonry, dedicated to Thèmis, goddess of law, was built in 490 BC, most likely to celebrate the Athenian victory at Marathon. Inside the temple are copies of two small thrones dedicated to Nemesis and Thèmis in the 4th century BC as well as the inscribed base of the famous cult statue of the goddess Thèmis, a masterpiece by the Athenian sculptor Charièstratos (290-280 BC), now at the National Archaeological

BC on a natural rock 680 meters above sea level, it features bastions in isodomic masonry and encloses an area of almost 4000 square meters. The perimetral wall is interrupted by four towers (three rectangular and one circular), a main gate to the east and a small emergency exit to the south. It was here that the Athenian democratic politician Thrasybolos plotted the war to liberate Athens from the tyranny of the Thirty.

108 top The architectural and sculptural remains of the honorary arches of Demeter and Kore and of Marcus Aurelius stand on the west side of the vast entrance to the mystery sanctuary of the two goddesses at Eleusis.

The very important archaeological site of **ELEUSIS** (now Elefsína) lies close to Athens, facing the island of Salamìna (Salamis). At the foot of the acropolis of the ancient city stand the remains of one of the most important sanctuaries of the ancient world, dedicated to Demeter and Kore-Persephones. The sanctuary also included a large cult room known as the *Telestèrion*, where the famous Eleusinian Mysteries were celebrated. The ruins visible today are the remains of an impressive series of monumental building projects from the 6th

century BC to Roman times.

The entrance to the site lies at the spot where the ancient Sacred Way meets the partially porticoed square (1). The porticoes and two triumphal arches in honor of the Goddesses Demeter and Kore and of the Emperor Marcus Aurelius (2-3) were built in Roman times. The beautiful small Doric temple, amphiprostyle tetrastyle of Artemis Propylaia (4) stands in the center. After a brief visit to the remains of the turreted walls (5), rebuilt several times between the 6th and 3rd centuries BC, one should

proceed to the so-called Greater Propylaia (6), that clearly reflects the Propylaia at Athens. On the floor, the large marble bust of Marcus Aurelius in armor, enclosed in a circular frame, is still visible. To the right, devotees of the Eleusinian Mysteries held their ritual dances. The well, dating from 470-460 BC, is known as the *Kallìchoron* (7). The Sacred Way continues at a slight incline, meandering between the houses of priests and public buildings, up to the so-called Lesser Propylaia (8), built in the Roman period, and featuring a Caryatid distyle and a Doric frieze with motifs evoking Demeter (ears of wheat). The tour continues through a distressing tumble of ruins that is difficult to identify (the temple of Pluto, (Hades) god of Hell, who abducted and married Kore-Persephones, as well as other temples of uncertain attribution to the right, are barely recognizable), to reach the *Telestèrion* (9), a huge hypostyle room. The remains visible today date from the reconstruction undertaken in the second half of the 2nd

108 bottom Worn away by time, unfortunately, the bust of Marcus Aurelius wearing military armor sits in a round cornice (clipeus) but the features of the emperor-philosophe are recognizable.

108-109 A view of the entrance square to the Eleusian sanctuary. In the background we see the steps that lead up to the Greater Propylaia, designed in Doric order to resemble those on the acropolis in Athens.

109 bottom The northern tier of the Telestèrion was cut out of the rock of the hill behind; from here it was possible to watch the ritual of the celebration of the Eleusian Mysteries.

ELEUSIS

1   ENTRANCE SQUARE
2-3 ARCHES OF MARCUS
    AURELIUS
4   TEMPLE OF ARTEMIS
    PROPYLAIA
5   WALLS
6   GREATER PROPYLAIA
7   KALLICHORON

8   LESSER PROPYLAIA
9   TELESTERION

    PERICLEAN WALLS
    WALLS OF LYCURGUS
    PEISISTRATEAN WALLS
    WALL OF CIMON

N

110 A striking detail of one of the Caryatids from the Roman era on the Lesser Propylaia at Eleusis . These were a clear reference to the Caryatids on the Erectheion (Elefsína, Archaeological Museum).

111 top Marble sculptures from the Roman age are exhibited on the terrace of the archaeological museum at Elefsína; there are two headless statues of men in togas, a neo-Attic amphora and a composite capital.

*111 bottom left
The museum at the
sanctuary of Eleusis
also holds many objects
from the Archaic age; a
fine example of an early
Attic amphora can be
seen in the foreground
and, behind, an Attic
koùros.*

*111 bottom center
The marble Roman
sarcophagus on the
terrace of the Elefsína
museum is from the
2nd century BC; its
finely decorated
exterior depicts the
final scene of the myth
of the boar of Kalydòn.*

century AD. It was here that at night, by
orchlight, the Great Eleusinian Mysteries were
elebrated. The crowd of initiates sat along the
teps (only those hewn into the rocky slope of
he hill have survived) in a solemn atmosphere
endered even more ominous by the shadows of
he dense stone forest of the colonnade that,
vith heavy timber trusses, supported the roof. In
he middle of the room was an *àdyton*. The *àdyton*
leliberately reproduces the structure of the
ncient Mycenaean *mègaron* around which the
ult of the *Chthonian* (underworld) deities,
leveloped. The archaeological museum (10)
ouses, among other things, a statue of Demeter
y Agoràkritos of Pàros dating from about 420
3C, a series of votive relief sculptures and
tatuettes consecrated to the Eleusinian deities, a
ew excellent examples of Archaic, early
Classical and Classical statuary, Roman
culptures and series of ceramics from the
3ronze Age to the end of the 6th century BC.

*111 bottom right This
statue at Eleusis is one
of the many dedicated
by the grief-stricken
emperor, Hadrian, to
his beloved Antinoo,
who drowned in the
Nile at the age of 18
(Elefsína,
Archaeological
Museum).*

112-113 It is possible to see the accuracy of the isodomic construction technique in the walls and towers at Eleutheraì; isodomic means the use of rows of uniform, parallelepiped, rusticated ashlar blocks.

112 bottom left Seen from below, this is the view of the wonderfully preserved, turreted defensive walls of Eleutheraì, as seen also at Phylè and Aigòsthena, which were built at Athens on the border with Boeotia.

112 bottom right The wooden beams and floors of the many towers of Eleutheraì no longer exist, making a tour of the battlements impossible. The photograph shows a doorway that allows access between the battlements and a tower.

113 top The countryside of oak woods around the fort at Eleutheraì is unspoiled; this is the same view seen by the garrison that used to be stationed in the fort.

113 bottom One of the posterns at Eleutheraì opens onto the south side. So narrow that only one man could pass at a time, it was easily guarded by the soldiers on the tall tower next to it.

The tour proceeds from Eleusis along the road to Thebes, stopping off at the fortress of **ELEUTHERAI**. Standing in a spectacular location, it is the best preserved fortress of Athenian defenses on the Attic-Boeotian border. It was probably built in the second half of the 4th century BC and covers a surface area of over 35,000 square meters. The highlights of the fortress include its defensive walls, featuring masterful isodomic masonry, two scee gates and several smaller exits; communicating passageways; and two-story towers with doors, windows and stairs both inside and outside the structure.

The last stop on this tour of Attica is the bay of Ghermenó, on the Gulf of Alkyonídon, at the eastern extremity of the Gulf of Corinth. Besides the magnificent beach, the area also houses the excavation site of **AIGOSTHENA**, with the remains of a sturdy 4th century BC fortress. Long the subject of dispute between Megara and Athens, the stronghold was independent for a few decades near the end of the 3rd century BC.

The surviving defensive walls to the north that feature several rectangular towers in isodomic masonry are particularly interesting. Another highlight is the acropolis enclosed by a wall in polygonal masonry that predates the main defenses by about a century. This earlier wall also features at least eight towers.

114 left The statue of Athena Aphaìa stands armed between contending Greek and Trojan soldiers in the center of the west pediment of the temple of the goddess at Aegina; the temple was the last great example of Archaic sculpture (Munich, Glyptothek).

114-115 The lovely south side of the temple of Athena Aphaìa at Aegina was the result of a precocious attempt to combine harmonious proportionality and unusual lightness in the austere Doric order.

115 left Another lovely view of the temple of Athena Aphaìa at Aegina; in the foreground, the columns of the pronaos; behind, the double row of columns on two orders that divided the cella into three aisles.

The island of **AEGINA** (Eghina) located in the Gulf Saronikós between Attica and the Argolid has been inhabited since the Old Bronze Age. A small Mycenaean settlement at first, it later grew to become one of the main Archaic shipping trade centers (7th-6th century BC) that competed with such powers as Athens and Corinth in Levantine and western markets. Economic rivalry with Athens led to a series of wars that culminated, towards the middle of the 5th century BC, with the annexation by the Athenians who deported the entire local population and replaced them with Athenian settlers. The remains of ancient Aegina include a precious page in the history of Greek art and architecture, the highly evocative Doric peripteral temple hexastyle dedicated to Athena Aphaìa. Famous for its pediments, the temple is part of the sanctuary dedicated to the goddess, located about 7 km east of the modern town. The sanctuary was already known in Mycenaean times and features a trapezoid *témenos*

(sacred enclosure) housing service structures and religious buildings dating from the 8th to the 7th century BC. The archaeological stratigraphy of the various phases and renovations is distinguishable. The late Archaic temple of Athena Aphaìa was built around 510-500 BC in shell limestone covered with stucco. The structure is surrounded by a peristasis of 6 x 11 columns. The cella of the temple is divided into three aisles by two rows of Doric colums. The pronaos and opisthodomos are both distyle *in antis*. The proportions, already hinting of the future balance of Classical temples, are easy to see. The pediments, bearing almost life-size statues in local marble, were crowned by arcoteria (sculpted decorations) at the peak and the corners. The arcoteria at the peaks depicted two Ionic-style *kòrai* flanking an *anthèmion* (palmette-and-lotus design) while the corner decorations represent sphinxes. All the pedimental decorations are now at the Glyptothek in Munich, Germany. The pedimental statues are important to historians of Greek art because in the quarter century (510 – 485 BC) that separates the completion of the western and eastern façades (possibly damaged in an earthquake), the artistic style shifted from Late Archaic to Early Classical.

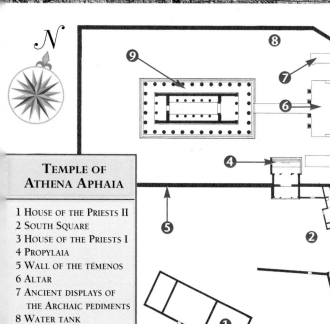

N

TEMPLE OF ATHENA APHAIA

1 HOUSE OF THE PRIESTS II
2 SOUTH SQUARE
3 HOUSE OF THE PRIESTS I
4 PROPYLAIA
5 WALL OF THE TÉMENOS
6 ALTAR
7 ANCIENT DISPLAYS OF THE ARCHAIC PEDIMENTS
8 WATER TANK
9 TEMPLE OF ATHENA APHAIA

The west pediment depicts the battle between Greeks and Trojans, while the sculptures on the east represent the previous expedition led by Heracles against the Trojan king Laomedon. It is possible that the older west pediment alludes to the war between the Greeks and Persians in Asia Minor as an allegory of the conflict between good and evil. The east pediment has been interpreted as an allegory celebrating Aeginetan victories against Athens at the beginning of the 5th century BC. In both pediments, the goddess, dressed and armed with a spear, shield and *aegis* (leather breastplate) bearing the image of the head of the Gorgon Medusa with her hair made up of snakes, stood in the midst of fighting or fallen warriors. The sequence is placed in the problematic triangular space of the tympanum that is over 15 meters long. Besides colored finishing, unfortunately much has permanently been removed by abrasion during brutal restoration work on the statues by B. Thorvaldsen in the first half of the 19th century. The same restoration work is also responsible for the loss of a great deal of details (weapons, ornaments, etc.) in gilded bronze that were fixed to holes in the marble.

Scant remains of ancient Aegina can be seen, northwest of the modern town, on the Kolòna hill, named for the sole surviving column of the Late Archaic Doric peripteral temple hexastyle dedicated to Apollo (circa 500 BC). Other remains can be seen along the coastline, and the ruins of two jetties of the ancient port can still be distinguished underwater. The small but interesting archaeological museum is close to the Cathedral of Aegina.

116 This beautiful head of a goddess, maybe Athena, was found in the sanctuary at Aegina; it was produced during the first half of the 5th century BC and has been attributed to an unknown island artist of superb skill.

116-117 bottom The famous figure of the dying soldier on the left corner of the east pediment of the temple of Athena Aphaìa at Aegina (490-480 BC) is one of the most beautiful examples of early Classical sculpture (Munich, Glyptothek).

117 top Another view of the temple from the southeast corner; this was the first view of the imposing white temple that was seen by visitors and pilgrims to the sanctuary after they passed through the Propylaia.

CORINTHIA AND ARGOLYS

The modern Greek province of Corinthia lies on the northeastern end of the Peloponnese and includes the narrow isthmus that links the peninsula to Attica. The local landscape does not differ much from that of neighboring Argolys and Achaia, while the coastline is particularly rich in harbors facing both the Gulf of Corinth and the Gulf Saronikós.

Visitors arriving from Attica are well advised to stop off at **PERACHORA** before crossing the Corinthian canal. Situated a little past the thermal baths and seaside resort of Loutràki, on the promontory of Irèo, lie the remains of the large Archaic, Classical and Hellenistic sanctuary of Hera.

The next structure, immediately to the west, is an altar decorated with triglyphs that was originally covered by a Ionic canopy (dating from the end of the 5th century BC). Still moving westwards, lying close to each other are the remains of the Geometric apsidal temple of Hera Akraìa followed by an Archaic apteral (i.e. not surrounded by columns on the outside) structure featuring a double row of Doric columns inside the cella and a marble roof. In front of the small pier stands a building dating from the second half of the 6th century BC with a courtyard and L-shaped portico that may have been used as a utilities building for the sanctuary.

118 The remains of the temple of Hera Limènia overlook the Bay of Perachòra in a setting of natural beauty in which the Mediterranean maquis and calcareous rocks slope gently down to the sea.

118-119 Most of the ancient structures of Perachòra are found in the lee of the bay. In the foreground, the ruins of the Archaic temple of Hera Akraìa are perfectly aligned east to west.

The remains of the *témenos* of the small apteral temple of Hera Limènia (protectress of the port) lie on the slope that descends towards the sea. Inside the temple, dating from the middle of the 8th century BC, are an altar and inscribed stelae. Excavations at the temple also unearthed a memorable series of votive offerings dating from the 8th up to the 4th centuries BC. Further to the west lies a large Hellenic reservoir based on an elliptical plan. The most interesting features of this complex are the nearby banquet hall and the pillars that supported the large beams that held the roof. The banquet hall was probably somehow linked to the sanctuary of Hera Akraìa ("protectress of the hill") on the upper reaches of the slope. The modern visitor will have some difficulty identifying the buildings of the sanctuary. The easternmost structure is a 4th-century BC L-shaped stoà with two floors, one in the Doric and the other in the Ionic style.

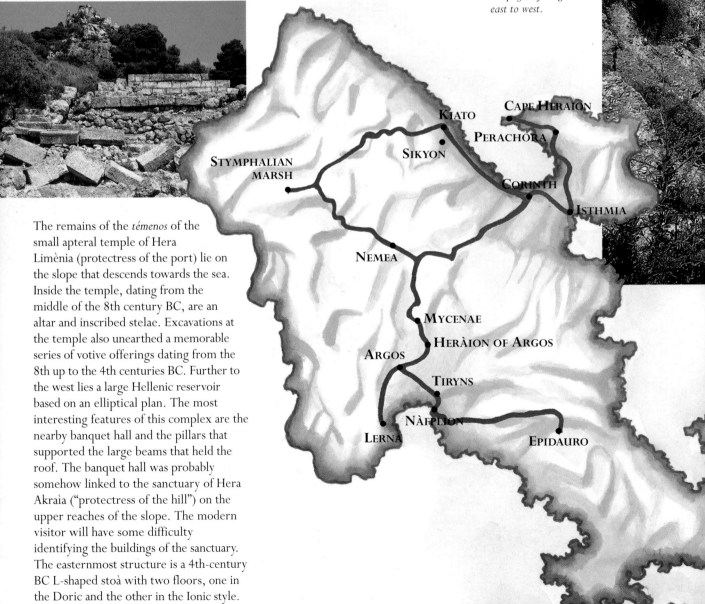

CAPE HERAÌON
KIATO
PERACHORA
SIKYON
STYMPHALIAN MARSH
CORINTH
ISTHMIA
NEMEA
MYCENAE
HERÀION OF ARGOS
ARGOS
TIRYNS
NÀFPLION
LERNA
EPIDAURO

119 bottom left The remains of a large rectangular water tank with short curved sides

(foreground) and a room for religious banquets (3rd century BC) have been found half way up Perachòra hill.

119 bottom right This is a suggestive detail of the Hellenistic water tank on Perachòra hill.

The problem of water supplies was often resolved in ancient Greece with this type of communal tank.

Just past the Corinthian Canal, however, towards the Aegean coast, lie the noteworthy remains of the Panhellenic sanctuary of Poseidon at ISTHMIA. Built between the end of the 8th and the early 7th century BC, it was embellished and renovated several times until Justinian dismantled it to scavenge building materials for a fortress (1) on the walls of the Isthmus built by the Peloponnesians during the Persian Wars. It is best to start the visit at the archaeological museum that houses precious remains from the sanctuary and the nearby Corinthian port

of Kenchrèai, before proceeding to examine the sanctuary of Poseidon (2), with its varied stratigraphy. Within the sacred enclosure stand the Doric peripteral temple hexastyle of the god (460-390 BC) and the remains of the nearby *Palaimónion* (3), dedicated to the cult of a hero and renovated in Roman times, featuring a small monopteral temple on a high podium. Close to the temple are the markings of the starting point of the more ancient stadium (6th-5th century BC) where the Isthmian Games were held every two years. The games were

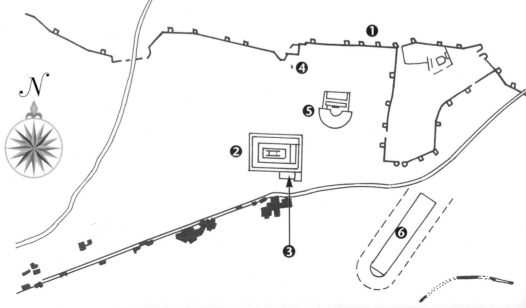

ISTHMIA

1 WALLS OF JUSTINIAN
2 SANCTUARY OF POSEIDON
3 HEROON OF PALAIMON
4 ROMAN BATHS
5 THEATER
6 STADIUM

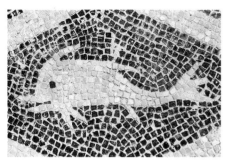

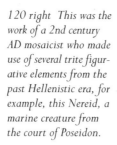

120 left The baths complex seen on this page is undoubtedly one of the most interesting sites in Isthmìa. Here you can see some of the chambers decorated with black and white mosaics.

120 right This was the work of a 2nd century AD mosaicist who made use of several trite figurative elements from the past Hellenistic era, for example, this Nereid, a marine creature from the court of Poseidon.

121 top left One of the marine symbols used in mosaic decoration of Roman baths in the 2nd-3rd centuries was that of dolphins.

121 top right A number of suspensurae *still remain in the* calidarium *of the Roman baths at Isthmìa. Suspensurae are the circular and square brick pillars that supported the floors heated by hot air from the* praefurnia.

121 center Another sea creature represented in mid-empire bath mosaics was the octopus, seen here at Isthmìa in a very stylized version.

121 bottom left Another Alexandrian-Hellenistic symbol of nimbleness was that of winged cupids with bridle and whip in hand, riding dolphins in a lighthearted parody of a horse race.

reformed in 582 BC and were second in importance only to the Olympic Games. Excavations to the northeast of the temple have uncovered a Roman Imperial thermal bath complex (4) with remains of mosaic flooring. To the south of the *thermae* lies the cavea of the theater (5) (5th-4th century BC, with refurbishments and extensions from the Roman period). The outline of the 4th-century BC stadium (6) is clearly visible on the other side of the road. Excavations at the site have uncovered stretches of paved road with parallel wheel ruts from the carts used to haul light ships over the *diólkos* between Kenchrèai (with interesting Hellenistic-Roman and Byzantine ruins now lying underwater, just south of Isthmìa,) and the Ionic port of the Lèchaion, very close and directly linked to Corinth.

122 left The fortifications of the Akrokòrinthos offer an unusual chance for some medieval and post-medieval archaeological trekking near Corinth, a city-state during the Classical age.

122 top right The courtyard in the archaeological museum in Corinth contains a number of sculptures and inscriptions from the Roman era but also an important sarcophagus from the 6th century and 2nd century BC decorative slabs from the theater.

The excavations at **CORINTH**, one of the largest cities of ancient Greece, are accessed by road from the modern city on the Corinthian Gulf, towards the very high acropolis, known as the Akrokòrinthos.

The almost total destruction of the city by the Romans led by Lucius Mummius in 146 BC, followed by reconstruction and the huge number of refurbishment projects by successive Roman emperors from Julius Caesar to Hadrian, have all but erased the architectural and artistic traces of the ancient city that, since the 8th century BC was a vital center for the crafts as well as the metallurgical and ceramic industries. At the same time, ancient Corinth was deeply involved in all the main events of

Greek history and dominated Mediterranean maritime trade in the Archaic period. It rose to become a colonial power and was governed by an alternating series of oligarchies and tyrannies.

A tour of the site should start from the Akrokòrinthos and proceed towards the Roman city. The Akrokòrinthos, housing the famous temple of Aphrodite, is enclosed by triple fortified walls that bear ample witness to successive Greek, Byzantine, Frankish, Venetian and Ottoman repairs. At the temple, about a thousand priestesses engaged in hierogamy or sacred prostitution,

demanding huge sums from the "pilgrims" who had to tediously climb up the long, steep slope to avail themselves of the privilege. Who knows if it is the great amount of effort involved in the climb that these ancient "sex tourists" had to go through or the high cost of the services that lies at the origins of the Latin proverb "Only few may venture to Corinth"! Halfway down the hill are the remains of the sanctuary of Demeter and Kore, built on terraces and fitted with rows of seats cut as steps into the rock. These graded seats were used to accommodate the congregation assembled for the ritual celebration of the mysteries.

The entrance to the excavations of the low city lies close to the very well-endowed archaeological museum (1) that houses a vast collection of Proto-Corinthian and

122 bottom right This is a view of Room III in the archaeological museum; it contains an extraordinary gallery of sculptures, reliefs, sarcophaguses and mosaics. Among them is the head of a Roman copy of the statue of Doriphoros by Polykleitos.

122-123 The head with flowing locks crowned with ivy may be that of Bacchus in a splendid circular polychrome mosaic framed with motifs "in perspective" (Corinth, Archaeological Museum).

123 bottom This fine mosaic showing a group of bulls and a shepherd playing a flute was a second century AD copy of an original by Pausìas at Sikyòn (Corinth, Archaeological Museum).

Corinthian ceramics (7th-6th century BC) as well as excellent examples of Archaic terracotta work and Roman statuary.

Next to the museum lie the remains of the *Capitolium* (2), a first century AD temple of Jupiter in the Roman city. This Corinthian peripteral temple hexastyle stands at the center of a double-porticoed peribolos. To the east it overlooks the forum-like *agorà*, dividing a long portico featuring shops (3). At the end of a short staircase lies the western terrace (4) that in Augustan times housed seven small temples – five of which were prostyle tetrastyle, one *thòlos* and one distyle *in antis* – dedicated to (from north to south), Venus, Neptune, Hercules (a small *Pàntheon*), and Fortuna. The long south side of the *agorà* extends over two levels. On the lower level lies a chapel with a circular cella

124 top left The results of the last three great monumental additions (Hellenistic, Augustan and Antonine) are visible in the view of the famous Peirene fountain.

124 top right The functional and decorative sections of the Peirene fountain from the Hellenistic age, with six tanks filled from a single source, are incorporated in the arcades of the face of the Augustan structure.

flanked by two small rectangular cellae, perhaps dedicated to Artemis and Dionysus (5) and a row of shops (6), interrupted at the center by a marble tribunal for public speeches and the administration of justice (7). The upper level was a wide square, bordered to the south by a double *stoà* (8) that opened onto administrative offices: at the center was the horseshoe-shaped *Curia* with a porticoed atrium tetrastyle flanked by archive rooms and meeting rooms for the magistrates of the colony. The side rooms probably served as meeting rooms for the powerful *collegia* (corporations) and – on the east side of the terrace – as offices for

the *collegium* of the *Augustals*, officials in charge of the imperial cult. Behind this complex lie the remains of the two-story South Basilica (9). This complex had a central peristyle hearth suggesting the existence of a clerestory. The Julian Basilica (10) to the east of the *agorà* was identical to the South Basilica, although only its underground structures are visible today. The north side of the square holds the modest remains of the north Portico (11) as well as imposing architectural fragments of a grand façade (14) decorated by statues of oriental prisoners, built to commemorate the victories of Septimius Severus against the Parthians. This façade

was interrupted by the monumental barrel-vaulted arch (12) that marked the beginning of the paved road (13) linking the commercial hub of the city to the port of Lèchaion. In the same area stands the complex of the Peirene fountain (15). The present layout of the fountain dates to the reconstruction by Herodes Atticus during the Antonine period. With a large basin in the center of the courtyard, the fountain featured a façade interrupted by arches framed by Ionic pillars in a combination of rustic ashlar and smooth marble. The façade was decorated by niches and statues of Atticus and his family. The spring, working today, used to provide water to the metallurgical workshops of the city.

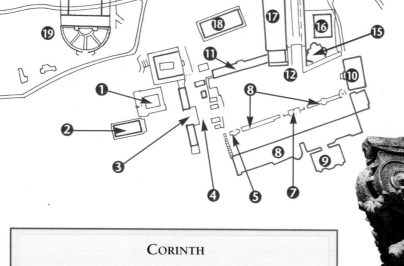

125 bottom The partial reconstruction of three columns in temple East at Corinth seems rather romantic; the temple should be considered the Capitolium of the city rebuilt by the Romans.

CORINTH

1 ARCHAEOLOGICAL MUSEUM	8 SOUTH STOÀ	15 PEIRENE FOUNTAIN
2 CAPITOLIUM	9 SOUTH BASILICA	16 SANCTUARY OF THE LECHAION
3 WEST PORTICO	10 JULIAN BASILICA	17 NORTH BASILICA
4 WEST TERRACE	11 NORTH PORTICO	18 TEMPLE OF APOLLO
5 SHRINE OF ARTEMIS AND DIONYSUS	12 ENTRANCE TO THE LECHAION	19 ODEION
6 SOUTH SHOPS	13 LECHAION WAY	20 THEATER
7 TRIBUNAL	14 FRAGMENTS OF THE ARCH OF SEPTIMIUS SEVERUS	

124-125 The splendor of the ruins and the decorative richness of the Corinthian capitals that marked the perimeter of the portico are all that remain of the shops in the west portico of the Forum.

125 top Corinthian capitals like the one in the photo crowned the columns of temple East, which was intentionally given a Hellenistic appearance.

126 top A lovely view of the cavea of the theater in Corinth which, it seems, was not built aligned with the peak of the Akrokòrinthos by chance; unfortunately, the building is in a poor state of repair.

126 center The ruins of the shops in the north portico of the Forum in Corinth stand at the foot of the low hill on which the *Archaic temple of Apollo stood; the temple is an excellent example of Doric architecture.*

126 bottom right The temple of Apollo bears architectural features typical of the Archaic era: heavy monolithic columns, a lengthened ground plan, and white plaster lining of the limestone (redone under the Romans).

The remains of a sanctuary (16) and a basilica (17) lie along the Lèchaion Road (13). At this point it is advisable to climb up to the modest enclosure to admire the remains of the peristasis of the sumptuous Doric peripteral temple hexastyle of Apollo (18). Built between 550 and 540 BC, the temple is a precious example of Archaic Greek architecture, featuring monolithic columns with pronounced *entasis* that surrounded a double tripartite cella opening onto a pronaos and opisthodomos. Some scholars believe that the smaller cella was used as an *àdyton,* either related to the oracular powers inspired by the god or serving as a small chapel dedicated to the cult of the god's sister, Artemis.

The remarkable *odeìon* (19) was built under the Roman Emperor Nero but was renovated in the Antonine period by Herodes Atticus and further modified in Severan times. The building could accommodate 7000 spectators and features structural and decorative aspects that are well in compliance with the architectural canons of the time. Further to the north lies the devastated theater, with its Classical foundations and circular orchèstra. It was refurbished in the Hellenistic period to accommodate 18,000 spectators. A sector in the theater was reserved for the priestess-prostitutes of the Akrokòrinthos, as indicated by an inscription on one of the seats.

126-127 The massive columns in the temple of Apollo decorated with the standard 20 sharp- *edged grooves are impressively high, over seven meters, and their diameter ranges from 1.30 to 1.75 meters.*

127 bottom left This interesting close-up of a column in the temple of Apollo shows the swollen line, typical of *Archaic architecture, of the echinus; the profile of the Doric capital is a sure method of dating buildings.* *127 bottom right Impressive remains of a paleo-Christian church of immense size (180 metres in length!)* *dedicated to St. Leonidas Bishop lie near the ancient Corinthian port of Lèchaion.*

128 top A lovely view of the theater of Sikyòn built during the Hellenistic era; the Romans added two covered entrances to the middle corridor (diàzoma), one of which can still be used.

128 bottom The historian and traveler Pausanias (2nd century AD) described several works of art at the gymnasíon at Sikyòn (in the photograph) that was still active as an educational center for the city's youth when he visited it.

128-129 Although only three columns of the temple of Zeus at Nemèa are still standing (the others were knocked down and broken during an earthquake), the architectural harmony the building must have emanated is still apparent.

The E65 highway leads from Corinth towards Patras. The next stop on the tour is, in fact, ancient **SIKYON**, home of the sculptor Lysippus, and also featuring a school of Classical painting. The city prospered under the rule of the Ortagorids (7th-6th century BC) and rose to a certain degree of prominence in the Hellenistic period. The most attractive highlights of the archaeological area open to the public are in the wide *agorà* flanked by the remains of the temple dedicated to Aphrodite Peithò, a long Doric double stoà (3rd century BC), a large (1600 square meters) Ionic hypo-style hall that served as the *bouleutérion* of the city, and the gymnasíon built on two terraces. The lower terrace is bordered by a triple Ionic colonnade and decorated with fountains and architectural elements. The upper terrace, accessible by well preserved side and central stairs, is surrounded by a triple Doric colonnade.

The large theater (circa 300 BC), features well-preserved *skenè* foundations and a large number of rows of the cavea. The Roman complex of thermal baths to the north of the *agorà* now houses a museum where visitors can admire some of the most ancient mosaic flooring of the Greek world (4th century BC).

129 bottom left The stadium at Nemèa — here seen from the sphendòne (curve) — is an impressive sight. The track on which the races in the Nemean Games were held is one of the best preserved in the Classical world.

129 bottom right The entrance corridor to the underground passage that led the athletes in the Nemean Games inside the stadium still has inscriptions on the walls left by participants.

NEMEA

1 ARCHAEOLOGICAL MUSEUM
2 TEMPLE OF ZEUS
3 ALTAR OF ZEUS
4 THESAUROI
5 XENON
6 HOUSES OF THE HELLANODIKAI
7 PUBLIC BATHS

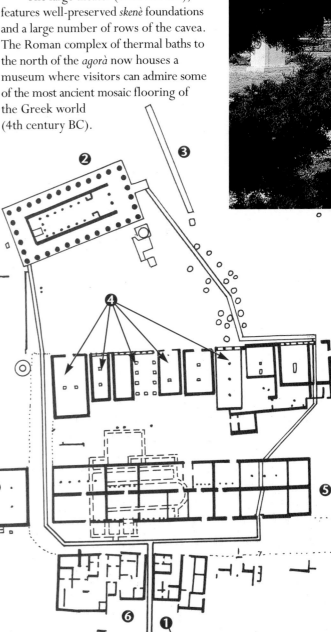

From nearby Kiàto, on the coast, a scenic road leads to the green valley of the mythical **STYMPHALIAN MARSH**, where Heracles completed one of the 12 labors. Winding through the wooded slopes of Mt. Killíni and Mt. Olìgyrtos, the road follows an unusual route up to another famous Peloponnesian sanctuary, **NEMEA**, already renowned in ancient times for the best red wine in all of Greece. It was here that the Panhellenic Nemean Games were held every two years in honor of Zeus.

It is advisable to start the tour of the site with a visit to the local museum(1) that is organized to provide the visitor with insight not only about the structures of the sanctuary but also about what life was like here in ancient times. Since the exhaustive material at the museum would make any detailed description in these pages superfluous, a summary outline of the site is provided below.

The splendid Doric peripteral temple hexastyle dedicated to Zeus (2) is the visual focus of the complex. Despite its

predominantly Doric layout, the temple features Ionic and Corinthian columns in the two overlapping rows of columns inside the cella. Three of the columns of the hexastyle, bearing a part of the pediment, still stand today on the massive stylobate (330-300 BC). An underground crypt at the back of the cella suggests that oracular prophecies were communicated here. A long altar to the east (3)was used for sacrifices. Athletes took oath at this altar before competing in the games. The way back to the museum passes by a series of *thesauroì* (4) (treasures), typical of

sanctuaries everywhere, built by certain cities (in some places the names of the donor cities are legible). Equally interesting are the remains of the large *xenòn* (5), the two-story inn where the athletes were housed. The nearby Hellenistic residences were occupied by the *Hellanodìkai* (6), the judges of the games. Excavations have recently been carried out on the stadium, recognizable along the road, not far from the museum. Access to the stadium was through an underground passage, over which stood a *própylon* that was used as a changing room for the athletes.

The provincial border with the Argolid is not far from the excavations at Nemèa. The landscape of the region features limestone highlands, smoothed by erosion and stripped bare by thousands of years of over-grazing and deforestation. The highlands alternate with a beautiful coastline incorporating many protected harbors.

The area has a rich architectural heritage. **MYCENAE** is by far the most famous site in the region. The city, which served as the backdrop to the legends immortalized by Homer and the Classical tragedies, also lent its name to the greatest of all pre-Classical Mediterranean civilizations, exquisite remains of which dating from the 17th to the 12th centuries BC have been found here. Since

remains. It is certain, for instance, that the walls were built (or rebuilt?) in the middle of the 14th century BC and were further extended about a century later.

The archaeological visit starts at the ramp that leads to the famous Lion Gate (2), the oldest existing example of monumental architecture in Europe. The gate is perpendicular to the wall and to its parallel defensive projection, in keeping with the traditional scheme, featuring a ramped, unroofed corridor leading to the door after a right-angled turn. The walls include a gate, a masterpiece of the application of the ancient *trilithon* (post-and-lintel) technique, with two heavy vertical support posts, and a massive, broad lintel stone

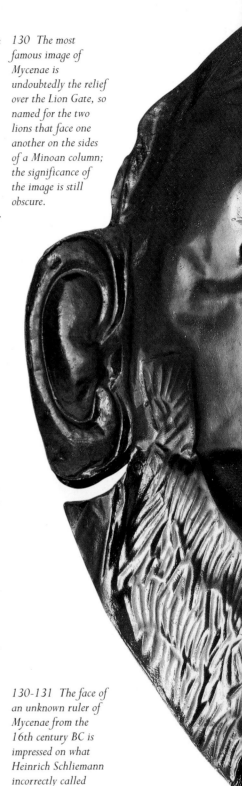

130   The most famous image of Mycenae is undoubtedly the relief over the Lion Gate, so named for the two lions that face one another on the sides of a Minoan column; the significance of the image is still obscure.

the city fell into rapid decadence and the destruction wreaked by the Dorian invasion and the raids by the "Sea Peoples" choked its trade-based economy, Mycenae has been left untouched by the recovery programs that erased all traces of previous civilizations in many other protohistoric cities.

Perched on top of a hill overlooking the plain of Argos and the Gulf of Nàfplion, and protected from behind by Mts. Sàra and Aghios Ilìas as well as the gorges of the Chàvos and the Kokorètsa, Mycenae impresses the visitor with its grandiose walls (1), mostly in polygonal and Cyclopean masonry. The walls extend for about one kilometer, the more recent parts being in pseudo-isodomic masonry. The original height and many details of the walls as they were in antiquity can be calculated from the

that thickens in the center. Above the lintel stone is a "relieving triangle," a Mycenaean Cyclopean architectural technique used to avoid excessive stress on the architrave just above the opening: the blocks above the opening are shaped and corbelled such that the forces exerted on them are discharged as vertical stresses on the piers and not directly onto the lintel. The triangular open space created above the lintel was filled with decorations in relief, in this case in stone, but of a much lesser thickness than the wall. The decorative slab, a rare example of Mycenaean figurative naturalism, depicts two heraldic lions facing each other from either side of a Minoan column on a high plinth, perhaps a seal or symbol of the royal house representing the Atridae, the ruling dynasty.

130-131   The face of an unknown ruler of Mycenae from the 16th century BC is impressed on what Heinrich Schliemann incorrectly called "Agamemnon's Mask" (Athens, National Museum).

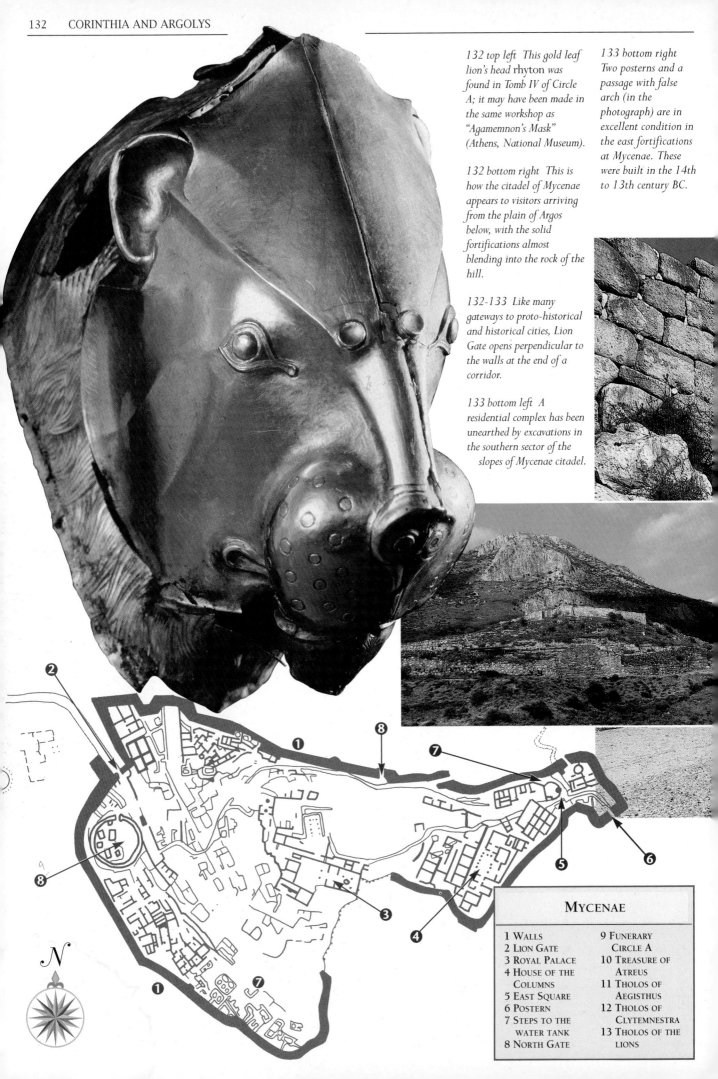

132 top left This gold leaf lion's head rhyton *was found in Tomb IV of Circle A; it may have been made in the same workshop as "Agamemnon's Mask" (Athens, National Museum).*

132 bottom right This is how the citadel of Mycenae appears to visitors arriving from the plain of Argos below, with the solid fortifications almost blending into the rock of the hill.

132-133 Like many gateways to proto-historical and historical cities, Lion Gate opens perpendicular to the walls at the end of a corridor.

133 bottom left A residential complex has been unearthed by excavations in the southern sector of the slopes of Mycenae citadel.

133 bottom right Two posterns and a passage with false arch (in the photograph) are in excellent condition in the east fortifications at Mycenae. These were built in the 14th to 13th century BC.

MYCENAE

1 WALLS	9 FUNERARY CIRCLE A
2 LION GATE	10 TREASURE OF ATREUS
3 ROYAL PALACE	11 THOLOS OF AEGISTHUS
4 HOUSE OF THE COLUMNS	12 THOLOS OF CLYTEMNESTRA
5 EAST SQUARE	13 THOLOS OF THE LIONS
6 POSTERN	
7 STEPS TO THE WATER TANK	
8 NORTH GATE	

A steep staircase leads to the summit of the natural acropolis with the remains of the royal palace (3), built between 1350 and 1330 BC. The palace centers on a wide, long *mègaron*, organized over several levels, with entrance structures (*propylaia*) and courtyards. The utility areas and residential rooms are partly spread over two floors, served by stairs. This is all that remains of the rooms that were the scene of the vicissitudes of the reigning dynasty, the Atridae, founded by the mythical king Atreus. Apart from stone that was mainly used for supporting structures, building materials included wood, mud, brick, and plaster. Beyond the rather unimpressive remains of other aristocratic residences, such as the House of the Columns (4), lies the East Square (5) opened on its east side by a postern (6) featuring a splendid corbel-vaulted roof. Here starts a long protected stairway leading down 18 meters to a well/cistern that provided a secure source of water if the city were under siege. In the northern wall of the acropolis is another ramped postern gate, known as the North Gate (8), the other smaller entrance to the walled city.

On the way back to the Lion Gate lies the first large cemetery of the city. This is known as Funerary Circle A (9),

134-135 This is an
imaginary
reconstruction of
Mycenae. This may
have been the
appearance of the city of

the Atridae at the time
of Agamemnon when
the last enlargement of
the defensive wall had
encircled Funerary
Circle A.

the 16th-century royal burial site. The site was enclosed by the citadel walls in about 1250 BC and transformed into a circular funerary sanctuary with cult structures very similar to a *heróon*. The archaeologist Heinrich Schliemann and his team excavated six shaft graves here. The site was especially rich in grave treasures. The shaft graves are large underground burial chambers (or *hypogea*) with pebble flooring, walls of rubble masonry and roofing (now lost), made up of wood or thin stone slabs resting on timber joists. After a burial, the shaft above the wood or stone roofing was covered with earth. The low mound was reinforced by sturdy rubble walls, delineating a circular sacred enclosure featuring a *dròmos* (entrance passage) with a *trilithon* (post-and-lintel) doorway. Within the enclosure 11 stelae, some decorated and others bare, marked the position of the graves that were opened and resealed for each new burial. 19 bodies were found in the shaft graves (eight men, nine women and two children). The very precious treasures unearthed here, including the famous gold death masks, are now at the National Museum in Athens.

135 Another example of the fervid imagination of Heinrich Schliemann was his naming of "Nestor's Cup" (16th century BC), a valuable gold chalice found in Tomb IV of Funerary Circle A (Athens, National Museum).

136 top This is an unusual view of the central nucleus of the royal mègaron at Mycenae; this was where the Atridae had their official seat and private residence and it was here, according to legend, that Agamemnon was assassinated.

136-137 top Funerary Circle A, dated to the 16th century BC, contained the royal tombs of at least three generations of the royal family. In the 14th-13th century BC, it was transformed into a heroic sanctuary.

136-137 bottom A lion hunt, perhaps by a Cretan artist, is represented on the blade of this bronze dagger decorated with gold and silver niello and found in Tomb IV of Circle A (Athens, National Museum).

137 top This delicate gold leaf diadem embossed with stylized floral motifs, in typical Mycenaean style, comes from Tomb III of the same funerary complex.

The tour of Mycenae continues with a visit to the burial sites outside the citadel walls, starting with the most famous and refined *thòlos* tomb of the ancient world, the so-called "Treasure of Atreus" dating from about 1250 BC. The circular corbel-vaulted chamber is preceded by an uncovered *dròmos* that was 36 meters long and six meters wide. The *dròmos* was flanked by ashlar walls made up of huge roughly rectangular blocks arranged in regular layers. Access to the corbel-vaulted chamber was through a high doorway (roughly 5 x 3 meters), the door of which, found shattered into fragments, was flanked by columns in green marble with a

smooth shaft bearing spiral decorative motifs. The relieving triangle, in turn framed by small columns in green marble, was filled by a slab bearing geometrical and architectural decorative motifs. The lintel (9.5 x 1.2 meters) made up of a single slab, weighs about 120 tons. The circular tomb chamber rises more than 13.5 meters in height and is 14.5 meters in diameter. The tomb chamber is corbel-vaulted, that is to say, made up of horizontal rows of finely cut stone blocks placed one on top of the other in such a way that each row slightly overlaps the one below, so that the structure gradually tapers upwards to the capstone that sealed the vault at its summit. To the side of the vaulted room, the small burial chamber was hewn into the bedrock that lies under the earth mound that, from the outside, is seen also to slope along the sides of the entrance walkway or *dròmos*.

The so-called *Thòlos* of Aegisthus is very ancient (ca. 1550 BC). Although part of the corbel vault has collapsed, scholars have calculated that the burial chamber was about 12 meters high and 14 meters across. Like part of the circular burial chamber itself, the 22-meter-long *dròmos* of this tomb is cut into the rock.

137 bottom The ramp that leads up to the palace of the Atridae is one of the most stirring sections in the city of Mycenae; knots of tourists tramp the same stone steps, worn by time, that Agamemnon walked upon.

138 top left A detail of the niello bronze dagger found in Tomb IV of Circle A: the stylized naturalistic outlines of the hunters appear to be miniatures of the figures seen in the frescoes of the Minoan palaces from the same era.

Not far from here lies the *Thòlos* of Clytemnestra dating from 1250 BC, with a 37-meter-long *dròmos*. The façade of the doorway, including the relieving triangle, was adorned by half-columns and decorated and painted chalk slabs. The round burial chamber measures 13.5 meters across. Other corbel-vaulted tombs have been found at Mycenae, dating from 1400-1250 BC. The *Thòlos* of the Lions that has lost its corbel-vault roofing is similar in size to the *Thòlos* of Aegisthus.

138 top right The underground tunnel in the northeast sector of Mycenae is an extraordinary example of the construction technique using the false arch method; a short stretch can still be visited.

138 bottom Miraculously intact in spite of the wear of time and weather, the false dome of the

"Treasure of Atreus" is a masterpiece of Mycenaean architecture that can only be admired.

138-139 The entrance to the large mound below which the "Treasure of Atreus" lies is solemnized by the long access corridor built with enormously heavy parallelepiped blocks.

139 bottom left Somewhat the worse for wear is the so-called "Thòlos of Clytemnestra," whose large monolithic architrave was too slender to support the pressure of the dome, despite the relieving triangle above it.

139 bottom right Less well-known, but still of interest for the presence of an access corridor partially dug out of the rock, is the Thòlos of Aegisthus, whose false dome collapsed.

The old road leading from Mycenae to **TIRYNS** and Nàfplion allows for a brief stop at the Heraìon of Argos, built at the site of the Mycenaean settlement of Pròsymna. The sanctuary stands on artificial terraces once adorned by sumptuous stoaì. The central terrace holds the foundations of the Doric peripteral temple hexastyle dedicated to Hera and rebuilt in 420 BC. It has a long cella that once held a chryselephantine (gold and ivory) cult statue of the goddess, by Polykleitos.

Unfortunately, the remains of ancient Greek and Roman **ARGOS**, the powerful *pòlis* that constantly fought with the major Helladic powers, are meager and disappointing. Today, it is a chaotic town of little archaeological interest except for its interesting museum, the spectacular fan-shaped cavea of the rock-hewn theater with a seating capacity of 20,000 (4th-3rd century BC) and the remains of the nearby Roman hot bath complex (2nd century AD) that includes sports structures.

Located on a bare mound close to the Gulf of Argos, the protohistorical site of **LERNA** is on the other hand, very fascinating. Under a modern protective structure lie the seven archaeological strata, ranging from the Neolithic age to the Mycenaean period. The site features the archaeologically important House of Tiles (2500 BC) one of the earliest examples of

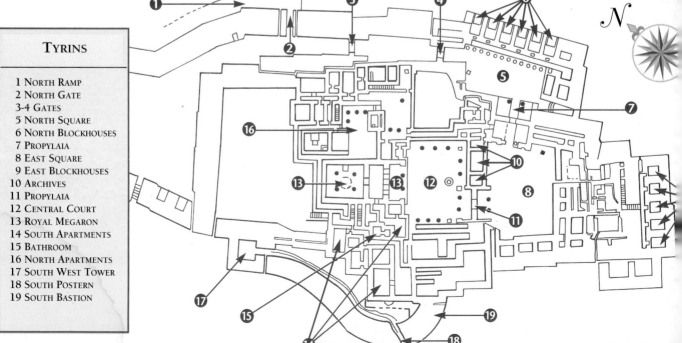

TYRINS

1 NORTH RAMP
2 NORTH GATE
3-4 GATES
5 NORTH SQUARE
6 NORTH BLOCKHOUSES
7 PROPYLAIA
8 EAST SQUARE
9 EAST BLOCKHOUSES
10 ARCHIVES
11 PROPYLAIA
12 CENTRAL COURT
13 ROYAL MEGARON
14 SOUTH APARTMENTS
15 BATHROOM
16 NORTH APARTMENTS
17 SOUTH WEST TOWER
18 SOUTH POSTERN
19 SOUTH BASTION

extensive roofing in durable material. The surviving structure of this house rises over 70 centimeters above the ground.

Continuing towards Nàfplion, one is well-advised to stop at the ruins of **TIRYNS** (2600-1100 BC), a powerful Helladic and Mycenaean city. The low acropolis extends from northwest to southeast and houses the *anáktoron* surrounded by a stupendous Cyclopean circuit wall, eight meters high and six meters thick. Access to the *anáktoron* is through a labyrinth of sloping ramped passages, and a sort of lower citadel built in the area below the acropolis. The "palace" was surrounded by walls that included, to the east and south, corbel-vaulted corridors linked to corbel-vaulted chambers built into the thickness of the walls. It is still uncertain whether these structures were used as storerooms or covered military outposts for archers during defensive and counteroffensive operations, since some of the chambers are equipped with window-like openings that could have been arrow slits.

141 top left The walls of Tyrins are an example of Mycenaean fortifications. Notable is the presence of sturdy towers and protected communicating passages.

141 top right The residential quarters of the fortified citadel at Tyrins; the heights of structures are better preserved here than at Mycenae and demonstrate the layout of the complex.

141 center right Despite being much less-known than Tyrins, the magnificently constructed cyclopean walls of Midea were also made using the polygonal technique.

141 bottom left Following a devastating fire of unknown origin, the precious and very fragile remains of the stone and unbaked brick walls of the houses at Lerna (2500 BC) are protected by every possible means.

140 top The corridor in the photo, in the background of which we see part of the cavea of the theater at Argos, was an internal passageway in the Roman baths complex.

140 bottom The "fan" shape of the rock-hewn theater of Argos is also to be seen in other Hellenistic theaters, e.g. Pergamum (Bergama, Turkey).

140-141 The baths at Argos were built during the Trajan era, restored in the 5th century and transformed into a Christian church. Here is the frigidarium, the room used for cold baths.

The *mègaron*-style layout is rather articulated: a large courtyard precedes a wide porticoed atrium that leads to the throne room, around which lie the private residential quarters and utility areas. The bathroom is surprising for its size and luxury, with a monolithic limestone floor. As at Mycenae, this site also features an ingenious system of protected access to underwater cisterns and a long staircase that connects a defensive tower of the western bastion with a well-camouflaged postern in the wall.

The museum of **NÀFPLION** is housed in an 18th-century AD Venetian palace at the heart of the city's historical center. The collection is made up of material from all over the region, including treasures from Funerary Circle B at Mycenae, the bronze armor from Midea late Mycenaean architectural decorations, and fragments of frescoes from Mycenae and Tiryns.

The last stop on this tour is the archaeologically very important site of **EPIDAUROS**, with its sanctuary of Asklepios, famous throughout the ancient world. Long an unrivaled cult and healing center, it flourished from the end of the 5th century BC up to the end of the Roman period. Athletic games as well as music and drama competitions were held here during the great festival of Asklepios. All this came to an abrupt end with the Edict of Theodosios I (395 AD) which incited Christians to completely destroy the site where the god of healing miraculously cured the sick.

The route of the visit today runs opposite to the itinerary followed by pilgrims in antiquity. Immediately after the entrance lies the famous, magnificent theater (1),

perhaps the best-preserved of the ancient world. The structure incorporates harmonious proportions with exceptional acoustics. Visitors should feel free to experiment directly and follow the advice of tourist guides who invite people to throw a coin on the stone at the center of the circular orchèstra, at the base of the altar of Dionysus – the tinkling sound of the coin as it hits the stone can be heard perfectly throughout the vertiginous cavea that leans against a hillside. The enormous cavea can accommodate between 12,000 to 15,000 spectators. The theater was built around 350 BC by Polykleitos the Younger. Only pale traces remain of the very simple skenè, while the corridors (parodòi) connecting the chorus to the orchèstra featured high

doors with Ionic pillars. The cavea, accessed through parodòi with decorated doors, opens out like a fan and comprises 55 rows of stepped seats, divided at the 34th row by a two-meter-wide diàzoma (horizontal passage). The seats above the diàzoma were added when the structure was extended in about 170 BC. The first three rows with finely decorated seats were reserved for city officials. The cavea is divided vertically by 13 staircases (the 7th staircase runs through the central point of the theater) below the diàzoma and 23 staircases above. The ratios between the individual parts of the structure are obvious, since the theater envelops the space of the spectacle, suggesting by its very shape, a quest for mutual understanding between the actors and the audience.

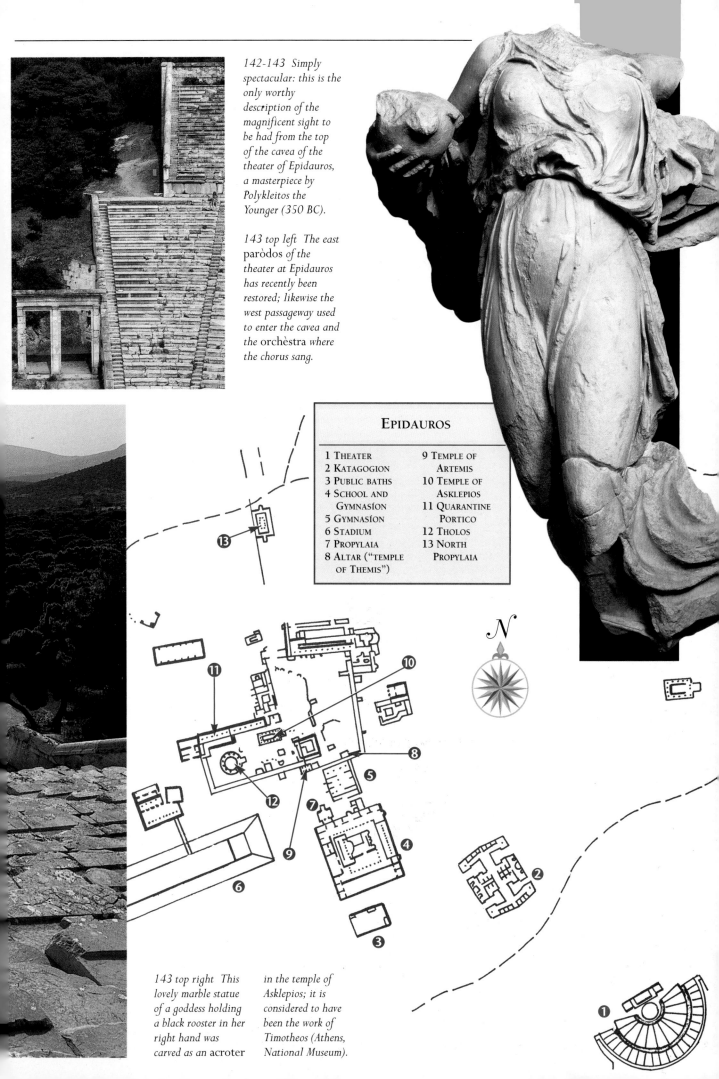

142-143 Simply spectacular: this is the only worthy description of the magnificent sight to be had from the top of the cavea of the theater of Epidauros, a masterpiece by Polykleitos the Younger (350 BC).

143 top left The east paròdos of the theater at Epidauros has recently been restored; likewise the west passageway used to enter the cavea and the orchèstra where the chorus sang.

EPIDAUROS

1 THEATER	9 TEMPLE OF
2 KATAGOGION	ARTEMIS
3 PUBLIC BATHS	10 TEMPLE OF
4 SCHOOL AND	ASKLEPIOS
GYMNASÍON	11 QUARANTINE
5 GYMNASÍON	PORTICO
6 STADIUM	12 THOLOS
7 PROPYLAIA	13 NORTH
8 ALTAR ("TEMPLE	PROPYLAIA
OF THEMIS")	

143 top right This lovely marble statue of a goddess holding a black rooster in her right hand was carved as an acroter in the temple of Asklepios; it is considered to have been the work of Timotheos (Athens, National Museum).

144 top left This rosette was chosen by Polykleitos the Younger for the metope of the Thymèle (or Thòlos) of the round temple erected in 350 BC to the southwest of the larger temple (Epidauros, Archaeological Museum).

144 bottom The ruins of many buildings at Epidauros are very eroded and almost unrecognizable; this is what remains of the Hellenistic gymnasíon and its many rooms.

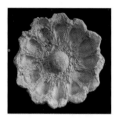

144-145 The bases of many votive offering containers erected in honor of Asklepios stand along the south edge of the temple dedicated to the god; many are based on a semi-circular exedra with seats.

The tour continues towards the heart of the sanctuary, at the foot of the hill against which the theater rests. The first structure to visit here is the *xenòn* or *katagògion* (2), a sort of official guest house for visiting VIPs in antiquity. The guest house, built in polygonal masonry towards the end of the 4th century BC, was equipped with 160 rooms spread over two stories as well as peristyle gardens with fountains and a decorative water system. The nearby heavily devastated public baths (3) date from the 3rd century BC. The same century saw the completion of the grandiose gymnasíon complex (4) covering about 5,300 square meters, with a peristyle courtyard and about 20 rooms of varying sizes, including hypostyle halls, used as training rooms, banquet halls and meeting rooms. After the construction of a small *odeíon* at the center

new materials, if necessary). Immediately to the right lie the remains of a 4th century BC altar, long mistaken as a temple of Themis (8). To the left, one can see the foundations of the small *pòros* Doric temple prostyle hexastyle dedicated to Artemis (9), featuring a cella with Ionic columns. The open-air altar, surrounded by a balustrade, was linked to the temple by a ramp.

Also accessible by a sloping ramp, the temple of Asklepios (10), the highlight of the sanctuary, stands at the center of the sacred enclosure. Built by the architect Theodotos in 380 BC to replace a more ancient structure, this *pòros* Doric peripteral temple hexastyle once boasted pediments and *acroteria* (sculpted pediment decorations) by the great Timotheos (all surviving elements are now at the National

145 top The thòlos *has recently undergone heavy restoration and partial anastylosis; the reconstruction is due to continue for some time.*

145 bottom One of the magnificent Corinthian capitals designed and sculpted with unequaled refinement by Polykleitos the Younger for the cella of the Thymèle *is in almost perfect condition (Epidauros, Archaeological Museum).*

of the complex in Roman times, a smaller additional gymnasíon (5) was built against the wall of the sacred enclosure (*témenos* wall).

The gymnasíon was closely linked to the nearby stadium (6), which was built by leveling a natural depression. Access is through an underground passage (as in Nemèa and Olympia). At the north side of the gymnasíon, a Hellenistic Doric *própylon* hexastyle with a ramp sloping towards the *témenos* marked the athletes' and judges' entrance to the sacred enclosure of the god (7).

The visitor crosses the *témenos* wall in the midst of a chaotic tumble of buildings, monument bases, inscriptions and architectural debris, soon to be reconstructed by anastylosis (the reconstruction of ancient ruins using original architectural debris combined with

Museum in Athens). A large number of building materials were used to construct the temple, ranging from Pentelic marble to ivory, gold and highly prized wood as well as stone in various hues.

To the north of the temple lies the Hellenistic Ionic *àbaton-enkoimetérion* (11), the porticoed "incubation" dormitory where pilgrims, having completed the preparatory rights, waited for the god to cure them through their dreams. Many votive epigraphs donated to the sanctuary in thanksgiving for cures were found at the site and are now in the museum. The most beautiful building in Epidauros is the *Thòlos* or *Thymèle* (12), a round monopteral temple, designed by Polykleitos the Younger, unprecedented, except perhaps for the temple of Athena Pronaìa at Delphi. The structure that evokes the elegant round huts of the protohistoric Helladic period,

rested on six underground concentric rings. The three outer rings were designed to support the peristasis while the three inner, intercommunicating rings, accessible from the cella of the temple, perhaps alluded to the coils of the snake sacred to Asklepios.

The peristasis featured 26 slender Doric columns crowned by a frieze of triglyphs, alternating with metopes adorned by rosettes in relief. The eave gutter or *sìma* was decorated with water spouts in the shape of lion-head *protoma* that alternated with refined palmettes resting on a bed of intricately intertwining sculpted plant branches. The cella boasted a peristasis of 14 Corinthian columns designed for the building by Polykleitos the Younger, and a decorated lacunar ceiling that featured large flowers within a wide variety of frames contained in its coffers. Polychrome plaster decorations and alternating white and

black marble completed the effect of a highly tasteful structure, suggested by the liveliness and depth of the relief sculptures. The conic roof was adorned by *acroteria* (pedimental decorations) depicting plant motifs.

To complete a visit to the site, it is worthwhile taking the long walk up to the elegant north Propylaia (13) built in 330 BC or a little later. In ancient times, pilgrims entered the sanctuary through these gate structures built with Doric hexastyle fronts supported by a high stylobate with sloping access ramps. Corinthian columns decorated the inside of the entrance buildings.

The archaeological museum close to the theater houses a wide and rare collection of beautiful architectural and sculptural decorations taken from the main buildings of the sanctuary.

146 top A lovely detail of the marble barrel vault of the Thymèle; the decorations of large fleshy flowers were

originally very colorful, as were many other parts of the building (Epidauros, Archaeological Museum).

146-147 Here is another example of the refinement of the work of Polykleitos the Younger; these are eaves decorated with palmettes, acanthus volutes and lion-head gargoyles (Epidauros, Archaeological Museum).

147 The photograph of the elevation of the cella of the Thymèle shows the slenderness of the column and capital and the lightness of the entablature (Epidauros, Archaeological Museum).

ACHAIA, ELIS AND MESSENIA

The northern region of the Peloponnese, Achaia, faces the long arm of the Ionian sea that stretches up to the Corinthian Isthmus. The rocky shoreline is often interrupted by white pebble beaches. The Mediterranean pines on the upper reaches of the steep Panachaikón, Erymanthos and Aroània mountains, cut by valleys, make way, on the lower slopes, for dense woods of oleander, cypress and eucalyptus trees that cover the coastline from Eghira to Kàtos Achaìa in a lush coat of greenery. To the west of Kàtos Achaìa, neighboring Elis extends over a less-rugged landscape.

PATRAS (Patra), the largest center of the entire Peloponnese, today shows scant traces of ancient Pátrai, whose origins are lost in the mists of prehistory. Often neutral in the rivalry between the Hellenic *pòleis*, the ancient city was to become the focus of the Achaian League (280-146 BC) before reaching the peak of its glory under the Romans, especially after its re-foundation as an Augustan colony. Although a large number of exhibits at the modern city's museum indicate that the area was populated from the Bronze to the Iron Age, the only monument visible today – apart from architectural debris from the ancient city's temples, recycled to build the Medieval castle – is the *odeíon* (160 AD), a concert hall that had a roof in ancient times. Although other parts of the structure required heavy restoration, the proscenium with small niches as well as the built-up *skenè* façade with three doors and niches, have survived almost intact. A large number of sarcophagi dating from the Middle Roman Empire lie around the site.

From Patras, it is worthwhile to take the time to make the trip to Eghira (70 km east, along the E65 highway), known in antiquity as **AIGEIRA**. Built in the

148 top The small green archaeological park that surrounds the odeíon *in Patras allows us to appreciate the time-worn building from many angles along the outer perimeter.*

148 center A few rooms of a building with polychrome mosaics from the third century BC have been discovered near the concert hall; the picture shows a detail with geometric motifs.

148 bottom Another view of the outer perimeter wall of the odeion in Patras; a vast third century AD polychrome floor *mosaic in the foreground is decorated with figured squares between wave-shaped and entwined frames.*

148-149 Numerous figured Roman sarcophagi, architectural elements and marble seats stand outside the restored concert room built *during the Roman era; this is the most important building from Patras's archaeological heritage.*

Geometric period, the city was still a flourishing center in Roman times. The main highlights of this site are the recently excavated areas of the rock-hewn theater (3rd century BC). The cavea and the orchèstra, cut into the rock, as well as the remains of the *skenè*, are easily recognizable. A little to the north lie the remains of several small Hellenistic temples, two of which feature floors decorated with pebble mosaics, inside the cella.

From Patras, the E55 highway continues southwest towards the border with Elis, heralded by long stretches of fertile plains interrupted by low hills that, more to the south, give way to mountains and valleys. The Ionian sea bathes the shoreline, tracing wide bays interrupted by saltwater lakes and marshland, up to the mouth of the river Nèdas.

149 top A high relief of vigor and expressiveness by an anonymous mid-empire Roman artist shows a spread eagle holding festoons in its beak.

149 bottom left A mid-empire Roman sarcophagus decorated in high reliefs shows a hunt in a forest and is therefore *indicative of the rank of the deceased; hunting was the prerogative of the nobility.*

149 bottom right A colossal lion in this *rather poorly executed sarcophagus hurls itself at a tiny rider. "Heroic" themes were favored by aristocratic clients of this kind of work.*

At Pyrgos, the tour continues eastward, heading for the most famous sanctuary of the ancient world, renowned today as one of the most important archaeological sites ever excavated. Even the most blasé visitor soon succumbs to the powerful charm of enchanting **OLYMPIA**, nestled at the heart of the flat river valley where the Alphiòs (Alpheus) and Kladiòs (Cladeus) rivers meet. The site lies at the foot of the low Krònion hill, covered by Aleppo pines and shrubs, evoking, albeit in a modern version, the Altis, the mystical grove consecrated to Zeus. The origins of Olympia date back to the end of the 2nd millennium BC, although the area had been settled since 2800 BC, about a thousand years earlier. All of Hellas used to gather at the non-oracular sanctuary for the Olympiads, the games held every four years. All conflicts were suspended and a truce (the Olympic

Truce) was declared to discuss and peacefully resolve disputes between the various *pòleis* during the games. The ruins are intertwined with ancient myths. The legend of the love story between the river god Alpheus and the nymph Arethusa, consumed in Syracuse, bears witness to the ideal ties between the Peloponnese and the Greeks of the western colonies. On the other hand, the myth of Pelops symbolizes the equally strong bonds that linked the sanctuary to remote Greek colonies. According to the myth, Pelops came from a distant eastern land and defeated the cruel king Oenomaus in a chariot-race to affirm the values of justice, humanity and respect for divine laws. As a reward for his pains, the region was named after him. Another myth recounts that Heracles brought the sacred olive branch from the land of the Hyperboreans and founded the Olympiads, the games held in honor of Zeus to celebrate the labors of Pelops.

The flat landscape of Olympia allowed structures to be widely spaced rather than concentrated around a compact core. Spread over the vast area of the sanctuary are a large number of structures, such as the sacred buildings, with annexes that served as residences for priests and administrative offices, the architectural and artistic commemorative monuments, the structure for the games and accommodations for athletes, visitors, and travelers, as well as political and diplomatic delegations. At first glance, even in ancient times, Olympia may not have appeared as overwhelmingly spectacular as the dense construction at the sanctuary of Apollo at Delphi. The modern day visitor should however bear in mind that the Olympian sanctuary remained one of the greatest epicenters of Greek art until the end of the 4th century AD, when its fate was sealed by the Christian Roman Emperor Theodosios I who banned all pagan cults, games and festivals. Earthquakes, landslides and devastating floods completed the destruction by burying the entire sanctuary under a thick layer of mud.

150 One of the greatest masterpieces of all time is the sculpture of Hermes with Dionysus as a child; it has been attributed to the sculptor Praxiteles (circa 340 BC) who infuses it with a discreet degree of pàthos (Olympia, Archaeological Museum).

150-151 The beauty of the ruins at Olympia is heralded by the elegant Doric column in the palaìstra (third century BC) around which stood training rooms for boxing and wrestling.

151 This fine capital was part of the South Portico, an elegant stoà to the south of the bouleutérion built around the mid-4th century BC with a Doric front and Corinthian colonnade inside.

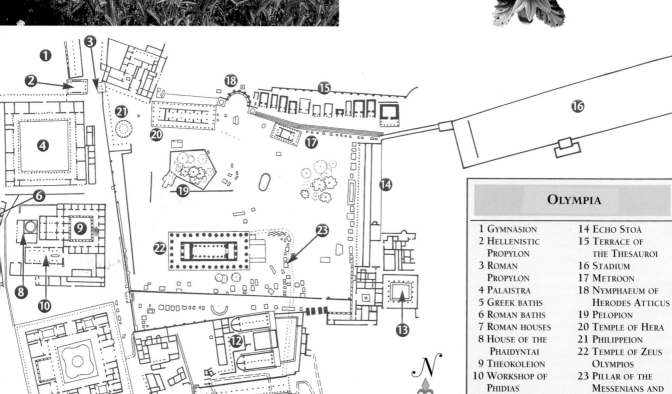

OLYMPIA

1 GYMNÀSION	14 ECHO STOÀ
2 HELLENISTIC PROPYLON	15 TERRACE OF THE THESAUROI
3 ROMAN PROPYLON	16 STADIUM
4 PALAISTRA	17 METROON
5 GREEK BATHS	18 NYMPHAEUM OF HERODES ATTICUS
6 ROMAN BATHS	19 PELOPION
7 ROMAN HOUSES	20 TEMPLE OF HERA
8 HOUSE OF THE PHAIDYNTAI	21 PHILIPPEION
9 THEOKOLEION	22 TEMPLE OF ZEUS OLYMPIOS
10 WORKSHOP OF PHIDIAS	23 PILLAR OF THE MESSENIANS AND OF THE NAUPACTIANS
11 LEONIDAION	
12 BOULEUTÉRION	
13 SOUTH-EAST BUILDING	

152 top The ruins of a paleo-Christian basilica stand over the Workshop of Phidias where the colossal gold and ivory statue of Zeus Olympios (circa 430 BC) was produced.

152 bottom The helmet worn by Miltiades at the battle of Marathon (490 BC) is of inestimable value; it was dedicated by the Athenian strategist to Zeus, as indicated by the engraving on the edge (Olympia, Archaeological Museum).

152-153 View of the palaìstra at Olympia. The large central space (about 4000 square meters!) was used for open-air training in certain athletic disciplines and relaxation.

153 top right It is difficult to imagine the original elegant layout of the Leonidàion, *the accommodation provided for the top athletes, with its internal gardens embellished with fountains and a winding canal (350 BC).*

153 bottom right The Leonidàion *was adorned with a Ionic colonnade; the building was in part converted into the residence of the Roman governor for the province of* Achaia.

cult statue of Zeus Olympios. These are followed by the *Theokoleion* (9), which may in fact have served as a wrestling school before being transformed into a residence for the priests in charge of organizing the Olympiads. The Workshop of Phidias (10) was a vast (nearly 500 square meters) rectangular hall in which the famous artist sculpted the colossal 12-13-meter high chryselephantine (gold and ivory) statue of the father of the gods. Excavations of the workshop brought to light a large number of rejected pieces as well as the famous mug inscribed with the words "I am (the property) of Phidias." The Early Christian basilica (400-410 AD) built over the workshop of the Athenian sculptor is also recognizable.

Further south stood the *Leonidàion* (11), a large luxury hotel built by Leonidas of Nàxos towards 350 BC to accommodate

Access to the site is from the parking lot, located near the museum. The remains of a large Hellenistic *gymnàsion* (1) dating from the end of the third century BC, are recognizable to the right of the path past the entrance. The double portico on the east side of the structure has been spared by the swells of the Kladiòs. This portico, known as the *xystos*, was used for indoor training by sprinters and covers the distance of one lap of the *stàdion* (220 meters). In ancient times this area was accessed through a graceful *pròpylon* (2) in the form of a small temple amphiprostyle tetrastyle with Asiatic Corinthian capitals. In Roman times, a rather melancholic *pròpylon* tetrastyle (3), breaching the *témenos* wall that delineated the sacred enclosure of the Altis, was built on an east-west axis with the earlier entrance structure. South of the *gymnàsion* lies the well-preserved vast *palaìstra* (training area for wrestling and boxing) (4), consisting of a large square enclosed by a portico. Access to the *palaìstra* was through the Doric *pròpylon* in the northwestern corner. The Doric peristyle

courtyard was flanked by 19 rooms preceded by Ionic columns. The functions of some of these rooms are still recognizable.

To the southwest corner, side by side and partly overlapping, lie the remains of a Greek bath complex (5), that served the *gymnàsion*/wrestling school. The baths, dating from 450-350 BC, were fitted with individual rooms and tubs for hot baths and showers as well as an open-air swimming pool. The current ruins also include the remains of a Roman hot bath complex (6), the so-called Kladiòs Thermal Baths, built under the Emperor Trajan. The Roman structure features mosaic flooring and rooms for both collective and individual baths. To the south, linked to the thermal baths stood two luxurious residences with peristyle courtyards, dating from the Antonine and Severan periods (7).

To the east of this residential-bath complex, lie the remains of what may have been the main office and cult building (8) (5th century BC) of the association of the officials in charge of the maintenance of the

the famous athletes competing in the Olympic Games. In Roman times, the structure was converted into the official residence of the governor of the province of Achaia. The structure featured a peristyle courtyard and wings with rooms of various sizes. A splendid garden with fountains and a deep decorative canal rendered the vast 6000 square meter complex a real delight. The remains of three *thermae* baths around the building indicate the great care taken in ancient times to ensure that the hotel provided full comfort.

To the east lie the remains of the *bouleutérion* (12). The building has a porticoed entrance porch and an enclosed courtyard used as a cult and assembly area (4th century BC), between two elongated Archaic structures each featuring a vestibule tristyle *in antis*, two naves and a bipartite apse. The South Stoà, a double Doric-Corinthian portico with a central *própylon* hexastyle on its south side, is scenically located on the road that led to the sacred *témenos* of Zeus. Equally interesting is the South-East Building (13), a complex that, between the 5th century BC and the Severan period, was frequently modified not only in form but also in use. It was probably also once used as the Olympian residence of the Roman Emperor Nero and as a luxurious bath complex that

154 top right The stadium used in the Olympic Games had only the simple grassy mounds that still ring the track for spectators to watch.

154 center left The temple of Hera is a perfect reference for the development of the Doric capital; the original wooden columns were in fact replaced over the course of nine centuries.

154 bottom left Only part of the barrel vault (4th century BC) remains in the underground passage that led into the stadium at Olympia; it has similarities with the passage at Nemèa.

featured mosaics depicting marine motifs. While the remains of the long Echo Stoà (14) may seem ridiculous today, the modern visitor should bear in mind that the structure was dismantled in 267 AD to provide the building materials used to fortify the sanctuary during the Herulian invasion. The original structure, famous for its echo effects was a double portico, almost 100 meters long. It was started in the 4th century BC and only completed during the Augustan period.

Past the Echo Stoà, to the right and along the Treasury Terrace (15) lie the bases of the *Zànes*, votive statues to Zeus, built using the proceeds of fines inflicted on athletes for cheating and fouls during the games. They served as a warning to competing athletes, since participants had to file past these statues to enter the Stadium (16). The current remains of the stadium date from 330-320 BC, with the tribune

and seats for the judges.

Going back to the Treasury Terrace, one passes 12 small buildings, nearly all *in antis* and intended to serve as small temple-like museums, housing offerings donated by city-states. Built between the middle of the 6th and the end of the 5th century BC, the treasuries were dedicated, in order from east to west, by the city-states of Gela, Megara, the inhabitants of an unknown city, Iblea, Metapontium, Selinos, the inhabitants of another unknown city, Cyrene, the inhabitants of another unknown city, Sybaris, Byzantium, Epidamnus, Syracuse and Sikyon.

At the foot of the complex lie the remains of the *Metròon* (17), a Doric peripteral temple hexastyle dating from the beginning of the 4th century BC, and converted to house the imperial cult in Roman times. Close by stand the ruins of

154-155 Not much of the base remains of the splendid Philippeìon, the round temple built in the most important sanctuary in the Peloponnese by Philip II of Macedonia after his victory at the battle of Chaironeia (338 BC).

155 bottom A view of the nymphaeum of Herodes Atticus (170 AD); tapping the waters of the river Mourìa 20 kilometers to the east, the fountain resolved the problem of water supplies that afflicted Olympia in summer.

the nymphaeum of Herodes Atticus, a fountain house, originally in marble, built in 170 AD (18). The structure became a memorial to the "divine" glories of the Roman Antonine Emperors and of the Athenian philanthropist (*euergetes*) who built it, in front of the ancient altars of Hera and Zeus (the latter included a mound of ashes from sacrifices, compacted using water from the Alphiòs). Close by lies the *Pelòpion* (19), an enclosure (4th century BC) dedicated to the cult of Pelops.

To the north of the *Pelòpion* stand the ruins of the temple of Hera (*Heraion*) (20), one of the earliest examples of Doric architecture. Founded in 650 BC and rebuilt near the end of the same century, it was so highly venerated that it was continuously repaired and replaced if necessary. Pausanias, writing in the 2nd century AD, recounts that he saw one of the original wooden columns. Within the peristasis of 6 x 16 columns lies the pronaos distyle *in antis* and the cella, with four internal spur walls and eight columns that provided support to the flat roof. Housing votive offerings from the outset, after the consecration of the larger temple, the *Heraion* was transformed into a museum. The statue of Hermes carrying the young Dionysus that was found here and controversially attributed to Praxiteles, is now at the museum. Not far from the *Heraion* stands the *Philippeìon* (21), a circular monopteral structure built by Philip II of Macedonia after the victory at Chaironea (338 BC). The structure was completed under Alexander the Great. While the outer peristasis was Ionic, the columns inside the building were Corinthian. The building housed five gold and ivory statues representing Philip II, a masterpiece by Leochares.

156 top left Many works of art built on bases of all shapes and sizes were spread around the main buildings of the Altis over the centuries without much thought given to their order.

The last structure on this tour of Olympia is the religious and architectural highlight of the entire sanctuary. Although it original, grandiose structure was literally taken apart by Christian zealots during the 5th century AD and further devastated by the natural cataclysms that hit the region later, the temple of Zeus Olympios (22), built in 470-460 BC by the architect Libon o Elis still undoubtedly retains a lot of its ancient charm. The largest temple of the Peloponnese (about 64 x 28 meters, with a height of 20 meters), it was built in shell limestone covered by imitation marble stucco The temple stands on a sturdy crepidoma

156 bottom left Damaged but not enough to prevent appreciation of its gracefulness, this is the Winged Victory of the Messenians and Naupactians (425-420 BC) by Paiònios of Mènde (Olympia, Archaeological Museum).

156 top right The Centauromachy is a masterpiece of proto-Classical pedimental sculpture (460 BC) by an unknown artist; it was positioned on the west pediment of the temple of Zeus (Olympia, Archaeological Museum).

156-157 The massive rocks of the Doric columns of the temple of Zeus collapsed at the sides of the building following an earthquake.

157 The master who decorated the east pediment of the temple of Zeus with the myth of Pelops personified the river Kladiòs with the face and body of a worried youth (Olympia, Archaeological Museum).

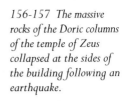

with three steps breached by an access ramp on the east side. The cella and other rooms as well as the impressive remains of the peristasis (6 x 13 columns) provide a good idea of the temple's imposing dimensions. The gabled roof was covered by large marble tiles and bordered by eaves with lion *protoma* water spouts. The column drums, each about 1.5 meters high and 2 meters across, that made up the columns were held together by sealed joints. The pediments and 12 metopes (six on each side) in Parian marble that decorated the Doric frieze of the pronaos and opisthodomos were the work of Peloponnesian artists and some

modern experts attribute them to Hageladas and his school. The frieze of the peristasis was bare. The east pediment depicted the chariot race between Oenomaos and Pelops, while the west pediment represented battles between Lapiths (humans) and Centaurs at the wedding of Pirithous. The metopes depicted the 12 Labors of Heracles.

Around 435 BC, the famous colossal chryselephantine (gold and ivory) cult statue (now lost) of Zeus by Phidias was placed in the cella.

In front of the entrance to the temple is the restored Pillar of the Messenians and Naupactians, commemorating their joint

victory over Sparta in 425 BC. The pillar was crowned by a statue of the goddess Nike or Winged Victory by Paiònios of Mènde (now at the museum).

A visit to the Archaeological Museum of Olympia is an absolute must for all visitors to the sanctuary. The museum's collection includes exceptional works of art, excavated at the sanctuary, dating from the Geometric period through to Roman times. Some of the highlights are the pediment sculptures and metopes of the temple of Zeus Olympios, absolute proto-Classical masterpieces, the Nike by Paiònios and the famous Hermes with the young Dionysus, attributed to Praxiteles.

From Olympia, the tour continues along the coast through Krestena. It is worthwhile to stop off at **KAIÀFAS**, with its dual grotto consecrated to the Anygrìdes Nymphs. According to myth, the mortally wounded Centaur Nessus, struck by Heracles' poisoned arrow, washed his injuries in the water, forever tainting it with the smell of his rotting blood.

At Tholò on the coast the tour deviates inland, continuing about 50 kilometers to the well-preserved Doric peripteral temple hexastyle of Apollo Epikoùrios ("the helper") at Phigáleia, modern **VÀSSES** (Bassae), the product of the genius of Ictinus and Callicrates, the architects of the Parthenon at Athens, who rebuilt this temple in 425 BC to commemorate the end of the pestilence.

Built in local limestone with details in marble, the temple features several stylistic contradictions resulting from the use of building materials recycled from earlier structures. The plan is elongated, dimensioned in keeping with the Archaic proportional ratio of 5:2 instead of the 9:4 ratio applied at the Parthenon. The optical effects built into the columns and stylobate are, on the other hand, very Classical. The cella features innovations and interesting contaminations, with its internal transversal spur walls, and typically Peloponnesian

158 top left The smell of the sulphurous waters of the grotto of Kaiàfas is said to have come from the Centaur Nessus who washed his mortal wound here.

158 bottom left The hill on which the temple of Apollo Epikoùrios stands at Vàsses retains remains of structures erected around the building.

158 top center The outer colonnade of the temple of Apollo Epikoùrios at Vàsses was built in the Doric order, whereas the cella has Ionic counterforts .

doors, an "Athenian" mix of architectural styles experimented with in Athens. Furthermore, the entablature of the cella bore a high-relief frieze depicting scenes from battles with Amazons (amazonomachy) and Centaurs (centauromachy). The frieze is now at the British Museum in London.

After crossing the Nèdas, one enters Messenia with its jagged coastline featuring beaches of fine sand, and more rarely, pebbles. The landscape is more rugged than in Elis, with mountain chains interrupted only by the brief Pàmissos plain. The border with Laconia to the east is marked by the heights of Mt. Taygetos.

A little before Kyparissìa, a brief deviation off the E55 highway leads to the Late Mycenaean necropolis of **PERISTERIÀ**, with collapsed rubble-walled *thòlos* tombs.

No tourist to the region should miss an opportunity to visit, further to the south, the hill of Epáno Englianós, where excavations, commenced in the 1930s, have unearthed the remains of the "palace-manor house" of ancient **PYLOS**, identified by modern scholars as the *anàktoron* (royal palace) of the Homeric King Nestor of Pylos. The vast complex was undefended except for a sort of low protective ring made up of escarpments and completed by modest ramparts. The site appears as a large rustic manor house, which obviously developed and prospered thanks to the cultivation of the fertile surrounding countryside, seconded by palace workshops. All this was revealed from the interpretation of accounting records on tablets referring to the last year of the palace's lifespan. The clay tablets were stored in the archive room at the entrance of the complex, written in a script known by modern researchers as "Linear B", the

alphabet of the Mycenaean language. These tablets have survived only because they were cooked into tile when the palace was destroyed by fire around 1190 BC. The discovery of the tablets marked a watershed in modern archaeology.

The map provides an indication of the various functions of the rooms and dependenci· of the complex. Arranged on a longitudinal axi stands a *própylon* (1) (entrance structure) flanke by guardrooms (3-4) and the royal archives (2-3), followed by a Tiryns-style courtyard (4) leading up to a double vestibule (5) (*pròdomos*) that opened onto a hall (*dòmos*). The latter had fixed throne at one end (6) and a central fixed hearth between four wooden columns that supported an open tower-like structure rising above the roof for light and ventilation (clerestory). Corridors led to various smaller rooms all around. These served as residential quarters and utilities or storage areas (such as, for instance, the room to the northwest (17), fitted with well-preserved hollowed-out

158 bottom center Callicrates used Corinthian capitals to decorate the column at the center of the far wall and the two oblique counterforts at the sides of the cella in the temple of Apollo.

158 right The Mycenaean thòlos tomb near Pylos palace dates from the 15th century BC; at over 9 meters in diameter, it is one of the largest Mycenaean tombs in the region.

158-159 One of the most attractive corners in the Mycenaean palace at Pylos is the bathroom in the residential wing where there is a painted terracotta tank with an access step.

159 bottom The residence of the ruler of Pylos was fitted with a living room with a low round hearth at the center of the room, used to provide heat and light and for cooking.

stuccoed benches intended to store a series of oil or wine jars). The remains of staircases suggest that the structures had two stories, with balconies and well-lit high-ceilinged rooms. Building materials were mainly timber and stucco, perhaps also mud-brick in the *pisé* technique, over a low stone foundation. The light weight of the structures therefore allowed for an upper floor. The buildings, dating from the 15th (the large *thòlos* tomb) to the 13th (the entire palatial complex) centuries BC, provide precious insight into what life was like in a flourishing Mycenaean city.

Many of the objects found at the *anàktoron* are on show at the archaeological museums of **Chora Trifylias** and Pylos. Discerning tourists would also enjoy a short stop at Chòra Trifylìas, to visit the Mycenaean necropolis of **Volimidia**, just outside the modern town.

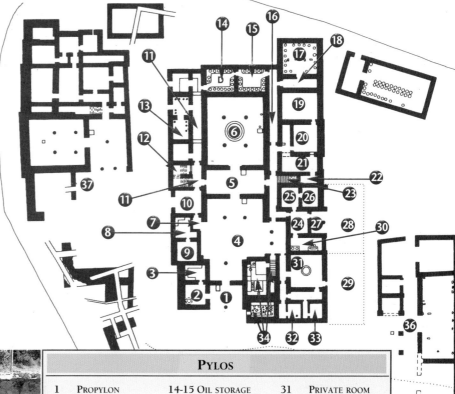

PYLOS				
1	PROPYLON	14-15	OIL STORAGE	31	PRIVATE ROOM
2-3	ARCHIVES	16	CORRIDOR		WITH HEARTH
4	CENTRAL COURT	17	OIL STORAGE	32-33	BEDROOMS
5	VESTIBULE	18-22	FOOD STORAGE	34	GUARD TOWER
6	THRONE ROOM	23	STAIRWAY	35	WINE STORAGE
7-10	DISPENSERS	24-26	PRIVATE AREAS	36	CRAFTS DISTRICT
11	CORRIDOR	27	VESTIBULE	37	RESIDENCE OF
12	STAIRWAY	28-29	PRIVATE		THE LAWAGETAS
13	STORAGE		COURTYARDS		(MILITARY CHIEF)
		30	BATHROOM		

Ancient **MESSENE** lies further north, in the heart of the region, on the slopes rising up to the summit of Mt. Ithòmi, close to the modern village of Mavrommàti. The current remains date from the Classical period although the ancient city was a proud, albeit unsuccessful, rival of Sparta even in Archaic times. The Classical city was founded in 370 BC by Epaminondas, the dictator of the short-lived Theban hegemony. The city flourished until 395 AD, when it was destroyed by the Goths.

160 left The cavea of the odeìon at Messene is well preserved; the building was not used purely for musical events at the festivals in honor of Asklepios but also for meetings of the religious council.

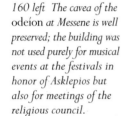

MESSENE	
1 ODEION	6 ALTAR OF
2 PROPYLON	ASKLEPIOS
3 BOULEUTÉRION	7 PROPYLON
4 SCHOOL	8 TERRACE OF
5 TEMPLE OF	THE SEBASTEION
ASKLEPIOS	9-13 SHRINES

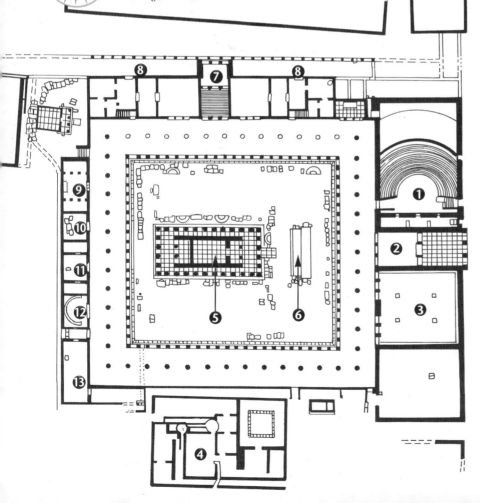

The city is encircled by beautiful walls in pseudo-isodomic masonry (9 kilometers long, 2.5 meters thick and 4.5 meters high). The walls are entirely recognizable and visitors may walk along them on the north side, which is breached by the Arcadian Gate, the most refined example of a fortified city gate in Greek architecture. Flanked by six-meter-wide protective towers, the gate opens onto a perfectly circular area measuring nearly 20 meters across! The curtain wall is interrupted at regular intervals by semicircular and square towers, with fortified sloping access ramps. Stretches of road paved with volcanic basalt and marked by wheel ruts are clearly visible at various points of the vast city area that is still under excavation.

The spectacular sanctuary of Asklepios (*Asklepieìon*) lies close to the *agorà*. The sanctuary features remains of the rectangular porticoed courtyard opening on to a large number of Late Classical, Hellenistic and Roman chapels. Overlooking the courtyard stand the graceful *odeìon* and – placed in an emphatically central location – the Doric peripteral temple hexastyle dedicated to the god of healing and the divinities associated with him (Hygieia, Machaon and Podalirius). In front of the temple stands a large hypaethral (open-air) altar for sacrifices. Other temple ruins can been seen on the summit of Mt. Ithòmi and to the east Mavrommáti, while the remains of a theatre and stadium lie closer to the *Asklepieìon*.

160 right The photo shows the walls of Messene (4th century BC), one of the greatest examples of ancient fortifications.

160-161 The Arcadian Gate based on a tenaille layout of a circumference of nearly 20 meters can still be explored. One of the 30 towers in the walls is on the right in the background.

161 bottom left The elevation of the hypostyle room used as the bouleutérion of the Messenians was built using the rustic ashlar technique, common in the Hellenistic age; it was lit by sunlight from windows high in the walls.

161 bottom right A view from the southeast corner of the porticoed courtyard of the Asklepieìon at Messene; the remains of the temple in the center formerly held famous statues by the sculptor Damophòn.

ARCADIA AND LACONIA

Visitors approaching Arcadia, from the modern Greek province of Corinthia, are greeted by the bastion of Mt. Mènalon, on whose wooded slopes Dionysus is said to have led frenzied processions of Bacchantes.

The unimposing remains of ancient **ORCHOMENOS**, which flourished between the 7th and 3rd centuries BC, are nestled in this setting. At the end of the road leading to the acropolis stand the well-preserved 4th century city walls in trapezoid isodomic masonry, interrupted by a large number of quadrangular towers. The walls run 2,300 meters around the site. Within the walls lie the *agorà* bordered by two long stoaì — one of which perhaps served as the city council hall. Both the *stoaì* feature Doric and Ionic orders in a combination that was popular during the 4th century BC. Further south lie the foundations of an Ionic temple prostyle tetrastyle dedicated to Artemis Mesopolitis (550-500 BC) preceded by the remains of an altar. The site also features an elegant theater dating from the 4th to 3rd

centuries BC, with marble paneling in the *prohedría* (front row of seats reserved for priests and high officials) and two unusual thrones placed symmetrically at a 60-degree angle in the orchèstra.

The tour of Arcadia continues towards Trìpolis with the site of **MANTINEIA**, set in a shell-shaped depression in the midst of high mountains. The area was thrice the scene of decisive battles in Greek history (in 418, 362 and 207 BC). The great Boeotian military strategist Epaminondas fell in the second of these battles in which Thebes won a victory over Sparta. Excavations have uncovered the almost two-meter-high stone socle of a well-defended city wall (370 BC) that ran for about 3.5 kilometers. The defensive circuit was made up of two

parallel lines of stone walls in Archaic-style polygonal masonry, with rubble in between, and a superstructure in mud-brick masonry, now lost. Also in the Archaic style and keeping with the tradition of the times are the 10 entrance gates with sloping access ramps featuring a sharp bend, so that any attacker was exposed to the city's defendants. The most amazing feature of the walls are their 122 square towers. The roads from all the gates converge at the *agorà*, the Roman version of which can be seen today, with remains of sacred and civil buildings as well as barely recognizable porticoes, which still reflect the lines of the Hellenistic plan. To the west lies the lower part of the cavea of the theater, dating from the same period as the walls, and built, unlike nearly all other Greek theaters, on an artificial terrace in polygonal masonry with an outer staircase leading to the highest rows of seats.

Just seven kilometers southeast of Trìpolis lies **TEGEA**, where Heracles is supposed to have ravished Auge, triggering the sad sequence of events narrated in the myth of Auge and Telephos, her son by Heracles. The site is of archaeological interest because of the remains of the Doric peripteral temple hexastyle, dedicated to Athena Alèa. Built in local white marble, it was constructed and decorated between 370 and 350 BC by Skopas, one of the greatest sculptors in all of ancient Greek history. The temple's proportions are expressed through the ratios between various architectural components and the overall dimensions. The slender columns of the peristasis, the light entablature, the cella adorned by half-columns, and the optical corrections, all combine to render the temple one of ancient Greece's best architectural experiments, second only to the Parthenon. The short sides of the temples were decorated by sculpted metopes, depicting on the east side, the fight between Heracles and Kepheus and on the west, the myth of Telephos. The pediments by Skopas, depict to the east, the hunt for the Calydonian Boar and to the west, the battle between Achilles and Telephos at Kaikos. Some of the surviving sculptures are housed at the museum attached to the site, while the rest are at the National Museum in Athens. Modest remains of the theater, the *agorà*

162 left Fragments carved by the great artist, Skopas, were taken from the pediments of this unspectacular ruin of the temple of Athena Alèa at Tegèa, originally a 4th century BC masterpiece of architecture.

162 right The theater at Megalopolis dates from the short period during which the Arcadian city flourished; like all the remaining buildings, it was designed on a monumental scale to reflect the "greatness" of the city.

162-163 Another fine example of a theater is at Mantineìa, where the lack of a hill to set the building against meant that earthworks contained by Cyclopean substructures had to be raised.

163 top left It is just possible to recognize the ruins of the Thersileion in this view of Megalopolis; the Thersileion was the huge hypostyle room in which a gallery was reserved for the assembly.

163 top right These are the remarkable ruins of the temple of Demeter Despoìna at Lykossoùra in the impassable mountains of Arcadia; the temple contained four cult statues sculpted by Damophòn of Messene.

and an Early Christian basilica with mosaic flooring (5th century AD) can be seen in the park of the Church of the Sleep of the Mother of God (Kìmissis tìs Theotòkou), in the nearby village of Paleà Episkopì.

Thirty-four kilometers from Trìpolis along the E65 highway to Kalamata lies the important site of **MEGALOPOLIS**. The city was founded during the Theban hegemony as part of its Sparta-containing campaign and was destroyed in 222 BC by the very Spartans it was designed to hold back. It was resurrected in the Roman period. Decades of excavations have uncovered the ruins along both banks of the narrow Helison river. Living up to its name, the "Great City's" main buildings seem to reflect grandeur. The

third century BC theater, with a seating capacity of 20,000, was fitted with a stage with grooves for changing the backdrop scenery. The Thersileion, a large (over 3,000 square meters) hypostyle hall used for public political meetings, incorporated the technique of radiating the columns outwards by varying the intercolumniate intervals, so as to afford the audience an unimpeded view of the platform. In the *agorà* stand the sanctuary of Zeus Sotèr (the "Savior") a Ionic-Doric structure, and the massive (155-meter long) Philippian Colonnade, the *stoà* (4th-2nd century BC) that adorned the north side of the town square.

To the south of the rocky mass of the

Lykeon (the sacred "Mountain of the Wolves" dear to Apollo), the ancient sanctuary of Demeter Despoìna at **LYKOSSOURA** is well worth a visit. Built in the 4th century BC, the site features remains of the foundations of the temple, a few altars and the *témenos*. The sanctuary once housed the famous cult statues of Demeter, Despoìna, Artemis and Anytos, sculpted by Damòphon of Messene in the second century BC.

It is rather difficult, on the other hand, to get to the archaeological site of **GORTYS**, on the border with Elis, close to Dimìtsàna. The site features a 4th-3rd century BC dual defensive wall and rather scant remains of a temple of Asklepios and thermal baths, dating from the same period.

Having enjoyed the delights of ancient Arcadia, the tour returns to Tripolis to head for Laconia, a mountainous region with highlands that roll from the heights of Mt. Taygetos and Mt. Parnònas towards the Eurotas river valley. The hilly landscape extends into the sea at the center and to the southeast of the Peloponnese, to form two "fingers" featuring a rugged coastline rich in natural harbors.

SPARTA, linked to Tripolis by the E961 highway, is the main historical and archaeological site of the region. The remains, which are not terribly awe-inspiring, are steeped in the midst of a concrete jungle that has seriously hampered archaeological research. Surveying the sad scant remains of the ancient city, now encroached by urban sprawl, modern visitors may find comfort in evoking its glorious history and peculiar political features.

Founded by the Dorians in the 10th century BC, Sparta started nurturing ambitions to dominate the southern Peloponnese in the 8th century BC and acquired full hegemony between the 7th and the 5th centuries BC. The city-state did not however seem to be interested in colonial expansion, with Taras (modern Taranto) as its one and only colony. Its famous constitution, drafted, according to tradition, by the lawmaker Lycurgus (the "illuminator") provided for a society divided into castes based on an ethno-aristocratic system. Only full-blooded Spartans descended from the founding warriors were allowed full citizenship. The political structure was very simple. The city was ruled by two kings, controlled by a board of supervisory magistrates (*ephors*) and advised by a small senate (the *gerousia*), seconded by an assembly (*àpella*) that included all full citizens over 30 years of age. The city's economy and organisation was based on a sort of atypical communism (equality was

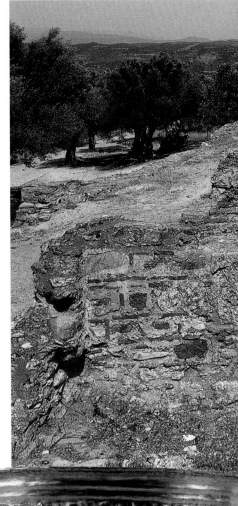

absolute, but only within each caste, without any possibility of upward mobility between castes). The city-state's main preoccupation was to maintain a colossal military force. From a very early age, all Spartans were almost exclusively subjected to a military and civic education under strict discipline and in practice, the family played no role in the training and education of children.

Production and trade that provided the community with considerable wealth were carried out by semi-free citizens (*perioikoi*) who had few rights. Agriculture and cattle-

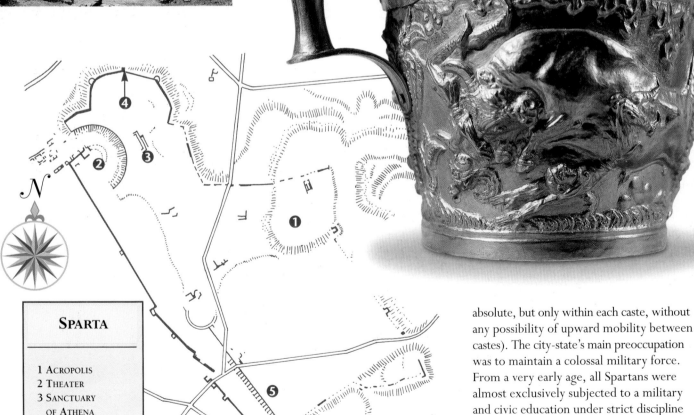

SPARTA

1 ACROPOLIS
2 THEATER
3 SANCTUARY
  OF ATHENA
  POLIOUCHOS
4 LATE-ANCIENT
  WALLS
5 SUBSTRUCTURES OF
  THE AGORÀ

VAFIO, lie the remains of a Mycenaean *thòlos* tomb that contained the famous collection of gold and silver grave goods now at the National Museum in Athens. The rich collection of the Archaeological Museum at Sparta includes a large number of epigraphs, Archaic and Classical votive relief sculptures, including the early 5th-century BC bust of Leonidas sculpted in Parian marble, as well as an extraordinary series of Laconian ceramics that were exported throughout the Greek world between the 7th and 6th centuries BC.

GYTHION, the last stop on this tour of Laconia, is conveniently located both for those who wish to continue towards the stupendous region of the Mani and those who prefer embarking for Crete and Kythira. Used in early times as a Spartan naval base, it became the capital of the league of the "Free Laconians" released from their slavery as helots of Sparta by the Roman Emperor Augustus. The site features noteworthy remains of a small theater dating from Late Roman Imperial times. The cavea built in local limestone was divided into four *kerkides* (wedge-shaped blocks of tiered seats). The front row of each block of seats, the *prohèdria* or seats of honor reserved for priests and high officials, was in marble. The orchèstra bears traces of a fountain, probably used for water ballet spectacles.

farming were entrusted to slaves (*helots*), who were considered human merchandise and doomed to their unenviable destiny from generation to generation. They were, in fact, descendants of the peoples conquered within the surrounding region of Laconia and prisoners of war from neighboring regions (especially Messene).

From a town planning viewpoint, Sparta was very similar to other Hellenistic cities built before the "Hippodamean" grid-plan became widespread. There were several sanctuaries and other places of cult worship dating from very ancient times, in and around the city. The large quantity of votive objects uncovered during excavations highlights the importance and long tradition of the various cults over the centuries.

The acropolis (1) was heavily refurbished in Hellenistic-Roman and Byzantine times and as a result, the foundations of the temple and the enclosure of the Sanctuary of Athena Polioùchos (3) ("Lady of the City") or Chalkioìkos ("Of the House of Bronze") are barely visible close to the *summa cavea* of the theater (2). The temple was built in the 6th century BC by the Spartan architect, sculptor and poet Gitiàdas. The building was completely paneled with decorated bronze slabs, many

bearing relief sculptures, that Pausanias admired and described a full seven centuries later.

The theater, with a diameter of over 140 meters, leans against the southwest slope of the acropolis hill. The remains visible today date from the 2nd century BC and later renovations under the Roman Emperors Augustus, Hadrian and Constantine. The Archaic sanctuary of Artemis Orthia (the "Just"), heavily vandalized in Roman times, lies on the banks of the Eurotas river. Here young Spartans were put through tests of endurance that involved ritual floggings. To the southeast of the city lie the meager remains of the 5th century BC *Menèlaion*, a sanctuary dedicated to the heroic cult of Menelaos and Helen.

Five kilometers to the south, at

164 left The remains of the theater of Athens' great rival, Sparta, are a Hellenistic-Roman construction.

164 right This gold cup decorated with scenes of the capture of a bull was found in the tomb of an unknown Mycenaean "prince" of the 15th century BC at Vafiò, near Sparta.

164-165 The ruins of the Christian basilica of Aghios Nìkon clutter the acropolis of ancient Sparta; the buildings from the Archaic and Classical ages have disappeared.

165 bottom left This is a view of the ruins of the sanctuary-heróon of Menelaos and Helen, built in the 5th century BC; it was evidently constructed to recall Sparta's legendary past for purposes of political propaganda.

165 bottom right These are the few remains of the princely tomb at Vafiò, popularly known as "Menelaos' Tomb," but in fact it was built for someone who died roughly 200 years before the husband of the beautiful Helen of Troy.

KEA

166 top The ruins at Aghìa Irini at Kea are a superb starting point for knowledge of Cycladic architecture that flourished for much of the Bronze Age (2nd millennium BC) in the principal Aegean archipelago.

The westernmost of the Cyclades, KEA, ancient Kèos, home to the sixth century BC lyric poet Simonides, features interesting archaeological sites. Close to Vourkári to the northwest lies the Cycladic settlement of AGHIA IRINI, which flourished between 2800 and 2000 BC. The settlement was abandoned for three centuries but was refounded and

separated by narrow lanes, with sewers running under them. To the south of the square is a residential complex, House A (3), which originally had an upper floor. In the southeastern sector, at the shoreline, archaeologists have uncovered the remains of a temple (4). Dedicated to Dionysus, it is the most ancient temple in the Aegean and was revered in Hellenistic and early Roman times. Just a kilometer to the northwest of Kea lies a colossal funerary lion, sculpted into a rock face in the 6th century BC. Along the southeastern coast lie the ruins of KARTHAIA. The site features the foundations of several temples (including a 5th century BC Doric temple dedicated to Athena) and the remains of a theater as well as turreted city walls built in the Classical period.

AGHIA IRINI

1 WALLS AND BASTIONS
2 SMALL SQUARE
3 HOUSE A
4 TEMPLE/SANCTUARY

became prosperous once again thanks to the influence of the Minoan civilization (1700-1450 BC). Redesigned in Mycenaean times (14th-13th century BC) it was probably destroyed by the "Sea Peoples." The site was colonized by the Ionians (1050-1000 BC) and had a sizable population during the Classical and Hellenistic periods. The remains of the walls with towers (1) at the corners, enclose a central square (2) surrounded by residential city blocks. The houses, made up of aligned rooms, were

166 bottom Worn away by weather and time, the 6th-century BC funerary lion carved in the rock close to the island capital still maintains an air of menace.

Minoan lines, provides evidence of the wealth of the region. Several tablets (perhaps accounting records) written in the "Linear A" script of the ancient Minoans that has not yet been deciphered, were found in the palace. The addition of a thick wall in the 15th century BC suggests the beginning of a traumatic transition towards the Mycenaean civilization, further corroborated by the transformation of the "palace" into a Mycenaean royal *mègaron*.

In the main center of Pláka (Mìlos) lie the remains of the city walls and the turreted East Gate in polygonal masonry (6th century BC), together with the ruins of the Hellenistic theater (third-second century BC), and a Roman Imperial building used perhaps for the gatherings of clubs dedicated to Dionysiac practices. The 65 square meter *andrón* (men's banquet hall) of the building features a mosaic floor depicting Dionysiac themes and the humorous inscription "Give us everything, except water!" The Christian catacombs on the Tripitì hill, dating from the third century AD, are the largest outside Rome.

MÉLOS

The volcanic island of *Mélos* (in modern Greek **MILOS**) was an important center for the mining and export of obsidian and perlite from the Neolithic through the Bronze Age, under both the Minoan thalassocracy (maritime supremacy) and Mycenaean domination. Independent in the Archaic period, it was subjected to repression by the Athenians during the Peloponnesian War. Liberated by Sparta, it flourished through the Hellenistic and Roman periods.

PHYLAKOPI on the north coast, is the most interesting archaeological site on the island. Between 2000-1500 BC, an early city, based on a grid plan with houses decorated by frescoes like those at Akrotìri (Thìra), was built over the Cycladic settlement that was set up during the third millennium BC. The remains of the "palace" built around 1600 BC along

166-167 *The seats in the elegant Hellenistic theater of Tripití on the island of Mìlos were lined in white marble with gray veins; the theater overlooks one of the superb panoramas that the island offers.*

167 bottom left *A view of the Cycladic town of Phylakopi that was dominated by the Minoans in the first half of the 2nd millennium BC and later conquered by the Mycenaeans; it lies on the north coast of the island.*

167 top right *The large Christian catacombs of Tripití certainly do not match the artistic quality of the more famous tunnels below Rome, but they make up for this deficiency by their length.*

167 center *Entirely dug from the volcanic rock on the island of Mìlos, the catacombs of Tripitì were divided into chambers, niches and arcosolia.*

DELOS

DELOS

N

The ancient religious heart of the Cyclades, venerated sanctuary of Apollo and his sister Artemis who, according to myth, were born there, and florid "free port" during the Roman era (from 166 BC), the bare and windy island of **DELOS** is one of the most important archaeological sites in the world. Those wishing to visit the island must know that the ferries that leave from nearby Mykonos only run in the early morning and early afternoon because of the strong countercurrents. Given the vastness and importance of the excavations, the visitor is advised to

spend a couple of days on Delos, either staying overnight in the small and only hotel or returning to Mykonos. Do not neglect to leave aside an hour to visit the archaeological museum, which houses sculptural and mosaic works of exceptional historical and artistic value.

The ancient port leads directly to the late-Hellenistic *agorà* of the "Compitaliasts" or "Hermaists" (1); these were the two powerful guilds of Italic merchants that dedicated numerous works of art there (the bases are still in situ).

Dated from 130 BC are the remains of a small circular monopteral temple

with a rectangular enclosure and conical roof with false scales, a rectangular (Ionic?) temple on a tall plinth dedicated to Hermes and Maia by the Hermaists, and a small, Ionic prostyle tetrastyle temple in the northeast corner of the square dedicated by the Compitaliasts to *Lares Compitales*, the tutelary deities of crossroads and borders. This marks the beginning of the Sacred Way, crowded with the foundations of dozens of containers for offerings, which passes through the ruins of the Doric Stoà of the Attalids of Pergamum (2) built around the mid-3rd century BC to house commercial workshops, and through those of the even longer Stoà of Philip V of Macedonia (3), built in 210-200 BC for propaganda and decorative reasons. Here you can take a quick glance at the *Agorà Tetràgona* (4), a porticoed square with one or two floors and workshops

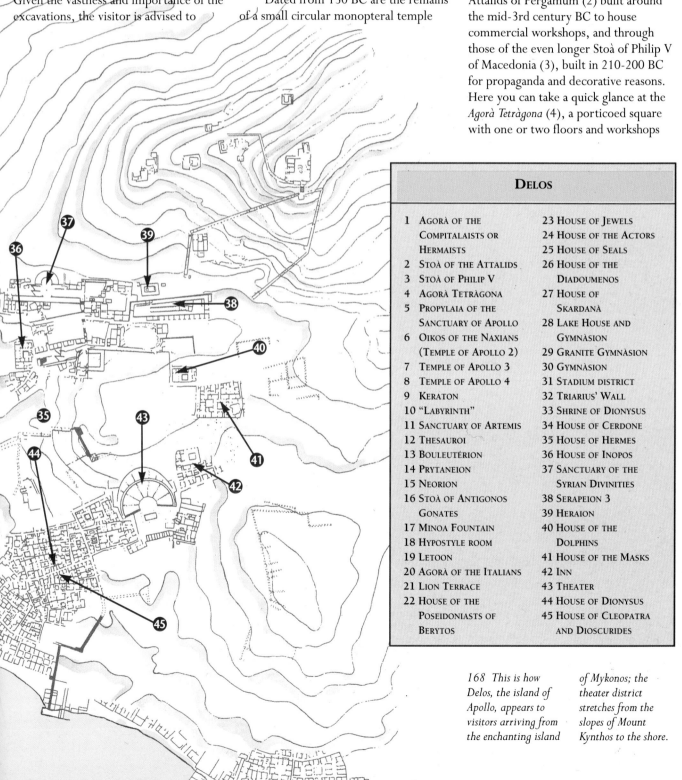

DELOS	
1 AGORÀ OF THE COMPITALAISTS OR HERMAISTS	23 HOUSE OF JEWELS
	24 HOUSE OF THE ACTORS
	25 HOUSE OF SEALS
2 STOÀ OF THE ATTALIDS	26 HOUSE OF THE DIADOUMENOS
3 STOÀ OF PHILIP V	27 HOUSE OF SKARDANÀ
4 AGORÀ TETRÀGONA	
5 PROPYLAIA OF THE SANCTUARY OF APOLLO	28 LAKE HOUSE AND GYMNÀSION
6 OIKOS OF THE NAXIANS (TEMPLE OF APOLLO 2)	29 GRANITE GYMNÀSION
	30 GYMNÀSION
7 TEMPLE OF APOLLO 3	31 STADIUM DISTRICT
8 TEMPLE OF APOLLO 4	32 TRIARIUS' WALL
9 KERATON	33 SHRINE OF DIONYSUS
10 "LABYRINTH"	34 HOUSE OF CERDONE
11 SANCTUARY OF ARTEMIS	35 HOUSE OF HERMES
12 THESAUROI	36 HOUSE OF INOPOS
13 BOULEUTÉRION	37 SANCTUARY OF THE SYRIAN DIVINITIES
14 PRYTANEION	
15 NEORION	38 SERAPEION 3
16 STOÀ OF ANTIGONOS GONATES	39 HERAION
	40 HOUSE OF THE DOLPHINS
17 MINOA FOUNTAIN	
18 HYPOSTYLE ROOM	41 HOUSE OF THE MASKS
19 LETOON	42 INN
20 AGORÀ OF THE ITALIANS	43 THEATER
21 LION TERRACE	44 HOUSE OF DIONYSUS
22 HOUSE OF THE POSEIDONIASTS OF BERYTOS	45 HOUSE OF CLEOPATRA AND DIOSCURIDES

168 This is how Delos, the island of Apollo, appears to visitors arriving from the enchanting island of Mykonos; the theater district stretches from the slopes of Mount Kynthos to the shore.

that lies behind the portico of the Attalids and was constructed in the 3rd-2nd century BC on the south side of the Archaic and Classical *agorà*, before heading towards the heart of the sanctuary.

From here you pass into the magnificent Propylaeum (5) with its Doric tetrastyle façade to the south and distyle façade to the north, rebuilt at the expense of Athens in the 2nd century BC. Note what remains of the famous Naxian *Oìkos* (6), the second temple dedicated to Apollo in the sanctuary and a gift from the inhabitants of nearby Nàxos (550 BC). It was built with a bipartite Ionic cell under which were found the remains of an earlier building (650 BC) that had, in turn, substituted for the first temple of which the gneiss foundations still remain. On the north side of the *Oìkos* stands the colossal marble base of Nàxos on which the 8-meter-tall Archaic cult statue of Apollo was placed. Note the hollow in the upper surface where the plinth rested. Around 530 BC, the Naxian *Oìkos* was converted into a *thesauròs* when, on the probable initiative of the tyrant Peisistratos who was aiming to establish Athenian hegemony over the Aegean, the *porinòs nàos* was built, the prostyle tetrastyle Ionic temple with stereobates in Attic *pòros* limestone (7). The same fate befell the third cult building which became the famous *thesauròs* of the powerful Delian League in 470 BC. A fourth temple dedicated to Apollo (8) was built, a classical Doric peripteral hexastyle *hekatòmpedon* which was never finished (the still un-

grooved rocks can be seen). Around 420 BC, the fifth temple of Apollo appeared, a Doric amphiprostyle hexastyle temple on a tall platform with four pillars *in antis* in the pronaos, of which two magnificent pedimental acroters with rape scenes remain in the museum.

All the temples except for the first were entered on the west side towards the center of the sanctuary where apsidal foundations (9) supported (perhaps) the canopy that protected and drew attention to the famous *Keratòn*, the altar built by Apollo using the horns of wild goats hunted by Artemis on the slopes of nearby Mount Kynthos. It was around this altar that the Athenians celebrated the ritual "Crane Dance" in commemoration of the ceremonies performed by Theseus in honor of Apollo after his victory over the Minotaur. If this

hypothesis were true, the large adjacent structure (10), a rectangular room of roughly 400 square meters with a decastyle Ionic pronaos, would have been the Labyrinth in which the dance began with a meaningful allusion to the adventure on Crete.

The south and west sides of the square are lined with the remains of the late-Archaic, Ionic Stoà of the Naxians with an internal colonnade, in the corner

of which lies the base of the bronze palm dedicated by Nicias in 417 BC (epigraph).

The smaller sanctuary enclosure, dedicated to Artemis, was built during a renovation in the 2nd century BC. It has an L-shaped stoà on the north and east sides, a coeval prostyle hexastyle Ionic temple dedicated to Artemis which was the last version of a cult building during the Mycenaean age, and a heroized tomb indicated by Herodotus as the tomb of two of the Hyperborean maidens who

170 The ruins of Delos are at times hardly noticeable; for example, a damaged sector is the commercial and port area to the west of the sanctuary of Apollo.

170-171 View of the theater district looking in the direction of the ancient port; it is characterized by many magnificent Hellenistic peristyle houses.

171 bottom left The remains of the statue of Apollo, sculpted during the Archaic era, can be seen in the sacred area of the temple-sanctuary of Artemis to the west.

171 top right Following the Sacred Way, it is easy to recognize the remains of the white Doric portico erected by the Attalids of Pergamum (3rd century BC).

171 bottom right The agorà of the Compitaliasts is ringed by the remains of the bases of many works of art dedicated by Roman and Italic merchants to the gods.

came to venerate Apollo. The maidens used to place a lock of their hair here before getting married.

To the north are the remains of the *ekklesiastèrion*, the room used for communal assemblies of the Delians, and the nearby banquet rooms aligned with a communal Doric peristyle court (5th century BC).

To the north and east of the temples of Apollo can be seen the foundations of five *thesauroì* (12) which have been dated to between 520-475 BC, and, more importantly, the island's administrative buildings: the double nave *bouleutérion* (13), and the *prytaneìon* (14) with a tetrastyle Doric entrance and paved court. Both buildings have a vestibule, a shrine dedicated to Hestia and banquet rooms.

Also very interesting is the nearby *Neòrion*, better known as the "Hall of Bulls" (15). This is a large celebratory structure built by Demetrios Poliorcetes in 306 BC and completed by his son Antigonos Gonates in 255 BC to thank Apollo and to celebrate their respective victories against the Egyptian Ptolemies. The structure (67 meters opens to south with a hexastyle prothyrum that leads into a long covered gallery decorated with a lovely frieze of sea creatures (Nereids and sea horses) now visible outside the building. The gallery ended in a bay, in which a triangular base supported a marble prow, that could be

reached via two narrow corridors with half-pillars decorated with bulls' heads. The function of the gallery was purely honorary: the lowered floor was filled with a pool of water in which the flagship of Antigonos' fleet dedicated to Apollo rested.

The *témenos* appears particularly magnificent on the north side. Here, in an area dotted with bases and exedras for monuments from the Hellenistic and

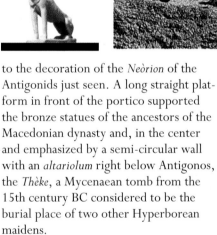

172 top The bosses on the plinth of the 4th temple of Apollo (475 BC) show that the building had not been completed when work was begun on construction of the 5th temple in 420 BC.

Roman eras, stand the remains of the long (119 meters.) Stoà of Antigonos Gonates (16) erected in the second quarter of the 3rd century BC; it consists of a winged portico with 47 Doric columns on the outside and 20 Ionic columns inside. The Doric entablature has metopes decorated with bulls' heads that clearly bear a similarity

to the decoration of the *Neòrion* of the Antigonids just seen. A long straight platform in front of the portico supported the bronze statues of the ancestors of the Macedonian dynasty and, in the center and emphasized by a semi-circular wall with an *altariolum* right below Antigonos, the *Thèke*, a Mycenaean tomb from the 15th century BC considered to be the burial place of two other Hyperborean maidens.

To the north of the Stoà lies the monumental pool of the Minoa Fountain (17) that is still fed by the spring. A flight of steps with a porticoed entrance (6th-5th century BC) descends to the pool. Heading west from this point, one reaches the commercial area to the north of the port, Theophrastos' *Agorà*, named after the magistrate who financed its paving (125 BC), and containing many monuments that were dedicated during the Hellenistic and Roman ages. The 2000 square meters of the ruins of the 208 BC Hypostyle Room (18) are very

172 bottom The north side of the Neòrion, *the proclamation pavilion that held the flagship of the Antigonids; the ship was consecrated to Apollo and exhibited* ad imperitura memoria.

172-173 Another view of the Neòrion *offers an appreciation of its size, which was remarkable even during an era (3rd century BC) in which grandiose and dramatic works were not unusual.*

173 bottom left Caius Billienus, the proconsul of the Roman province of Asia, erected this marble monument near the long portico of Antigonos Gonates around 100 BC.

173 bottom right A worn herma (342 BC) with the face of Hermes Propylaios stands on the steps of the Propylaia, which formed the entrance to the sacred enclosure of the sanctuary of Apollo.

impressive. This was used to store
Egyptian grain and, perhaps, the goods
in transit through the Aegean free port.
It used to be a rectangular building with
a façade on the south side, embellished
by 44 columns, an earthen floor, a
central court illuminated by a skylight,
and four concentric peristyles: the
external one Doric and the others Ionic
(capitals and bases *in situ*).

Returning eastwards, one passes
the *Dodekàtheon*, the hexastyle
amphiprostyle Doric temple, built circa
300 BC, and dedicated to the 12 major
gods of Olympus, and the *Letòon*, the
marble temple dedicated to Leto (19)
built around 540 BC. The honeycomb
decoration of the outer bench was an
Archaic Apollonian theme from Delphi.
The *Agorà* of the Italians (20) – the
largest monumental complex on Delos
and so-named because it was dedicated
to Apollo by Roman-Italic merchant
guilds with the contributions of several
rich financiers (circa 120 BC ca) – was a

structure entered from two narrow and
easily controlled passageways. It was in
fact used to buy and sell slaves, the
workforce on which the ancient
economy was based.

Having explored the square, return
to the *Letòon* and then continue north
with the foundations of the "Granite
Monument" to the left. This vast
building was originally a two-story
structure containing storerooms, offices
and the accommodations of a Roman-
Italic merchants' association.

Next comes the Lion Terrace (21), an avenue monumentalized by the Naxians with a row of at least nine statues of roaring lions squatting on their haunches. They were made from Nàxos marble around 550 BC and appear to be guarding the sacred place similar to the long avenues that led the faithful to the temples in Egyptian sanctuaries. It is probable that there was an Egyptian influence given the visits made by merchants from the Cyclades to the trad-

ing center of Naukràtis in the Nile delta. From the terrace, look east and try to imagine the blue sheet of water, today dried out, of the Sacred Lake where legend has it that Leto gave birth to Apollo and Artemis.

A short path rises to the northern area of Delos, built between 120-90 BC on an orthogonal plan. Stop at the House of the Poseidoniasts of Berytos (22), an association of merchants, ship owners and hoteliers from what is now Beirut in Lebanon, who were accommodated there under the protection of Poseidon, Astarte-Aphrodite, Roma and a fourth deity (Heracles-Melqart?). Passing through the narrow corridor, you reach a rectangular court with four altars and, on the west side, a Phoenician-type domestic sanctuary with four shrines that used to contain cult statues. On the east side of the court stood the accommodations with rooms arranged around a Doric peristyle with a central

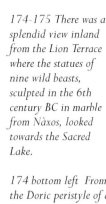

174-175 There was a splendid view inland from the Lion Terrace where the statues of nine wild beasts, sculpted in the 6th century BC in marble from Nàxos, looked towards the Sacred Lake.

174 bottom left From the Doric peristyle of a house in the theatre quarter, to the south of the central nucleus of Delos, the view sweeps out in the direction of the bay which contains the modern quay.

174 The arches of the large water tank of the Inn, in the theater district, were made from local gneiss like many structures in Hellenistic Delos.

175 top Standing up on their front paws and snarling, the marble beasts on the Lion Terrace have been worn away over the centuries and made even more mysterious by the erosion of the salty sea breezes.

175 bottom left The magnificent House of the Poseidoniasts of Berytos was originally embellished with many works of art, including this fragmentary statue of the goddess Roma in a sober Hellenistic form (100 BC).

175 bottom right The domestic architecture of Hellenistic and republican Roman Delos produced large, spacious houses with numerous rooms arranged around a colonnaded atrium and set on different levels.

water tank that was originally covered. A triple gateway leads into the west courtyard that used to be a meeting place, while the south side was lined with shops and storerooms, one of which produced the sculptural group of Aphrodite and Pan now in the National Museum in Athens.

After a glance at the remains of the four houses in the residential block to the west, go over the crossroads and turn into the blind alley on the right. Here you can explore the inside of the superb House of Jewels (23) – where jewelry and a mosaic showing Athena and Hermes were found (now in the museum) – and the nearby House of the Actors (24), named for the theatrical paintings found there. After admiring the peristyle, originally Doric and Ionic on two stories, pass into the adjacent House of the Tritons to look at the wonderful polychrome mosaic depicting a female Triton and a winged Eros in the banquet room on the north side.

Another group of houses stands on the west side of the street and the isolated House of Seals (25) in which 15,000 seals were found that related to an archive of papyrus documents from the age of the Roman republic. The atrium of the house contains a sun dial.

Further west, at the top of the rise, is the interesting House on the Hill in which a large water tank can be seen.

Descending the slope to the east, stop at the large House of the *Diadoùmenos* (26) where the replica of the masterpiece by Polykleitos and the so-called Pseudo-Athlete of Delos were found (both now in the National Museum in Athens). The quantity of works of art found in these houses is explained by the number of reception rooms they had, in addition to the residential quarters, and is evidence of the rapid development of the taste of their inhabitants, mostly Roman and Italic, for Hellenic art.

176-177 Many large Delian houses have been unearthed on the slopes of Mount Kynthos; the House of Hermes, perhaps the most beautiful of all the houses in the ancient center, can be seen in the center of the photograph.

176 bottom left The Hellenistic House of the Tritons is a very lovely house; here we see the north banquet room paved with a mosaic floor depicting a female Triton and a winged Eros.

176 bottom right Colossal phalluses on bases with Dionysiac reliefs adorned the entrance to the shrine dedicated to the god of wine and pleasure; they stood on the northeast corner of the sacred enclosure of Apollo.

177 top left The
impressive upper loggia
of the House of Hermes
overlooked the peristyle;

it still has many of the
slender Ionic columns
between which a wooden
balustrade probably ran.

phallus. The one on the right was
dedicated by Karystios for a courageous
victory around 300 BC and is decorated
with delicate reliefs of Dionysiac motifs.
In the south-east corner of the *témenos*
stands the peristyle House of Cerdone
(34), built in the 2nd century BC.

From here you can climb up to the
peristyle House of Hermes (35), one of
the most interesting on the island. It has

A short diversion north allows one to
admire the polychrome mosaics in the
luxurious House of Skardanà (27), in the
bay of the same name. This building had
two floors, a corner tower and a porticoed peristyle on two orders.

The route now requires a pause at
the Lake House and at the rather run-
down Lake Gymnàsion (28), a 3rd-2nd
century BC complex with a courtyard and
water tanks. Of similar size but much
better preserved is the nearby Granite
Gymnàsion (29), with a peristyle
courtyard and *xystos* with a portico on the
north side.

From here you can complete the tour
of the sanctuary's sporting structures; across
from the large trapezoidal expanse linked
with the horse track, the gymnàsion (30)
built circa 300 BC with a square plan, 48
Ionic columns and propylaia to the south,
is worthy of examination. A vestibule in
the northeast corner leads to the *xystos*,
the covered training track, and to the
stadium near which there stands a
residential area (31) containing some
lovely examples of Hellenistic peristyle
houses along the road parallel to the east
side of the gymnàsion. The remains of the
oldest surviving synagogue built following
the Diaspora stand almost on the shore of
the sea.

Return to the Granite Gymnàsion,
then continue south along Triarius' Wall
(32), a defensive structure built by an
officer under Pompey the Great to protect
the sanctuary from pirates (second quarter
of the first century BC). Then proceed
outside the east wall of the Hellenistic
témenos as far as the Shrine of Dionysus
(33) which can be recognized by its pillars
each topped by an enormous erect

been dated to somewhere between the
3rd-2nd century BC and has taken its
name from the statue of the god that was
found there. The house is multistoried as
it is built on the slope of a hill. Like
almost all the Hellenistic residences on
Delos, it was built using blocks and
overlapping tiles of gneiss with white
plastered walls. The inside walls were
further decorated with an experimental
lining that imitated variegated marble
enclosed by false moldings, some of
which were embellished with figured
decorations in an example of the first
Pompey style. The nucleus of the house is
reached via an atrium, off of which
bathrooms lead. This central section of
the house is made up of relaxation and
service rooms arranged around a Doric
peristyle from which natural light is
filtered into the rooms. The upper balcony
is reached via stairways cleverly cut in the
structure and fitted with landings to form
intermediate floors on which additional
rooms were made available. The Ionic
loggia leads into the proper *oìkos* where
there is a large banquet room; it was this
that suggested the house was used by a
guild or association for receptions and
providing hospitality.

177 top right The
size and variety of the
subjects depicted in
the mosaic floors of
the Hellenistic houses
is quite remarkable;
here the mosaic is
made from pebbles.

177 bottom left Make
sure you visit the Ionic
peristyle House of the
Lake; in accordance with
the canons of Hellenistic
domestic architecture, the
main rooms of the house
faced towards the peristyle.

Climbing higher up the hill you will notice the arrangement of the *Serapeìon 1*, the oldest building of worship dedicated to the Egyptian god Serapis (third century BC). Approach the summit of Mount Kynthos with a pause at the House of Inopòs (36), which has several small rooms with mosaics, and at the *Samothràkeion*, a remarkable sanctuary dedicated to the gods of Samothrace. The building is divided into two terraces (4th-2nd century BC) in accordance with the customary dramatic criteria of Hellenistic architecture.

The even higher Sanctuary of the Syrian Divinities (37) is impressive for its position and grandeur. Its construction was financed by the rich mercantile associations of Hellenistic Syria during the third quarter of the 2nd century BC. The cult area is to the south in a square courtyard with shrines and service rooms; the long porticoed terrace that faces west houses the cavea of a theater that was used for ritual worship of the goddess Atargatis who became syncretized with Aphrodite. Equally impressive and large is the *Serapeìon 3* complex dedicated to Serapis, Isis, Anubis and Harpocrates (38) and built around 180 BC. Adapted to the terrace dug out of the hill to the south of the previous sanctuary, the most remarkable and original feature of the complex divided into two sections and entirely surrounded by porticoes is the avenue of

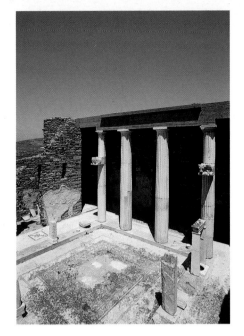

peak of the hill (from where there is a lovely view) through the ruins of several other cult buildings which are not worth dwelling on.

From the *Heraion*, you can descend directly to the southern quarter of the sacred city passing by the splendid House of the Dolphins (40), another memorable example of a peristyle Hellenistic house. Its floor mosaics include the one in the central courtyard that shows Eroses bearing symbols of divinity as they ride pairs of dolphins; this was the work of the mosaic artist Asklepiades of Arados (Phoenicia), who also produced the floor decoration in the vestibule with the magical-religious sign of the Phoenician goddess Tanit whom the unknown house owner clearly worshipped.

A little further down the hill in a sort of square, reached by an elegant colonnaded street, stands the very large House of the Masks (41) that is similar in design to the Roman House on Rhodes with magnificent Dionysiac mosaics in the four banquet rooms that overlook the raised wing of the peristyle. Past a threshold on the left in which dolphins are seen facing one another, there is an emblem of a large amphora, a palm and a bird. A small room decorated with a mosaic of a dancing Silenus follows, then

178 center View of the cella of the temple of Isis. The shrine was built on Mt. Kynthos overlooking the town below and still contains the cult statue.

178 bottom left The two entrance columns of the temple of Hera are still almost intact; they date from the mid-sixth century BC when the complex was built, perhaps on the orders of Polykràtes, the ruler of Samos.

178 top right The House of the Trident can no longer be visited; it is a fine example of a Delian Hellenistic house built with a peristyle. The columns had projecting consoles decorated with the heads and shoulders of animals.

178 bottom right The House of the Trident is one of a block of houses along the Theater Way.

179 Heavily restored, the distyle front of the small temple of Isis (135 BC) offers a glimpse of the statue of the goddess inside; like all the most important Egyptian deities, Isis was much worshipped on Delos.

Sphinxes (70 meters) that imitates the hypetral processional ways of Egyptian sanctuaries. The reconstruction of the distyle Doric temple *in antis* was built by the Athenians in honor of Isis in 135 BC and still holds its cult statue of the goddess, which is unfortunately headless. Meanwhile, the ruins of the *Heraion* (39) that stand above are visually very dramatic; this is also a distyle Doric temple *in antis*, built between 520 and 500 BC.

A steep flight of steps leads to the

180 top The House of Dionysus, perhaps the loveliest on Delos, was decorated with *superb mosaic floors; the photograph shows the Ionic marble peristyle in the theater district.*

181 bottom right The Doric peristyle in the House of Cleopatra and Dioscurides; the incomparable blue of the sea and sky of Delos can be glimpsed in the background, the last gift of the god to those who visit his ancient seat.

180 bottom The statues of Cleopatra and Dioscurides in the Doric peristyle of the house of the same name are an unusual example of Hellenistic sobriety; they were named after their owners (the originals are in the museum).

180-181 This is the superb view from the theater on Delos; though not one of the largest in the Greek world, the theater was built with the customary harmony of proportions and high-quality acoustics.

181 bottom left The walls of the houses on Delos have lost their coating of white plaster and the frescoes that frequently adorned the most important rooms; the basic structure made from slabs of local gneiss is all that remains.

a larger room with a mosaic of cubes in perspective and masks of the New Comedy linked by shoots of ivy, and finally a room depicting the triumph of Dionysus.

Going down the street, note the rectangular marble portal of the building known as the Inn (42) which has a water tank capable of holding 27,000 liters of water. Enter the fine theater (43) that lies in a dramatic position and which can hold 6,000 spectators in its slightly curved cavea. Few remains of the decorated scenery can be seen in the *orchèstra* but you will see the huge tank that holds the eight supporting arches of the lost covering. Second to first century BC residential blocks line Theater Way including the House of Dionysus (44), named after the mosaic floor portraying the god of wine riding a tiger in the *impluvium* of the atrium, and the House of Cleopatra and Dioscurides (45), which contains copies in the Doric peristyle of the original statues (137 BC) now in the Museum. On your return to Mykonos in the caique, you will notice a third residential sector of Hellenistic and Roman Delos.

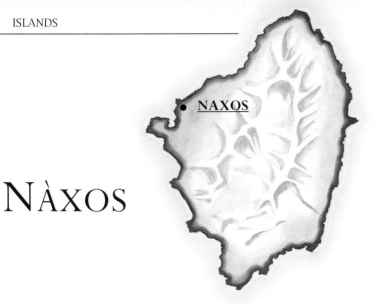

NÀXOS

182 left The Portàra, the portal of the cella in the Ionic temple of Apollo (540-530 BC), frames this lovely view of Nàxos and its sea; the temple was built as a result of the munificence of the leader Lygdamis.

182 right The greatest curiosity of the ancient world can be seen in the ancient marble quarry of Apolònas on the north coast of the island: a colossal and incomplete Ionic koùros.

Nàxos, the largest of the Cyclades, is now a tourist destination rich in archaeological treasures. It is the mythological birthplace of Dionysus, who courted and married the beautiful Ariadne after she was jilted by Theseus after she helped him escape from the Labyrinth of Knossos with a thread, or in other accounts, glittering jewels.

The island was an important center of the Cycladic civilization in the 3rd millennium BC, as indicated by the remains of the fortified settlement of **GROTA** on the north coast, over which a citadel defended by Cyclopean walls was built in Mycenaean times. The Mycenaean city was only abandoned in the 9th century BC when the Naxians moved to the acropolis currently occupied by a 13th century AD Venetian castle.

Thanks to its quarries of highly prized marble and its enterprising landed and merchant class, the island flourished between the 8th and 6th centuries BC. People from here set up the colony on **NÀXOS** in eastern Sicilty in 734 BC, together with Chalkidians from Euboea. The island affirmed its hegemony over the archipelago and at the same time, under the illuminated leadership of Lygdamis (550-524 BC), rose to become an important artistic center with a refined school of sculptors that promoted the Archaic style of the Ionian islands.

In Mitropòleos plaza in the modern city of Nàxos, visitors can admire the remains of the ancient *agorà*, with Doric colonnades on three sides, dating from the elegant Hellenistic renovation in about 200 BC. The highlight of the visit to the island however is a trip to the Islet of Strongyle, now Palàti, linked to Nàxos by a narrow artificial causeway, close to the ancient port. The site features the remains of the incomplete psuedo-peripteral Ionic Archaic temple of Apollo (540-530 BC), one of the most ancient examples of this architectural order. The cella of the temple is divided into three aisles by two rows of four columns, and opens onto a pronaos and an opisthodomos, both distyle *in antis*, and an *àdyton* (inner shrine) between the cella and the opisthodomos. The imposing doorway of the cella, the Portàra was reused and partially damaged in Christian times. The cornices bear Archaic motifs typical of the Ionian islands. The cornices are unfinished since they still bear the lifting bosses – outcroppings of stone used as grips for positioning the components. The museum, housed in the Venetian Ducal palace, has a good collection of Cycladic "idols" dating from the 3rd millennium BC, Mycenaean ceramics, and noteworthy examples of statuary dating from the 7th to the 2nd century BC.

The Archaic marble quarry with its unfinished statue of a *koùros*, perhaps depicting Dionysus, is open to visitors at **APOLONAS**. The statue is over 10 meters high and dates from the second half of the 6th century BC. Two other earlier *koùroi* from the same century can be seen at the ancient quarry of Melànes.

SANTORINI
(THIRA)

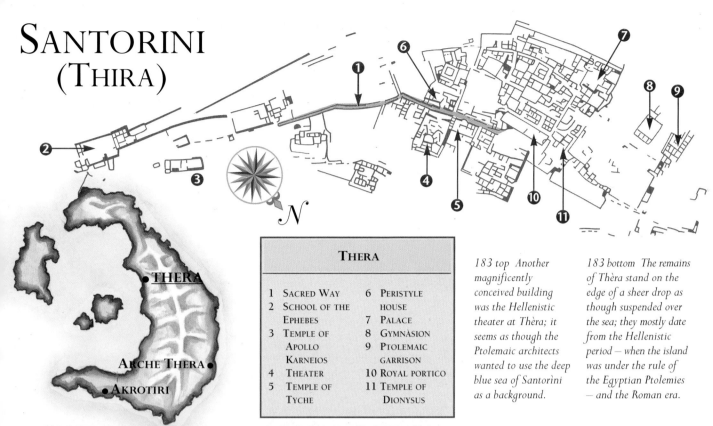

THERA

1 SACRED WAY
2 SCHOOL OF THE EPHEBES
3 TEMPLE OF APOLLO KARNEIOS
4 THEATER
5 TEMPLE OF TYCHE
6 PERISTYLE HOUSE
7 PALACE
8 GYMNÀSION
9 PTOLEMAIC GARRISON
10 ROYAL PORTICO
11 TEMPLE OF DIONYSUS

183 top Another magnificently conceived building was the Hellenistic theater at Thèra; it seems as though the Ptolemaic architects wanted to use the deep blue sea of Santorìni as a background.

183 bottom The remains of Thèra stand on the edge of a sheer drop as though suspended over the sea; they mostly date from the Hellenistic period – when the island was under the rule of the Egyptian Ptolemies – and the Roman era.

Ancient Thèra, now **THIRA** or Santorìni, considered by some as the most beautiful of all Greek islands, owes much of its charm to the volcano that, over the millennia, has sculpted its crescent-shaped outline. The island is sometimes called the "Aegean Pompei" because of a violent volcanic eruption that in the third quarter of the 17th century BC would have killed most of its inhabitants, had they not fled the island when it was rocked by an earthquake shortly before the eruption. At any rate, this natural disaster buried the abandoned, but previously flourishing Cycladic city with Minoan overtones, under a thick layer of volcanic ash. Excavations have been carried out at the site only recently, uncovering the ruins.

The very important site of **AKROTIRI**, lying on a north-south axis to a road, known as "Telchines Street," leading to the port below, has only been excavated to about half its estimated extent (some scholars place it at two hectares). Excavations have uncovered squares and several residential units with two or three floors, some of which were aristocratic residences while others were the independent dwellings of wealthy citizens and others were housing blocks shared by several families. All are now protected under sheds that, to some extent, diminish the charm of the site. *Xestè 3* seems to have been the home of a nobleman invested with priestly authority. The structure is divided into a private area, lying to the west, with service rooms on the ground floor and

residential quarters on the first floor, and to the east, a series of cult rooms with walls featuring several openings that could be closed using sliding panels, depending on the rite. The splendid frescoes found here, depicting the preparation of a woman before marriage in the vivid naturalism of Minoan art, are now at the National Museum in Athens (like all the frescoes from Akrotiri). "Telchines Street" continues towards the Square of the Mill, and the bottleneck caused by the overlapping of the Beta and Gamma city sectors. The Beta Sector features a sanctuary with frescoed rooms depicting initiation rites-of-passage of boys to adulthood, and the various competitions involved. Frescoes with motifs alluding to fertility and the continuation of life were uncovered in another cult room in the Delta Sector. The room that housed the mill is also clearly identifiable (D15). Further still is a triangular plaza, widely believed to have served as a sort of *agorà*, overlooking which is House O, probably the residence of a politically important city official. The fact that the window on the first floor opens onto the plaza as well as

the frescoes in room 5, that repeatedly allude to the ties between the population and the sea, suggest that the owner of the house and his family played a leading role in the small island community. Equally suggestive is the residential context of the House of the Women, Room 1 of which seems to have served as a household shrine with frescoes representing nuptial themes. A milling complex together with storage space for flour occupies the Alpha Sector, to the north of the area open to visitors. The store room contains Minoan-type storage jars.

The site of ancient **THERA** lies near Kamàri on the volcanic crest towards the east coast of the island. Founded as a Dorian

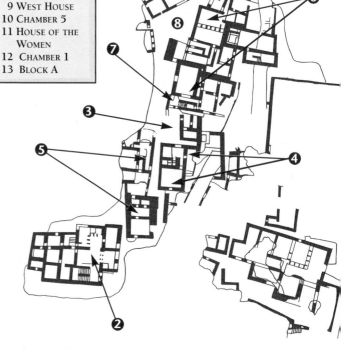

AKROTIRI

1 "TELCHINES STREET"	8 TRIANGULAR
2 XESTE 3	PLAZA
3 SQUARE OF THE	9 WEST HOUSE
WINDMILL	10 CHAMBER 5
4 BLOCK B	11 HOUSE OF THE
5 BLOCK G	WOMEN
6 BLOCK D	12 CHAMBER 1
7 CHAMBER D15	13 BLOCK A

colony in the 10th century BC, perhaps as a result of an as-yet-undefined interaction between Greeks and Phoenicians, the city became prosperous and in turn, set up its own colony at Cyrene on the Libyan coast in 631 BC. The remains now visible, however, all date from the golden age of the city when it was used as a Ptolemaic naval base in the southern Aegean. At the top of the steep path that leads to the excavation site, one can admire the cult complex dedicated to Concordia, the Dioscures (Castor and Pollux), Zeus, Apollo and Poseidon, by Artemidoros of Perge (Asia Minor), admiral of the Ptolemaic

184 top left Protection from the weather has guaranteed the survival of the "Aegean Pompeii," the nameless Minoan center at Akrotìri.

184 center The subjects of the 16th century BC frescoes in room B1, a cult room in Block B at Akrotìri, have been related to Minoan initiation rites (Athens, National Museum).

184 bottom This fresco (16th century BC) comes from Room 5 in House O, a domestic sanctuary the equivalent of which was found in houses of a certain status in the Minoan world (Athens, National Museum).

184-185 bottom This fresco with a rare representation of an exotic, perhaps Egyptian, river journey also comes from Room 5 in House O (Athens, National Museum).

fleet (250-240 BC). Inscriptions here attest to the importance of its donor.

Continuing along the stepped path, one reaches the *agorà*. A staircase to the right leads to the remains of the barracks of the garrison and, a little further, a small gymnasium for the troops. Further to the south lies the chaotic residential complex of the governor of the island, dating from the Ptolemaic period with refurbishments and extensions carried out in Antonine times. The south slope of the *agorà* features a row of workshops arranged in keeping with a pattern widespread in Hellenistic cities. A little further to the south, almost halfway between the southern and northern

plazas, stands the small temple that was first dedicated to the dynastic cult of the Ptolemies, before being transformed to serve the Roman Imperial cult. Beyond the plaza, with a Royal Portico on its west side, structured like a dual stoà, lie residential sectors and the theater within a square enclosure, which affords a scenic view of the sea. Built in Ptolemaic times, the theater was rebuilt and further embellished in the Julius-Claudius period. The last part of the visit follows the Sacred Way that runs, in the midst of remains of monuments and shrines, to the ancient sanctuary of Apollo Karneìos. The temple, partially hewn into the rock, has an apteral plan. The *Karneìai*, Archaic feasts of Spartan origin, linked to Thèra's colonial roots, were celebrated along the Sacred Way and in the square in front of the temple.

185 left The fresco shows crocus gatherers and alludes to the cult of Persephone (16th century BC); it comes from chamber 3 of Xestè 3, a domestic shrine in an upper-class house (Athens, National Museum).

185 right This lovely fresco of two boys dressed as boxers in Room B1 of Block B alluded to the spirit of competition that youths were encouraged to cultivate (Athens, National Museum).

RHODES

The largest island of the Dodecannese archipelago, **RHODES** was a Minoan settlement that later became a flourishing Mycenaean kingdom. It was colonized by the Dorians during the Greek Middle Ages. The already large Archaic settlements of Ialyssòs, Lìndos and Kàmeiros came together in synoecism to give rise in 407 BC to one of the most famous cities of the ancient world. Between the 4th and 2nd centuries BC, the city and the island attained impressive levels of wealth, population and living standards. A maritime and trading power, as well as a refined artistic and cultural center, the island played a major role in the diplomacy of the period. Rhodes started to decline in 167 BC when Rome, in retaliation for the island's political ambiguity during the conflict between the Romans and the Macedonians, opened the port of Delos, soon causing the collapse of the Rhodian trade-based economy. Throughout the Roman period, however, Rhodes remained a lively economic and cultural center.

LINDOS is by far the most attractive archaeological site on Rhodes, with its very high natural acropolis rising steeply from one of the most beautiful beaches in all of Greece. Defended by fairly well-preserved Byzantine and Medieval walls, the acropolis houses the fascinating remains of the Hellenistic sanctuary of Athena Lìndia.

The city, with the remains of a 4th-century BC theater near Aghios Pàvlos, was founded at least as early as the Mycenaean period (14th-13th century BC), and took part in the Rhodo-Cretan colonization of Asia Minor (Licia) and Magna Grecia (Gela, Agrigento and perhaps also Parthenòpe, which would develop to become Naples). It flourished for centuries and from the end of the 5th century BC, benefited from the political and maritime prestige of Rhodes during the Hellenistic period. The city features a 3rd-2nd century BC Doric colonnaded plaza, while in the surrounding area lie the remains of the tomb of Archokràtes and of Kleòboulos (4th-3rd century BC).

A temple and sacred enclosure dedicated to Athena Lìndia already stood in Archaic times (8th-6th century BC) at the edge of the dropoff directly above a cave that served for cult rituals in even more ancient times. The current remains date from the monumental facelift given to the sanctuary at some point between the end of the 4th and the beginning of the 2nd century BC. The refurbishment project included scenic combinations of stairways and colonnades, typical of Hellenistic architecture. The natural acropolis, which was molded using terraces that make it quite a climb to the temple, at the summit affords the visitor a breathtaking panorama, in a harmonious blend of natural scenery and architectural delight. A large number of works of art, votive offerings to Athena Lìndia, were placed between the columns and the open spaces, even along the very steep Sacred Way.

Beyond the Medieval walls, from the small square of the water tanks (1), the path gets even steeper. A semi-circular exedra (2) cut into the rock bears inscriptions

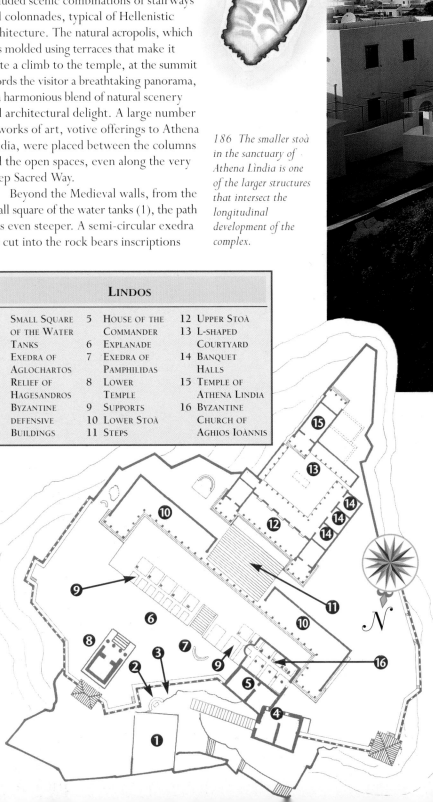

186 The smaller stoà in the sanctuary of Athena Lìndia is one of the larger structures that intersect the longitudinal development of the complex.

LINDOS					
1	SMALL SQUARE OF THE WATER TANKS	5	HOUSE OF THE COMMANDER	12	UPPER STOA
2	EXEDRA OF AGLOCHARTOS	6	EXPLANADE	13	L-SHAPED COURTYARD
3	RELIEF OF HAGESANDROS	7	EXEDRA OF PAMPHILIDAS	14	BANQUET HALLS
4	BYZANTINE DEFENSIVE BUILDINGS	8	LOWER TEMPLE	15	TEMPLE OF ATHENA LINDIA
		9	SUPPORTS	16	BYZANTINE CHURCH OF AGHIOS IOANNIS
		10	LOWER STOA		
		11	STEPS		

186-187 The modern town of Lìndos has a splendid view over the natural acropolis and massive medieval fortifications that ring the sanctuary of Athena Lìndia built between the 4th and 2nd centuries BC.

187 bottom left This view of Lìndos' medieval fortifications is taken from the east bastion with its barbican; note the steps to the lower terrace on the right.

187 bottom center Like many other points in the monumental complex, the avant-corps of the upper stoà have been rebuilt, often by Italian architects using the original materials.

187 bottom right The austerity of the Doric order seems irretrievably, and pleasantly, lost in the proportional elegance and lightness of Hellenistic buildings, as can be seen here at Lìndos.

from the Late Roman Imperial period by
the priest Aglòchartos who dedicated it.
On the same side, a little further, is a large
rock-carved relief of a warship (3), offered
to Poseidon by the Rhodian admiral
Hagesandros, and sculpted by Pythokritos,
to whom some scholars attribute the famous
statue of Nike (victory) at Samothrace.

Beyond the 15th-century AD
residence of the Commander (5) of the
local garrison of the Knights of Rhodes
(Knights of Malta), the steep stairway
passes through openings in the Byzantine
walls (4) to reach a flat area (6) at the foot
of the lower terrace. The flat area is
covered with marble bases, the largest of
which is the base of Pamphilìdas (7), in
the shape of a semi-circular exedra (250-
200 BC). The meager remains nearby are
of the lower temple (8) dedicated to the
Imperial cult (first-third century AD).

Facing this point, follow the architectural
sequence that is heralded by the arched supports (9), also from the Imperial period and
holding the lower terrace, served by a
central staircase. A small rectangular area
precedes the very long (88 meters) Lower
Stoà (10) with jutting wings. The stoà is
adorned by 28 Doric columns in *pòros* with
eight more for each wing. The portico
preceded the staircase (11) that led to the
upper terrace.

The smaller Upper Stoà (12), similar in
design to the lower stoà, served as an elegant
Doric *própylon* decastyle. The back wall had

188 top left A view of
the Hellenistic rock
necropolises of Akandià
(3rd-2nd century BC),
where large tombs were
given elaborate faces.

188 bottom left The
Doric Hellenistic temple
of Apollo Pythios was
built during the 3rd
century BC.

188 bottom right The
remains of the fountain
of the sacred enclosure
in the temple of Apollo
Pythios at Kàmeiros
before it was transformed
into a porticoed room
(3rd c. BC).

188-189 The southern
part of Kàmeiros, seen
here with the temple of

Athena, is characterized
by the imposition of the
Doric stoà between the
city and the sanctuary
in the acropolis.

189 top A rock
sanctuary known as the
"Grotto of the nymphs"
has been discovered to the
south of the cult complex
of Apollo Pythios.

189 bottom Aphro-
dite crouches as she
arranges her hair
after a bath (circa
100 BC); this is a
curious and some-
what lifeless variation
of the better-known
Aphrodite of
Doidàlsas (Rhodes,
Archaeological
Museum).

the 3rd century BC. No visitor would want to miss the chance to see the sanctuary of Apollo Pythios, known as the *Hyerotytheìon*, located here. It is enclosed within a colonnaded courtyard featuring other shrines, exedrae and a monumental 4th century BC fountain. The large north-south road is flanked by residential districts with peristyle houses. The acropolis, with its impressive Doric stoà and projecting side wings, stretches for 200 meters and is decorated with 87 columns on its façade, which served as a curtain behind which opened 46 rooms to accommodate travelers. The stoà also provided access to the Archaic and Classical sanctuary of Athena Kameiras, with its Doric peripteral temple hexastyle dedicated to the goddess, featuring a Classical design.

five doors, each flanked by a pair of columns, that opened onto a wide L-shaped courtyard (13) with Doric porticoes on its north, west and south sides. Three ritual banquet halls (14) opened onto the west portico, affording an oblique view of the elongated structure of the Doric temple, amphiprostyle tetrastyle (15), standing to the left of the axis of the complex.

RHODES, the island's capital, is a splendid town with a Medieval Venetian air that still preserves a few vestiges of its original Hippodamean grid plan, spread over terraces from west to east. From Eleftherías square at Mandráki, go through the Medieval Liberty Gate to admire the remains of the Doric temple of Aphrodite in Sìmis square and then continue to Arghirokástro square, which houses the archaeological site of the *Tetrápylon*, a monumental cube-shaped Corinthian arch dating from the 3rd century AD that opened from the military arsenal onto the city (only the foundations of the arch remain today). A visit to the rich archaeological museum housed in the 15th century AD Hospital of the Knights on the lower acropolis, is a must for

every discerning tourist. It was from here, within the sanctuary of Helios and in view of the mercantile port that one of the Seven Wonders of the Ancient World, the famous 30-meter-high bronze statue of the Colossus of Rhodes by Chares of Lìndos (292-226 BC), greeted incoming vessels. The Park of Mount Smith now stands on the location of the ancient acropolis with scattered remains of the Hellenistic city; including the Sanctuary of Apollo Pythios. Highlights here include the temple, the stadium and the *odeíon*. Lastly, the Park of the Rhodians houses a well-preserved Hellenistic bridge over the Karakónero stream and the rock-cut Hellenistic necropolis of Akandiá, with a few exceptional examples of mausoleums, extending up to the summit of the hill.

The scant remains of Minoan and Mycenaean Ialyssòs, close to Triánda, are not particularly interesting, in contrast to the ruins of **KÀMEIROS**, on the west coast. The surviving remains date from the town-planning project at the end of

KOS

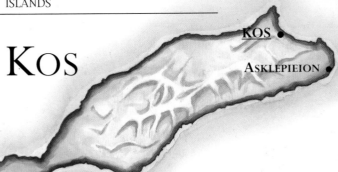

According to myth, the lovely Dodecanese island of **Kos** was dear to the heart of the god of health, Asklepios. It was also the birthplace of Hippocrates, the physician who revealed the ethical basis and practice of medicine to the ancients, thereby initiating the establishment of a medical school, that of the Asklepiads. The island was also loved by the ruler of Egypt, Ptolemy II Philadelphus who promoted a cultural development without precedent there, and by the poet Theocritus, the greatest exponent of bucolic poetry, and by the painter Apelles. Today it is an ideal place for a holiday thanks to its clean beaches and wealth of ancient and medieval archaeological treasures.

The island first flourished during the Minoan (17th-15th century BC) and Mycenaean (14th-12th century BC) epochs. The later arrival of the Dorians brought the development of Geometric artistic culture and the creation of an urban center which, in 366 BC, was refounded at the culmination of a period of prosperity that lasted until the 6th century despite a series of damaging earthquakes. During the Classical, Hellenistic and Roman eras, Kos was a busy trading port for traffic between Asia Minor and western markets as well as an exporter of its famous wines and high-quality fabrics throughout the Mediterranean.

Before visiting the ruins of the ancient *pòlis* in the historical center of the main town, you are advised to take an archaeological tour starting with the excavations of the huge *Asklepieìon*, the sanctuary of Asklepios four kilometers southwest of the town, constructed near a stand of cypress trees sacred to Asklepios and Apollo.

The complex appears as it was laid out between the second half of the 4th century BC and the end of the 2nd century BC, when embellishments were made by the Romans. It stands on four artificial terraces dug out of the slope of a hill, buttressed using the isodomic technique and connected by marble steps along a broken central axis. A rising *klìmax* in Pergamum style led the visitor on his pilgrimage up to the reassuring sight of the porticoes, fountains and temples that formed the

setting for a cure of his body or mind.

The remains of a first century baths complex, perhaps an expansion of the one that overlooks it, lie in the eastern sector of Terrace IV (1). From here, a ramp and Doric *propylaia* (2) lead to Terrace III (3), a square bounded on three sides by a Doric portico (4) along which lie a number of rooms used as a clinic and medical school. The water from a spring (5) in the upper terrace wall supplied the tanks and fountains – mostly visible in the section to the left – and flowed into the channels on the sheltered side of the portico.

On the right at the foot of the flight of steps (6) that leads to Terrace II, there are the ruins of an elegant Ionic temple (7) dedicated to the "new Asklepios" (Emperor Nero) by the Greek doctor who studied the poison that killed Claudius, Nero's predecessor. Terrace II (8), narrower than the others, was the center of religious activity; note the

190 bottom This view of Terrace III of the Asklepieìon shows the size of the space enclosed by porticoes and terminated by the solid series of arches set in the supporting wall of Terrace II.

190 top The remains of the peristasis of the second century AD Corinthian temple dedicated to the cult of Antoninus Pius stand in the east sector of Terrace II at the bottom of the steps to the larger temple.

190-191 Here we have another view of Terrace II with the columns of the temple of Antoninus Pius; the remains of a large Roman baths complex built in two phases (1st c. BC-1st c. AD) stand in the background.

191 top Only the base remains of what used to be a large semi-circular monument that probably supported an important work of art at the foot of Terrace I.

191 bottom The remains of the oldest temple of the god of medicine (300-270 BC) can be seen in the western sector of Terrace II; it was built in the Ionic order with two columns between the doors of the side walls.

N

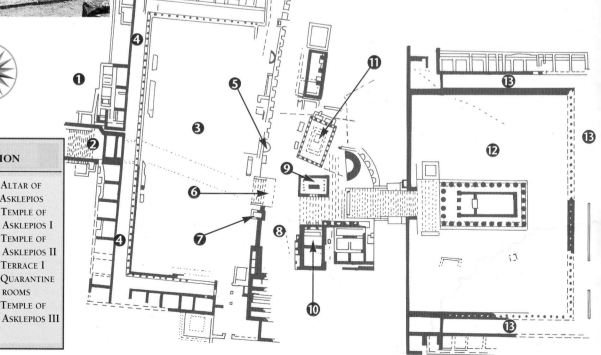

ASKLEPIEION

1 TERRACE IV	9 ALTAR OF
2 DORIC	ASKLEPIOS
PROPYLAEUM	10 TEMPLE OF
3 TERRACE III	ASKLEPIOS I
4 DORIC	11 TEMPLE OF
PORTICO	ASKLEPIOS II
5 SPRING	12 TERRACE I
6 STAIRWAY	13 QUARANTINE
7 TEMPLE OF	ROOMS
NERO-	14 TEMPLE OF
ASKLEPIOS	ASKLEPIOS III
8 TERRACE II	

foundations of the altar of the god (9) that was erected on a podium *in antis* and decorated with reliefs sculpted by the workshop of Praxiteles. Then there is the earliest temple dedicated to Asklepios (10), a Ionic distyle design *in antis* (300-270 BC) that was later transformed into a *thesauròs* where pilgrims offered tribute, and the foundations of a hexastyle peripteral Corinthian temple (11) built on the site of

the earlier temple of Apollo Delios from the Classical age that was dedicated to the imperial cult.

A magnificent stairway leads to Terrace I (12) lined on three sides by other porticoes (13) used in the cure of the sick; two of the porticoes were marble and Doric; the other was originally made from wooden pillars which were later replaced with marble ones. At the start of the 2nd century BC, the new temple of Asklepios (14) was constructed here, a hexastyle peripteral Doric model, with an unusually raised cell. To have an idea of the attractions of the layout of the sanctuary, it is necessary to imagine an internal garden matched by the frame of sacred cypresses around the outside.

Continuing west to a spot near Zipàri nine kilometers from the town of Kos, we come to the excavations of the Christian basilica of Aghios Pàvlos (6th century) with mosaic floors. A similar complex can be seen south at Kapamà.

From here, proceed to the beach at

Kefalòs, 43 kilometers southwest, where the attractive ruins of the 6th-century basilica of Aghios Stèfanos perch on a rocky outcrop accessible from the beach.

Returning to Kos, first visit the extensive excavation area of the *agorà* and the port starting from the sanctuary of Aphrodite which was rebuilt in 200-150 BC and enclosed by a vast four-sided portico. It contains twin Doric tetrastyle prostyle temples on a tall platform, both preceded by an altar and tetrastyle Corinthian propylaeum, commissioned by Roman merchants on the model of the twin temples of Fortuna and Mater Matuta in the cattle market (Foro Boario) in Sant'Omobono in Rome close to the river port.

The remains of the coeval sanctuary of Heracles lie near the large date palm that characterizes the landscape of this area of the excavations. The sanctuary has a small temple bounded by a trapezoidal portico built during the Mid-Imperial age. Of the ruins in the large Christian basilica nearby (circa 490), a number of columns still stand remaining from the renovation during the reign of Diocletian of the proto-Hellenistic stòa that bounded the sanctuaries. South of this area, you can follow the street network that touches on the northern residential area, in part adjacent to walls built during the Classical age, and containing blocks of houses and shops from the 2nd to 5th centuries. Looking west you will see the spectacular ruins of the *agorà,* fully 16,000 square meters in size and lined with marble porticoes of which only certain columns still stand.

From the *agorà*, head towards the restored Roman House, a luxurious and large two-story Hellenistic building that was modernized on several occasions until the

3rd century. The house contains a number of interesting sections: the windowed courtyard in front of the entrance, equipped with a water tank and decorated with the mosaic of a panther attacking a deer; the small room that faces onto the courtyard and the adjacent room that bears the remains of wall paintings; the *andròn* that looks onto the large Rhodian-Corinthian peristyle along which there are a number of rooms with frescoes and mosaics; the rooms reserved for the slaves; the splendid triclinium lined completely with high-quality marble; and the garden-*nymphaeum* with its polychrome mosaics. When you have looked at the remains of the large Central Baths, visit the residential area on the *decumanus maximus* of Roman Kos where there are impressive remains of 2nd-3rd-century houses and workshops on either side of the paved road (over 40 meters wide). Between the acropolis and the road, you can see the House of the Rat (100-120) which mixes elements of classical Greek design with a

192-193 A visit to the huge agorà at Kos is a moving experience (the remains of a Doric colonnade can be seen in the foreground); the agorà was mostly excavated by Italian archaeologists between 1911 and 1945.

193 top right View of the agorà; in the foreground are the remains of a marble entablature decorated with the twisting motifs that were used throughout the Classical era.

193 bottom The Doric columns with entablature and frieze of metopes and triglyphs are from the portico of the West Gymnàsion on Kos; they still mark the layout of the covered athletics track, the xystos.

Roman ground plan and contains a mosaic of the rat of Europe in a *cubiculum*. There is also the House of Silenus decorated with lovely figured mosaics of different subjects. Observe the dramatic advance of the *cardus maximus* towards the port and pause to admire the remains of the large Western Baths, built during the 3rd century with a perfectly restored public latrine, and those of the House of the Judgement of Paris, decorated with mosaics at the end of the second century. Then, consider the splendid parade of 17 trabeate Doric columns in the Western Gymnàsion which correspond to the portico on the *xystos*, the covered running track built during the second century BC. On the other side of the street, you can admire the Roman theater from the second century that has undergone heavy restoration. The six rooms of the archaeological museum on Kos hold important works of art: magnificent examples of late-Classical and Hellenistic statuary and two masterpieces of Hellenistic and Roman mosaics.

192 left The photo shows the two-story Ionic peristyle of the Roman House, completely excavated and restored.

192 right Floor mosaics that used to belong to houses and complexes from the Roman era have been moved to the agorà on the island of Kos; the view in the picture shows buildings from an earlier period in the background.

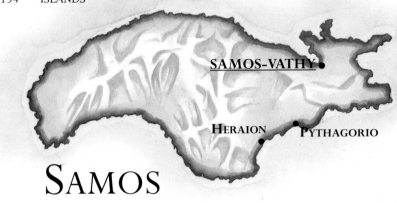

SAMOS-VATHY

HERAION   PYTHAGORIO

SAMOS

SAMOS, the homeland of Pythagoras, Epicuros, and Aristarchus and already inhabited during the Bronze Age, was the target of the Ionic colonization during the 11th century BC. Four-hundred years later, the advent of an aristocratic oligarchic government saw the beginning of the development in the Mediterranean part of the island, a change which was completed in the century that followed as a result of the beneficial effects of the tyrannies under Aiàkes and Polykràtes. The latter turned Samos into a great political and military power in the Aegean as well as an important cultural center in the fields of scientific philosophy and the arts. After a phase of political ambiguity, the help given against the Persians at Mykàle (479 BC) and the island's efforts as part of the Delian League

BC) made using the polygonal construction technique. They had circular towers and parapet walkways that have in part been preserved, and, along the western slope of the hill, an aqueduct that was dug out of the rock for at least a kilometer. It was designed by the architect Eupalìnos of Megara (6th century BC) to carry water from the Aghiàdes springs through clay pipes to the city.

A visit to one of the largest sanctuaries in Ionia, the **HERAION** that stands at the outlet of the Imbrasos river, is obligatory. This was where the birth of Hera was supposed to have taken place according to the myth that appeared around the 11th c. BC and which flourished in the Archaic age.

The marshy terrain does not make a visit easy and you are advised to start from

maintained Samos as among the most important *pòleis* in the 5th century BC. However, the not always peaceful alternation of democratic and oligarchic governments (440-320 BC) accelerated the political marginalization of the island, which continued throughout the Hellenistic and Roman eras when Samos was famous as a holiday destination.

Of the ancient city, partially covered by the modern Pythagòrio, one can see the remains of the Hellenistic walls (310-290

the temple of Hera (1), the largest Greek temple ever built (approximately 55 x 108 meters), which was faithfully reconstructed by Polykràtes (538-522 BC) to replace the previous model (circa 570 BC) designed by the architects Rhoìkos and Theòdoros of Samos and destroyed by an earthquake. A single column of this colossal octastyle dipteral Ionic temple (enneastyle on the west side) still stands, in the northeast corner. A true "stone

forest" stood around the deep *pronaos* and the huge long cell, both tripartite. A triple row of columns screened the short sides, and the capitals of the outer peristasis were in the standard volute design, while those of the inner peristasis followed the Ionic *kyma* model. A continuous frieze adorned the top of the walls of the pronaos and the cell. In the foundations, the bases of columns and other blocks from the previous *Heraion* can still be seen. Opposite the temple, a small coeval Ionic *monòpteros* (2) protected the base of the temple's cult statue (8th century BC). Nearby li the ruins of the small temple of Hera (3) built during the reign of Augustus and of the altar (570-560 BC) (4). To the south is the Exedra of the Ciceros (5), an honorary monument dedicated by the Samians to the Roman politician and his family in thanks for his support after the thefts of art by Gaius Verres.

Lying amid the remains of the cult buildings and logistical structures of the sanctuary from the Hellenistic and Roman eras is the Offering House designed by Ghenè-leos (6), one of the best artists from the Archaic period (560-550 BC), which housed copies of the statues of a local aristrocratic family. The Vathy (Samos) Museum holds splendid and colossal examples of Archaic statuary as well as excellent examples of votive materials from the sanctuary.

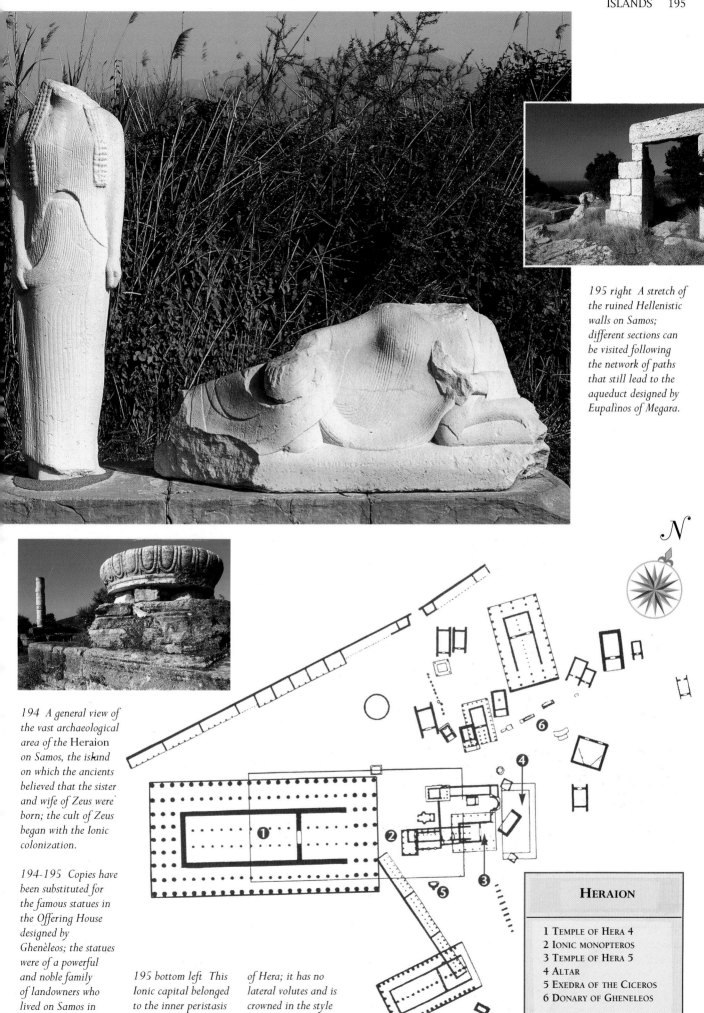

195 right A stretch of the ruined Hellenistic walls on Samos; different sections can be visited following the network of paths that still lead to the aqueduct designed by Eupalìnos of Megara.

194 A general view of the vast archaeological area of the Heraion on Samos, the island on which the ancients believed that the sister and wife of Zeus were born; the cult of Zeus began with the Ionic colonization.

194-195 Copies have been substituted for the famous statues in the Offering House designed by Ghenèleos; the statues were of a powerful and noble family of landowners who lived on Samos in the 6th century BC.

195 bottom left This Ionic capital belonged to the inner peristasis of the dipteral temple of Hera; it has no lateral volutes and is crowned in the style known as Ionic kyma.

HERAION

1 TEMPLE OF HERA 4
2 IONIC MONOPTEROS
3 TEMPLE OF HERA 5
4 ALTAR
5 EXEDRA OF THE CICEROS
6 DONARY OF GHENELEOS

CRETE

The landscape of Crete is home to many sites of great archaeological interest from the Minoan civilization (first half of the second millennium BC), but there are even centers from the Mycenaean, Greek and Roman ages.

For visitors who arrive at **KASTELI** in the gulf of Kìssamos from the Peloponnese port of Gythion, we suggest a visit to its small

(16th century) which gives an ample overview of the local archaeology.

If you are interested in archaeological-speleological sites, a long deviation into the province of Rèthymno via Anoghià and the slopes of Mount Idi takes you to the cave of **IDEO** at almost 1500 meters altitude; this was the place in which tradition says that Zeus was born and to which the mythical King Minos climbed every nine

museum displaying finds from a local Minoan "palace" and from the nearby Hellenistic cities of Polyrrhènia and Phalasàrna. One should also head to the south coast of the island, to the village of Soughià. About an hour's walk from here lie the ruins of the important Hellenistic and Roman sanctuary of **LISSOS** dedicated to Asklepios and Hygieia near a spring that gushes water with healing powers. The small Doric temple still retains its cella with a mosaic floor.

In **CHANIÀ**, the archaeology museum holds important finds from the main Minoan and Mycenaean centers in western Crete. Proceeding east, a brief stop can be made at **ARMENI** (14th century BC) with hypogean passage-tombs and, sometimes, with a central pillar, monolithic funerary stele and seats inside. At **RETHYMNO** you are advised to visit the archaeology museum in the elegant Sammicheli Loggia

years to know the wishes of the king of the gods. A much-worshipped place in the Minoan age, showing Geometric-eastern and Hellenistic-Roman influences, it had a vast open square and the cave itself, inside which stood the large Hellenistic altar on the left. Returning to Anoghià, follow the signs for Goniès and **TYLISSOS** where there are the remains of three Minoan villas from the 17th-16th century BC.

From the island's capital, Iràklion, head south to reach **GORTYNA**. Founded by Laconi of Amyklai in the Geometric age, it flourished from the 5th century BC until its hegemony over all of Crete was established (3rd-2nd century BC). It was the administrative capital and major economic center of the island from the Roman conquest (67 BC) until its destruction by the Arabs (824).

The Archaic and Classical *agorà* has been identified by the impressive remains

of the Justinian basilica of Aghios Titos that bears monograms of the emperor on its capitals. Not far from the museum, there is a well-preserved *odeíon* built during the Triumviral period and renovated during the reign of the Emperor Trajan. The semi-circular *cavea* rests on radial walls and walkways with vault coverings. The stage was straight with curved ends. Below the portico are curved blocks of stone on which a long text in Archaic Doric Greek known as the "Queen of Inscriptions" can still be read in full: this is the Code of Gòrtyna that detailed private and public rights and is the oldest and most complete collection of laws to have survived from the world of the Greeks. The blocks, which came from a circular *ekklesiastèrion*, were inserted into the new building which was later transformed into the *odeíon*. The cavea of the Hellenistic-Roman theater — 120 meters in width — can be seen on the slope of the hill.

196 The remains of the concert room (odeion) of Gòrtyna, built in opus testaceum (hollow brick) and lined with marble, belong to a renovation program from the 2nd century AD.

196-197 The ruins of the Byzantine basilica of Aghios Titos (circa 550) reflect the importance of Gòrtyna in the history of Hellenistic, Roman and Christian Crete until the 9th century.

197 top right The Roman statues that embellished the public and religious complexes of Gòrtyna are displayed in the local archaeological museum.

197 bottom left A fragmentary inscription from the age of Justinian (note the lengthened sections of the letters and the letter "S" in the form of a "C") lies near the ruins of the basilica of Aghios Titos.

197 bottom right This statue of a seated Roman figure from the second or third century AD may have come from a workshop of the famous sculptural school of Aphrodisìas in Caria (Asia Minor).

From Aghios Titos, descend towards Mitròpoli and turn east along the path that will take you to **AGHII DEKA**: the temple of Apollo Pythios, rebuilt in Hellenistic times and modified inside while under the domination of imperial Rome, can be seen next to the ruins of a Roman theater with a brick cavea 100 meters wide. Also interesting are the nearby ruins of a sanctuary of Egyptian gods that has a vast tripartite cella preceded by a portico with an architrave inscribed by its dedicants (2nd century AD).

The route can be terminated with a stop at the coeval monumental complex of the *Praetorium*, the administrative and private residence of the provincial governor during the Roman era. From north to south, note the remains of a basilica, a baths complex, and a temple inside a four-sided portico dedicated to the imperial cult. The large

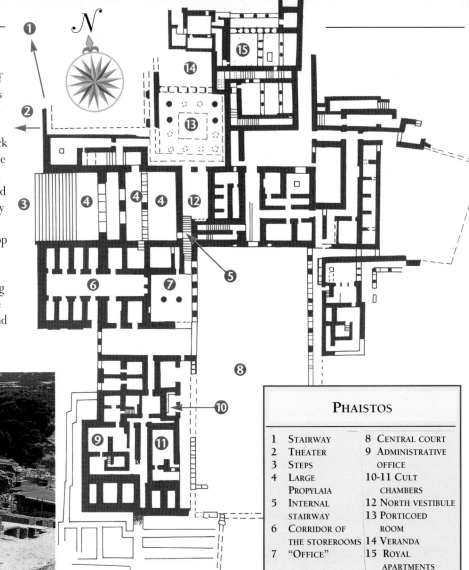

PHAISTOS

1	STAIRWAY	8	CENTRAL COURT
2	THEATER	9	ADMINISTRATIVE
3	STEPS		OFFICE
4	LARGE	10-11	CULT
	PROPYLAIA		CHAMBERS
5	INTERNAL	12	NORTH VESTIBULE
	STAIRWAY	13	PORTICOED
6	CORRIDOR OF		ROOM
	THE STOREROOMS	14	VERANDA
7	"OFFICE"	15	ROYAL
			APARTMENTS

rectangular tank of an Antonine fountain/*nymphaeum* can be seen on the *decumanus*. It was originally embellished with an octastyle Ionic front with wings and niches with statues. If you have time, make a side trip to the bay of Lèndas to appreciate the remains of the sanctuary of Asklepios at **LEBENA** which was built in the 4th century BC and then rebuilt in the Roman republican era. The building still has two columns and the mosaic *pronaos* floor.

A visit to the Minoan "palace-city" of **PHAISTOS** is essential. The site flourished between 1900-1700 BC; it was destroyed but rebuilt smaller and subordinate to the powerful "villa" of Aghìa Triàda nearby. Excavation has unearthed most of the second palace and important sections of the first. Stop to consider the complex from above. It was arranged around a huge central courtyard in accordance with a typical palace-city ground plan. The west and north wings, and part of the east wing, are still extant. Descending the steps (1) to the west square, also called the Theater Square (2) because of the eight long tiers on the north side, note the changes in level resulting from the different arrangements of the square for the two versions of the palace.

It is possible that this space in front of the main access was a sort of *agorà* for public meetings of one sort or another. The façade of the second palace stood on the east side of the square. It was originally a two-story building with walls made from stone, wood and unbaked bricks. A flight of steps (3) solemnized the entrance where the famous Large Propylaia (4) stand. The propylaia were formed by three partitions with openings embellished respectively by a column *in antis*, a pillar *in antis* and a tristyle portico (note the guard room on the right). They led into a court from which a door in the southeast corner led to a stairway (5). Go down the stairs for a visit to the storerooms that were arranged around a central corridor (6) in front of which there was an "office" with columns and alabastrine plastered walls (7). The office faced onto the courtyard (8) from which it was possible to pass to the palace's administration offices (9) and two rooms that may have had a ritual use (10-11).

After returning to the stairway (5), visit the royal quarter in the north wing via the vestibule (12) at the top of the ramp. This leads into a room with porticoes (13).

A veranda (14) on the north side was connected to the two-story royal apartments that can still be seen to the north. These included rooms for private worship and living accommodation and were arranged around skylight shafts to receive natural light (15). The rooms facing north and east onto the central courtyard have been identified as a banquet room and shops and workshops linked with the palace's productive activities.

198 left The west side of the Minoan "palace-city" of Phaistòs was the main entrance to the complex excavated for a century by the Italian Archaeological School of Athens.

198 right As in all Cretan palace-cities, Phaistòs too had a sizable area dedicated to the storage of food; the photograph shows several large pìthoi (jars) with ring handles.

A short distance separates Phaistòs from the "royal villa" of **AGHIA TRIÀDA** that stands on top of a pre-existing residence from the Proto-Palatial period which had been subjugated by the nearby palace-city. The villa was heir to the hegemonic role of the palace-city in the region from 1700 BC until the Mycenean conquest (1400 BC) when a *mègaron* and associated structures were added to the Minoan residence to accommodate a *wànax*.

The Aghìa Triàda was an L-shaped structure and therefore had an open square. To the left, the path flanks the remains of a 16th-century BC house (1) with a courtyard; the east wing had distyle porticoed bays, and the west wing was used for storerooms. A Mycenaean shrine (2) with a vestibule and cella fitted with an altar for idols lay behind the southern section of the building. Between the house and the large square onto which the north and west wings of the villa face, you can see what remains of the paved road that joined Aghìa Triàda with Phaistòs (3) and a flight of steps (4) that leads to the paved street and pavement (5) that ran along the outer northern edge of the villa towards the house. This will bring you opposite the north

AGHIA TRIÀDA	
1 NEO-PALATIAL HOUSE	7 WEST QUARTER
2 MYCENAEAN SHRINE	8 ROYAL MEGARON
3 PAVED ROAD	9 SHOPS AND STORES
4 STEPPED RAMP	10 AGORÀ
5 PAVED ROAD	11 BASTION
6 MYCENAEAN MEGARON	

199 bottom right This is a masterpiece of Minoan painting; it is the painted sarcophagus found at Aghìa Triàda decorated with scenes of religious rituals overseen by a priestess (Iràklion, Archaeological Museum).

wing of the complex where the remains of the Mycenaean *mègaron* overlaid by the Minoan structures (6) make understanding of the residential and service areas difficult (the 2-story storerooms are interesting however). Head for the West Quarter (7), arranged around a paved courtyard with an L-shaped portico and connected, via a bay with *polythyra* walls, to the royal *mègaron* (8). This is a large apartment with a vestibule, living room and bedroom at the back. Note the traces of alabastrine wall-plaster (the candelabras are copies). Pieces of fresco were found here and in rooms identified as archives and a sanctuary. To the south of the western quarter are the ruins of pottery workshops and stores (9). Descending the stairs (4), you will notice the separation of the villa from the Mycenaean *agorà* (10). It is not certain what the function of the bastion (11) was. Porticoes that housed shops and stores faced onto the square which seems to have been built especially for commercial purposes.

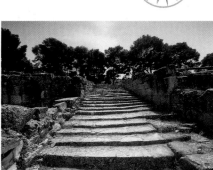

199 top right The view over the agorà of Aghìa Triàda; a porticoed front can be clearly seen related to the complex of shops on the right of the photograph.

199 bottom left The ramp of the Minoan "villa" of Aghìa Triàda seen from the paved road that crosses the village; the low steps were to allow pack animals to use the ramp.

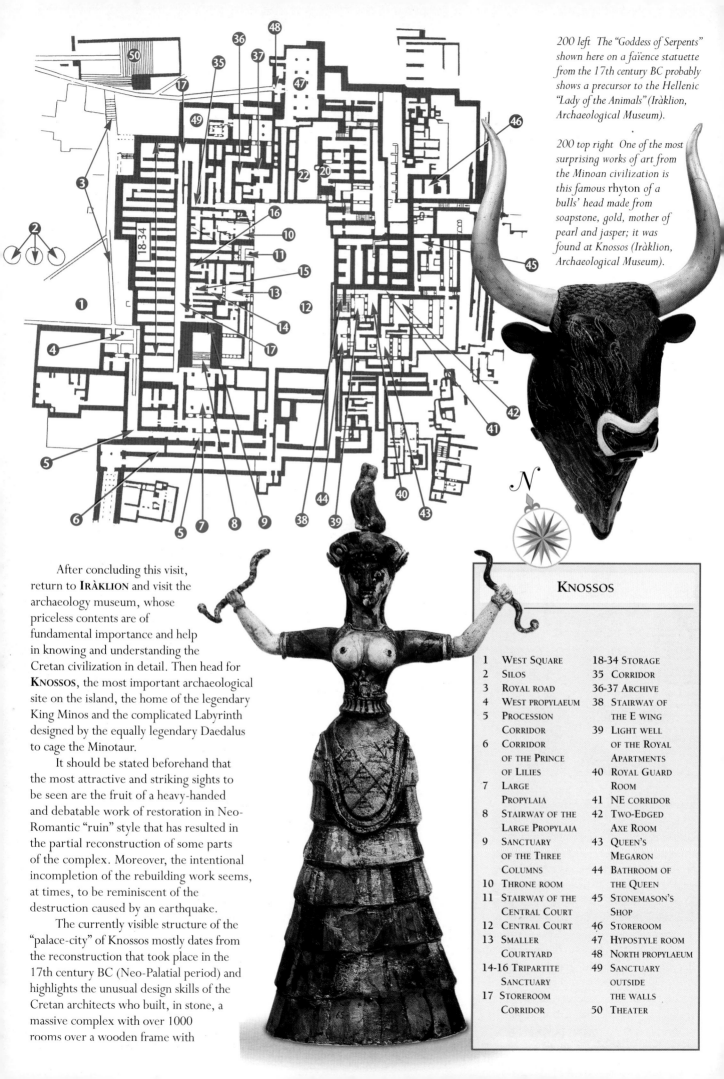

200 left The "Goddess of Serpents" shown here on a faïence statuette from the 17th century BC probably shows a precursor to the Hellenic "Lady of the Animals" (Iràklion, Archaeological Museum).

200 top right One of the most surprising works of art from the Minoan civilization is this famous rhyton of a bulls' head made from soapstone, gold, mother of pearl and jasper; it was found at Knossos (Iràklion, Archaeological Museum).

N

After concluding this visit, return to **IRÀKLION** and visit the archaeology museum, whose priceless contents are of fundamental importance and help in knowing and understanding the Cretan civilization in detail. Then head for **KNOSSOS**, the most important archaeological site on the island, the home of the legendary King Minos and the complicated Labyrinth designed by the equally legendary Daedalus to cage the Minotaur.

It should be stated beforehand that the most attractive and striking sights to be seen are the fruit of a heavy-handed and debatable work of restoration in Neo-Romantic "ruin" style that has resulted in the partial reconstruction of some parts of the complex. Moreover, the intentional incompletion of the rebuilding work seems, at times, to be reminiscent of the destruction caused by an earthquake.

The currently visible structure of the "palace-city" of Knossos mostly dates from the reconstruction that took place in the 17th century BC (Neo-Palatial period) and highlights the unusual design skills of the Cretan architects who built, in stone, a massive complex with over 1000 rooms over a wooden frame with

KNOSSOS

1	WEST SQUARE	18-34	STORAGE
2	SILOS	35	CORRIDOR
3	ROYAL ROAD	36-37	ARCHIVE
4	WEST PROPYLAEUM	38	STAIRWAY OF
5	PROCESSION		THE E WING
	CORRIDOR	39	LIGHT WELL
6	CORRIDOR		OF THE ROYAL
	OF THE PRINCE		APARTMENTS
	OF LILIES	40	ROYAL GUARD
7	LARGE		ROOM
	PROPYLAIA	41	NE CORRIDOR
8	STAIRWAY OF THE	42	TWO-EDGED
	LARGE PROPYLAIA		AXE ROOM
9	SANCTUARY	43	QUEEN'S
	OF THE THREE		MEGARON
	COLUMNS	44	BATHROOM OF
10	THRONE ROOM		THE QUEEN
11	STAIRWAY OF THE	45	STONEMASON'S
	CENTRAL COURT		SHOP
12	CENTRAL COURT	46	STOREROOM
13	SMALLER	47	HYPOSTYLE ROOM
	COURTYARD	48	NORTH PROPYLAEUM
14-16	TRIPARTITE	49	SANCTUARY
	SANCTUARY		OUTSIDE
17	STOREROOM		THE WALLS
	CORRIDOR	50	THEATER

*201 top left
An enthusiastic
reconstruction,
sometimes arbitrarily
selective and often
with little philological* *respect for materials
and techniques, has,
in any case,
conferred an easy
interpretation on
Knossos.*

wooden supports. It was split onto two or
three floors served by stairways, corridors,
porticoes and carriageable ramps. All of it
was arranged around a huge rectangular
central courtyard. The lack of fortifications
is surprising and is an indication of the
inhabitants' knowledge of their superior
power; the apparent lack of order in the
arrangement of the structure is misleading
and there is in fact a logical distribution of
functions in the various wings and on the
different levels. The palace-city was, in
fact, an administrative, economic,
productive and residential complex all at
the same time, not just for the king but

*201 top right The
theater outside the
northeast corner of
Knossos' palace was
strikingly large; it is
considered to have been
an area of collective use.*

*201 bottom left The
horns of a bull, symbol
of fertility and prosperity,
frequently appeared at
Knossos as decorative
elements charged with a
magical value.*

*201 bottom right
The northern access
ramp to the palace-
city of Knossos
connected the theater
with the north*

*hypostyle room and
central court; the
portico on the right is
of course, a
reconstruction.*

also for a large group of managing
functionaries and, one assumes, the priests
whose role it was to oversee the rituals
that accompanied the deeply held religious
convictions in every phase of community
life whether public or private. In addition
to the manifestation of a joyous sense of
life and the desire of expressing the
fundamental values and concepts of society
and its regal apex, it was to the presence of
the religious ceremonies that the striking
architectural, sculptural and pictorial
decorations of the palace-city and its
various areas (residential, private royal
sections, reception rooms, political halls,
shrines and porticoes) are owed.

202-203 *The many frescoes seen on the walls of the palace-city of Knossos are excellent copies painted in the 1930s and 40s; this scene shows a religious procession with offerings of food.*

202 left *The residential buildings in the palace-city of Knossos were often spread over several floors; the rooms were illuminated by light wells faced by low galleries and small windows.*

202 bottom right *Another view of the palace-city of Knossos; in the center, a reconstructed room has been decorated with copies of frescoes of procession scenes.*

203 top *Copies of frescoes depicting naturalistic — often marine — scenes can be seen on the walls of the galleries of the "Queen's Apartment," the residential nucleus of the east wing.*

entirely covered and without major sources of light, and painted decorations on either wall show over 800 figures bearing gifts to the king (symbolized by a priestess). Running adjacent to the Procession Corridor is what remains of the Corridor of the Prince of Lilies (6), so-called for the fresco (a copy) that perhaps shows a priestess on the wall where there may once have been a procession similar to the one in the other corridor.

203 bottom Like many of the frescoes found at Knossos, the famous "Prince of Lilies" dates from the 15th century BC and may represent a priestess guiding a court (Iràklion, Archaeological Museum).

Approach the palace from the vast West Square (1) with a quick glance at the three large sunken grain silos (2) from the Proto-Palatial era, and note the large paved road (3) that heads north towards the complex known as the Theater (much further ahead). Enter the palace through the West Propylaeum (4) where there used to be a guard room. You will quickly be made aware of the Cretan preference for axial ground plans with frequent right angles and changes of direction. The entrance to the Procession Corridor (5) is in the southeast corner of the west propylaeum. The corridor is

Having arrived at the Large *Propylaia* (7), ascend the grandiose stairway (8) that gives importance to the entrance and leads to the main floor of the heavily restored palace. Walk through the sequence of vestibules and rooms on this floor, including the well-known Sanctuary of the Three Columns (9), that was used prevalently for the performance of cult functions. Then go down the small service stairway to the Throne Room (10) named after the alabaster throne believed to have belonged to the king but which probably was used for formal religious rituals. The room appears to be more a place of worship; the copies of frescoes of cosmological

symbols and griffins squatting between lilies on a red background seem to favor this hypothesis.

Returning south along the west wing, you can admire the large stairway (11) and visit the Tripartite Sanctuary via the short flight of steps that leads from the central courtyard (12) to a smaller court (13) from which you can explore the cult area to the right. This comprises a room (14) that still contains a very tall clay jar (*pìthos*), typical of Cretan craftsmanship, and a cella (15) in which two important votive stores were found. The items they held included high-quality examples of art from places of worship in the earlier version of the palace-city that had been ritually buried under the floor at the time of the rebuilding. The cult area also includes the section to the west of the stores where the Pilaster Crypt is found; the supports of this crypt are marked by the omnipresent symbol of regal power, the two-edged axe (16).

It is only from here that it is possible to reach the long Storeroom Corridor (17), with the usual changes of direction. On the left you will pass 17 rectangular rooms (18-34) where large storage jars

were kept that held food under the direct supervision of the king and where cists were dug in the floor to increase the capacity of the building. The fact that another floor used to exist is shown by the various steps that can still be seen at various points. Another meandering corridor (35) leads to the archive (36-37) that shows brightly colored frescoes and tablets written in "Linear B" script.

Cross the central courtyard (12) and head for the east wing set against the slope of the hill. This is the location of the royal apartments that were built on an elegant and complex vertical plan.

204 left The central courtyard at Knossos leads to the famous Throne Room, but it was in fact probably a room in which stately religious ceremonies were held; this is the entrance seen from the east.

204-205 The Throne Room is decorated with copies of the original frescoes showing griffins and lilies; attention is quickly drawn to the alabastrine throne, perhaps used for divine epiphany.

205 bottom left A detail of the lovely griffins crouching among the lilies in the frescoes of the Throne Room at Knossos; the fluidity of the lines, typical of Minoan art, suggests volume and dynamism.

205 bottom right Curious bull hide shields in the shape of a figure eight, more suitable for ritual uses than fighting, were painted on the walls of one of the largest official reception rooms at Knossos.

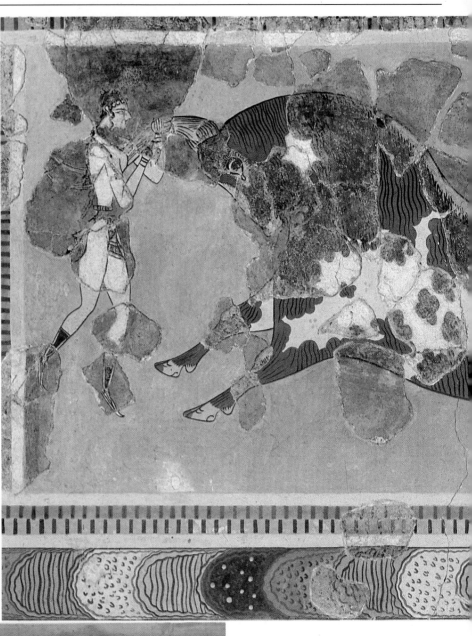

206 top left The fresco depicting the difficult exercise of taurokathápsia *in the central courtyard was also painted in the east wing of the palace-city, the wing mostly dedicated to the royal residence.*

206 bottom The so-called "Ladies in blue" are in fact three elegantly dressed dancers wearing contemporary jewelery and with their hair arranged in the styles of the time (15th century BC) (Iràklion, Archaeological Museum).

206-207 It has been hypothesized that the dangerous sport of vaulting over the back of an angry bull was part of a ritual that was concluded with the sacrifice of the animal (Iràklion, Archaeological Museum).

An impressive stairway (38) lit by a skylight (39) connected the two lower floors to the one at the level of the courtyard and that above it. Descend to the first floor to visit the Royal Guard Room (40) with its famous decorations of shields in bull hide in the form of an 8, and then to the ground floor to wander along the Colonnaded Court and the narrow northeast corridor (41). One of the rooms on the corridor is the Two-Edged Axe Room (42), probably used by the king for receptions (see the symbols of royal power on the walls); it was lit by a skylight and divided by a *polythryon* and was connected to a veranda to the south and east that overlooked a garden (no longer extant).

207 bottom The reconstruction of the palace-city of Knossos has recreated almost exactly the original proportions of light and shadow determined by the structure of the colonnades and light wells.

Next door there is the Queen's *Mègaron* (43) composed of a central room – with a portico leading straight into the garden – and a private bathroom (44) fitted with a bench, a skylight and a plant for drawing the water. The private rooms were all on the top floor (see the stairs in the corners of some rooms). Magnificent frescoes decorated the walls but only copies can now be seen.

Pass now to the northeast section of the palace which was reserved for workshops: the Stonemason's Shop (45) was given its name for the blocks of green marble that are still waiting to be worked, and large jars stand in the storeroom (46) that used to be part of the earlier palace.

Having left the area of the workshops, you can end your tour of Knossos by exploring the north wing where the large Hypostyle Room (47) was used to check and impose duty on incoming goods, and the north propylaeum (48) which seems to stand beside a sanctuary that lies outside the palace walls (49). The Royal Road ran from the propylaeum to the port; all of it was paved, like the central courtyard. The Theater (50) stands close to the north-west corner of the palace: it was an enclosed rectangular square with monumental tiers to the south and east and a speaking platform whose remains can be seen in the southeast corner. It was undoubtedly used for assemblies and meetings but of what nature we cannot know.

208 top Dozens of terracotta jars in excellent condition, some of them whole, have been found in the many stores of the west wing of the palace-city.

208 bottom left There is not a single sector of Knossos that the eagerness of Arthur Evans – the discoverer of Crete's most important palace-city – to rebuild the site has not terminated in debatable partial reconstruction.

208 bottom right A throne similar to the one found in the Throne Room has been restored in the Room of the Polythyra *in the official area of the palace-city where the king may have exercised his political power.*

208-209 The ruins of Knossos are set among luxuriant Mediterranean plant life that it is not difficult to imagine surrounded the site at the time of King Minos.

209 bottom One of the most famous Minoan frescoes at Knossos (here in a pair) is the one showing dolphins in a lively marine setting; it was painted in the area known as the "Queen's Apartment."

210 top left A view of the Hypostyle Room in the "palace" of Màllia; massive pillars support the roof on which there was a series of official reception rooms and banquet rooms.

210 bottom left This enormous reconstructed terracotta pìthos stands in the north courtyard of Màllia palace; it is decorated

with reliefs of wave and spiral motifs, racemes and impressions.

210 bottom right The most famous object to be seen at Màllia is the kèrnos, the wooden table used for ritual offerings of fruits and vegetables to the gods; it has a central cavity and 33 hollows around the edge.

The third from the last stop on the visit to Crete is **MÀLLIA** on the north coast where another imposing "palace" was built. It suffered the same phases of destruction and reconstruction as Phaistòs and Knossos, but it was not reoccupied following the Mycenaean conquest of the island. French excavations have uncovered a mostly two-story structure similar to those already seen in terms of ground plan and height.

A wide triangular expanse lies in front of the complex on the west side (1). You are advised to follow the paved road (2) to the southwest corner where you will see eight grain silos (3), all fitted with a central pillar to hold up the roof (no longer in existence). The public sanctuary (4) lies next to the silos and, in the center of the south side, the monumental entrance (5) to the palace is characterized by a long vestibule that leads into the central court (6). Entirely enclosed by balustrades and gates, it is centerd on a small altar with a sacrificial well (this is what suggested its function as an arena for the bloodless and ritual tauromachy of the Cretans). Access to the storage (7-9) is along its walls as well as to a shrine (10) containing the famous kèrnos, the large round stone table with a

central cavity and 33 hollows along the edge for offerings of early or rare vegetables and fruits.

The east wing is entirely filled with service structures and rooms. The southeast corner was the site of the stores for luxury items (11) while two rectangular storage areas (13-14) on the other side of the east portico (12) were used for food. Perhaps the complex of small rooms in the northeast corner of the court (15) was used as a kitchen.

The porticoed wing to the north seems to have been used for receptions, while banquet rooms on the upper floor were reached through a vestibule (17), hypostyle room (16) and a broad stairway.

The west wing, aligned along a monumental stairway that led to the upper floor (18), must have been extensive and impressive. On its left lay the audience room with one side opening on a portico and the whole surrounded by a number of service rooms (19). It was also connected to the stores on the west side (20) that lay

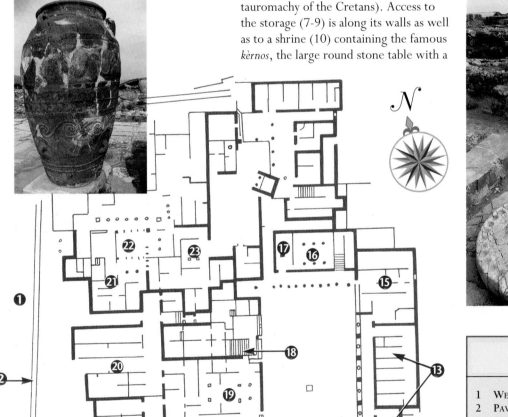

MALLIA	
1 WEST SQUARE	11 DEPOSIT
2 PAVED ROAD	12 EAST PORTICO
3 SILOS	13-14 STORAGE
4 PUBLIC SANCTUARY	15 KITCHENS
5 MONUMENTAL SOUTH ENTRANCE	16 HYPOSTYLE ROOM
	17 VESTIBULE
	18 STAIRWAY
6 CENTRAL COURT	19 ROOM OF THE AUDIENCES
7-9 DEPOSITS	
10 SHRINE OF THE KERNOS	20 STORAGE
	21-23 ROYAL APARTMENTS

behind. The private living quarters of the king (21-23), on the other hand, were spread across the whole of the northwest section of the complex.

Proceeding along the east coast of the island, you really must stop at **GOURNIÀ**, a rare example of a Minoan town (so far only seen in the guise of a "palace-city") which grew up around a small palace visible in the center of the residential area. A grid of paved roads crisscrossed the town.

The trip can be concluded with a visit to the palace of **KÀTO ZÀKROS** that stands in a magnificent position on Crete's east coast close to the famous palm groves

of Vài. The layout appears very similar to those already visited. The palace probably flourished as a result of its lying on a crossroads of the traffic with the Levant, as shown by discoveries of goods imported from Cyprus and Syria.

To end with, do not forget to pay a visit to the lovely archaeology museum in **AGHIOS NIKOLAOS** which specializes in the archaeology of eastern Crete.

GOURNIA

1 ROAD A
2 ROAD B
3 ROAD C
4 HOUSE OF THE CARPENTER
5 MYCENAEAN SHRINE
6 PALACE
7 RESIDENTIAL AREA
8 CENTRAL COURTYARD

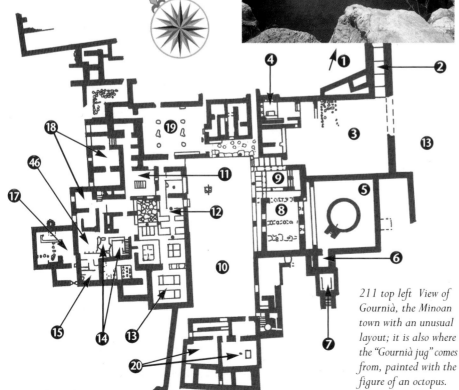

KATO ZAKROS

1	ROAD OF THE PORT	11	VESTIBULE
2	MAIN ENTRANCE	12	ROOM OF THE RITUALS
3	SMALLER COURTYARD	13	ROOM OF THE BANQUETS
4	LUSTRAL POOL	14	SANCTUARY
5	COURT WITH UNDERGROUND SWIMMING POOL	15	VOTIVE OFFERINGS
6	SPRING	16	ARCHIVE
7	MONUMENTAL FOUNTAIN	17	SHOPS
8-9	RECEPTION ROOMS	18	STORES
10	CENTRAL COURT	19	KITCHEN AND BANQUET ROOM
		20	SHOPS

211 top left View of Gournià, the Minoan town with an unusual layout; it is also where the "Gournià jug" comes from, painted with the figure of an octopus.

211 bottom left The pool of the palace of Kàto Zàkros is still fed by water from the spring beside it, probably part of a cult complex linked to the residence.

211 bottom right In this photograph one can observe the ruins of the residential nucleus of the palace at Kàto Zàkros.

GLOSSARY

ABACUS flattened cube crowning the echinus of a Doric capital

ACROTER decorative element at the top of a temple

ÀDYTON inaccessible chamber in the cella of a temple

AGORÀ central public square in a Greek city

AMBULACRUM covered corridor

ANÀKTORON Mycenaean royal palace

ANÀLEMMA supporting wall

ANÀTHEMA work of art offered to a god

ANDRON banquet room for men

AMPHIPROSTYLE temple with columns on the shorter sides

ANTHEMION floral decorative element

APODYTERIUM changing rooms in public baths

ASTYLE without columns

BOULEUTERION meeting room of the city council

CALIDARIUM hot water room in the public baths

CAPITOLIUM temple dedicated to Jupiter

CARYATID architectural support in the form of a woman

CAVEA semi-circular theatre auditorium for spectators

CELLA central shrine in a temple, the "holy of holies"

CENOTAPH commemorative monument to a person, without the body

CENTURIATION orthogonal division of fields during the Roman era

CERAMOGRAPHY painting on vases

COEVAL contemporary

ANGULAR CONFLICT problem related to coinciding the axis of the corner triglyph with that of the column below in a Doric temple

CHRYSELEPHANTINE made using gold and ivory

CRUX COMMISSA T-shaped

CHTHONIAN underground

DECUMANUS MAXIMUS main east-west street in a Roman city

DEDALIC founded on the conventions of early Archaic sculpture

DIAKONIKON sacristy of deacons

DIÀZOMA horizontal dividing corridor in a theatre cavea

DIPTERAL temple with double peristasis

DISTYLE having two columns

GARGOYLE figured discharge projecting from a gutter

DONARY votive monument

DROMOS entrance corridor

ECHINUS ovolo molding below the abacus of the capital of a column

EKKLESIASTERION seat of the citizens' assembly

EMBLEMA central figured square

ENTABLATURE set of support elements of a roof including the architrave, frieze and cornice

ENTASIS optical correction for thickening of the shaft of a column

EPISTYLE architrave on columns

HEXASTYLE having six columns

EX(H)EDRA semi-circular or rectangular room, open at the front

FICTILE made of terracotta

FORNEX the opening in an arch

FRIGIDARIUM cold water room in the public baths

GENS noble family clan

GYMNÀSION school of physical, literary, philosophic and musical education

HEKATOMPEDON 100-foot long temple

HEROON monumental complex consecrated to a dead hero

IMPLUVIUM marble tank embedded in the floor of the atrium of a Roman house to catch rainwater

IN ANTIS between the extensions of side walls, orthogonally in line with their corners

IN SITU in the original place

HYPETRAL uncovered

HYPOCAUST under-floor space heated with air

ISODOMIC TECHNIQUE construction technique using regular rows of large parallelepiped blocks

HYPOGEAN underground

HYPOSTYLE with columns inside

CARDUS MAXIMUS principal north-south street in a Roman city

KATAGOGION place for public hospitality, an inn

KORE statue of a young female in Archaic style

KOUROS statue of a young male in Archaic style

LÀRNAX urn

LITHIC made of stone

LOUTRON bath

LUSTRAL relating to purification rites

MACROTECTONIC structured on gigantic dimensions

MAGOULA low hill

MANTEION place the oracular responses of a deity are heard

MEGALITHIC made of enormous blocks of stone

MEGARON rectangular residential nucleus from protostoric era with porticoed vestibule, central room with hearth and small chamber

METOPE four-sided element, often figured, in a Doric frieze

MONOLITHIC made of a single block of stone

MONOPTERAL small circular temple or shrine with columns

MOLDING continuous strip of projecting plasterwork

MUSIVE made using mosaic work

NARTHEX vestibule across the western end of early Christian churches

NAVARCH admiral

ODEION covered concert hall similar to a theater

OIKOS small, rectangular sacred building

OPISTHODOMUS chamber behind the temple cella, symmetrical to the pronaos, of uncertain function

ORCHESTRA circular or semi-circular space used by the chorus and dancers between the cavea and the stage

OCTASTYLE having eight columns

PALAISTRA sports complex with internal four-sided portico

PANATHENIAN concerning all Athens and Attica

PANHELLENIC concerning all Greeks

PARASCENIUM projecting part of the stage

PÀRODOS side entrance to the orchestra in a theatre

PENTELIC white marble from Mount Pentèli

PERIBOLUS sacred enclosure

PERIPTERAL temple with single peristasis

PERISTASIS colonnade on all four sides of a temple

PERISTYLE having columns all around a courtyard

PILASTER rectangular pillar engaged in a wall

PISÉ construction technique of clay walls on a wooden structure

PLATEIA wide street in a Greek city

PLINTH parallelepiped support

POLEIC relating to the pòlis

POLIAD patron goddess of the pòlis

POLIS autonomous state in ancient Greece

POLYGONAL TECHNIQUE construction technique using large irregularly shaped blocks of stone

POROS type of porous limestone

POSTERN secondary gate, secret exit in a defensive wall

PRAEFURNIA heating rooms in public baths

PROEDRIA first row of seats in a theater

PRONAOS vestibule of the cella in a temple

PROPYLAEUM monumental entrance to a temple

PROPYLON (see propylaeum)

PROSCENIUM front part of the theatre stage

PROSTYLE temple with columns on the front short side

PROTOMA sculpture showing the head and chest of an animal

PRYTANEION seat of the prytanea, the highest magistrates in the pòlis

PSEUDO-DIPTERAL temple with single peristasis double the necessary distance from the walls of the temple

PSEUDO-ISODOMIC TECHNIQUE construction technique using irregular rows of large parallelepiped blocks

PSEUDO-MONOPTERAL small round temple or shrine with half-columns

REGISTER decorative space bounded by horizontal cornices

DRUM cylindrical element in the shaft of a column

STOÀ portico

STYLOBATE continuous basement supporting a row of columns

SUSPENSURAE terracotta floor supports in the hypocaust

SYNTHRONON sequence of priestly seats

TABERNA shop

THALASSOCRACY commercial and/or military supremacy at sea

TEMENOS sacred enclosure

TEPIDARIUM warm water room in the public baths

TETRARCHIC relating to the period of the Tetrarchy in imperial Rome (305 to 395 AD)

TETRASTYLE having four columns

THESAUROS small building for the preservation of valuable votive offerings

THOLOS round cult building

THOLOS TOMB tomb having a false (corbel) dome

TYMPANUM triangular space bounded by projecting cornices

TRABEATION set of support elements of a roof including the architrave, frieze and cornice

TRICLINIUM dining room in a Roman house

TRIGLYPH decorative element with three vertical grooves in a Doric frieze

TRISTYLE having three columns

VOLUTE a spiral-shaped decorative element

WÀNAX Mycenaean king

XENON inn

XYSTOS covered running track for training

ZOOPHOROUS continuous frieze with figured decoration with animals

INDEX

A

Abdera, 82, *82*
Acarnania, 50
Achaia, 46, 102, 118, 148, 153, *153*
Achaian League, 148
Acheans, 66
Achelòos, 84, 85, *87*
Acheron 46
Achilles, *12*, 17
Acropolis, 16, *22*, 23, 25, *25*, *26*, 27, 28, 32, *32*, 34, *34*, 37, *37*
Admirals, monument of, 90
Aeacus, 66
Aegean Pompeii, see Santorìni
Aegean Sea, *5*, 8, 77, *104*, 170, 172, 184
Aegina, *5*, 6, 11, 14, 114, *114*, *116*, *117*
Aegisthus, *132*, 137, *139*
Aetolia, 88
Aetolians, 94
Aetolic League, 84, *92*
Agamemnon's Mask, 44, *130*, *132*
Agamemnon, *134*, *136*, *137*
Agatharchos, 17
Aghìa Irini, 166, *166*
Aghìa Sophìa, 80, *81*
Aghìa Triàda, 199
Aghiàdes, 194
Aghii Deka, 196
Aghios Charàlambos, 82
Aghios Dimìtrios Lombardiàris, 41
Aghios Dimìtrios, *50*, 57, 70, 73
Aghios Gheòrghios , 73, 82
Aghios Ilìas, 130
Aghios Ioànnis Pròdromos, *46*, 47
Aghios Ioànnis, *186*
Aghios Nikòlaos, 56, 211
Aghios Nìkon, *165*
Aghios Pàvlos, 186, 192
Aghios Stèfanos, 192
Aghios Titos, 196, *197*
Aglòchartos, *186*, 188
Agorà, *22*, 38, 39, 40, *40*, 41, *48*,
Agoràkritos, 16, 26, 107, 111
Agoranomion, *22*
Agrigento, 186
Agrilèza, 105
Agrìnio, 84
Agrippa, *23*, 26
Aiàkes, 194
Aigaì, 18, 19, 63, *63*, *65*
Aigeira, 148
Aigòsthena, 105, *112*, 113
Akandià, *188*, 189
Akanthos, *95*
Akrokòrinthos, 122, *122*, 123, 126, *126*
Akrotìri, *9*, 44, 167, 183, *184*
Aktìa, 50
Aktion, 84
Albania, 70
Alcinous, 54
Aleppo, 150
Alexander IV, 65
Alexander the Great, 18, 19, *19*, 20, 21, 60, 61, 65, 66, 68, *68*, 69, 77, 100, 155
Alexandroùpoli, *82*
Ali Pasha, 48
Aliàkmon, 63
Alkamenes, 16, 41

Alkmeonìdai, 42, *43*, 94
Alkyonìdon, gulf, 113
Alkyson, *50*
Alphiòs, 150, 155
Altis, 150, 153, 156
Amazonomachy, *17*, 31, 158
Amazons, *12*, 91
American Archaeological School, 41
Ammoudià, 46
Amorini, 121
Amphiaraeìon, 107
Amphiaraòs, 107
Amphieìon, 100
Amphieìon, 100
Amphilochìa, 84
Amphìpolis, *76*, 77, *77*, 82
Amvrakikós Gulf, 49, 84
Anassagoras, 17
Anàvyssos, 42, *43*
Andronìkos M., 64
Andronikos of Kyrrha, 38
Annia Regilla, 34
Anoghìa, 196
Antènor, 11, *11*, 44, 97
Antigonids, 172, *172*
Antigonos Gonates, 172,˙*173*
Antikythira, Ephebus of, 44
Antiochos III of Syria, 20
Antiochos IV of Syria, 37, 41
Antiope, rape of, 103
Antoninus Pius, *191*
Anubis, 62, 178
Anytos, 163
Àpella, 164
Apelles, 19, 69, 190
Aphrodisìas in Caria, 197
Aphrodite Hypolimpìdia, 61
Aphrodite of Doidàlsas, *188*
Aphrodite of Milos, 20
Aphrodite Peithò, 128
Aphrodite, *30*, 52, 62, 175, 178, *188*, 192
Aphrodite, temple of, *51*, 122
Apollo Daphnephoros, 102
Apollo Delios, 192
Apollo Epikoùrios, 16, 158, *158*
Apollo Ismenios, 100
Apollo Karneios, *183*, 185
Apollo Làphrios, 87, 87
Apollo Ptòios, 99, *99*
Apollo Pythios, 84, 88, *89*, 90, 92, *188*, 189, 198
Apollo Sitàlkas, *89*, 92
Apollo Thérmios, 84, *85*
Apollo, *12*, 14, 50, *50*, 87, 88, *89*, 90, 91, 116, 123, 126, *126*, 129, 150, 163, 169, *169*, 170, 171, *171*, 172, 173, *173*, 174, 176, 182, 190
Apollo, temple of, *91*, 92, *93*, 94, 96, *125*, *127*, *159*, 170, 172, *182*
Apollodoros, 17
Apolòna, 182, *182*
Arákynthos, 86
Arcadia, 16, 158, 160, 161, *162*, *163*
Arcadians, 90
Archèa Kassòpi, 48
Archokràtes, 186
Ardetto, 37
Areopaghìtou, Dionisìou, 37
Areopago, *22*, 40
Arèos, 39
Ares, temple of, *40*, 41, 105
Arethusa, 150

Arghirokástro, 189
Argolys, 6, 114, 118, 130
Argos, 12, 14, *89*, 90, 130, 138, 140, *141*
Ariadne, 70, *72*, 182
Aristarchus, 194
Aristides, 41
Aristotle, 18, 66
Armenia, 73
Armenians, 196
Arne, 99
Aroània, 148
Artemidoros of Perge, 185
Artemis Brauronia, *23*, 27, 106, *106*
Artemis Làphria, 86, 87, *87*
Artemis Mesopolìtis, 162
Artemis Orthìa, 165
Artemis Propylaia, 108, *109*
Artemis, *87*, 123, *125*, 126, 145, 163, *169*, 170, 171, *171*, 174
Artemis, temple of, *55*, *143*
Artemìsion, 54, 86,
Asia Minor, 13, 116, 185, 186, 190, 196, *197*
Asia, 18, *173*
Asklepiades of Arados, 178
Asklepiads, 190
Asklepieìon, 161, *161*, 190, *191*
Asklepios, 56, 142, *143*, *144*, 145, 147, *160*, 161, 163, 190, 192, 198
Astarte-Afrodite, 174
Atargatis, 178
Athena Alèa, 162, *162*
Athena Aphaìa, *5*, 11, 14, 114, *114*, 115, *117*
Athena Chalkìoikos, 165
Athena Kameiràs, 189
Athena Lìndia, 186, *186*, *187*
Athena Nike, 16, *23*, 26, 27, *27*
Athena of the Varvakìon, *29*
Athena Parthénos, 16, 27, 29, *29*
Athena Poliàs, 32, *32*
Athena Polioùchos, 164, 165
Athena Pròmachos, 26
Athena Pronaìa, *94*, *95*, 96, 146
Athena Thinking, *22*
Athena, 25, *30*, *30*, 31, 33, *116*, 166, 175, *188*
Athenians, 27, 77, *89*, 98, *106*, 107, 170
Athens, *7*, 12, 13, 16, 18, 22, *25*, 28, 31, 34, 41, *89*, 90, 92, 99, 100, 102, *103*, 104, 105, 107, *112*, 113, 114, 116, *164*, 170, 198
Athens, Museum of the Acropolis, *11*, *14*, *22*, 31, 33, 42, *43*, 44, *44*,
Athens, National Archaeological Museum, *7*, *9*, 42, *42*, *43*, 105, 107, 130, *131*, 135, *135*, *137*, *143*, 145, 162, *164*, 165, 175, 183, *184*, *185*
Atridae, 133, *134*, *136*, *137*
Attalids of Pergamum, 169, *171*
Attica, 6, 8, 30, 33, 104, *104*, 105, 106, 107, 113, 114, 118
Augè, 162
Augustals, 124
Augustus Caesar, *23*, 26, 32, 50, 78, 79, 84,
Auriga of Delphi, *14*, *15*
Avdira, 82
Avrilìou Márkou, 38

B

Bacchantes, 162
Bacchiadai, 54
Bacchus, 122
Barbarians, 73
Basileùs, 8
Beirut, 174
Benàki Museum, 42
Beulé Gate, *23*, 25, *26*
Billienus, Caius, *173*
Bithynia, 94
Black Sea, 77
Boeotia, 6, 8, 98, *112*
Boeotia, Orchomenos, 99
Brancusi, 8
Brasida, 77
Brauron, 106
Bronze Age, 8, 111, 114, 148, 166, 167, 194
Bruce, T. of Elgin, 28
Bryaxis, 18
Byron, *104*
Byton, *96*, 97
Byzantine Museum, 42
Byzàntion, 70
Byzantium, 154

C

Callicrates, 16, 26, 27, 28, *28*, 158, *159*
Cape Artemísso, 15, 42, 44, *42*, 103
Cape Soùnion, 16, *104*, 105, 106, 107
Carthaginians, 92
Caryatids, 33, *33*, 91, *110*
Caspian Sea, 19
Cassander, 63, 70
Centauromachy, *12*, 28, 31, 41, 66, 105, 157, *157*, 158
Cerdone, 169, *177*
Chaironea, 18, 98, 99, *154*, 155
Chalcidic, peninsula, 60, 74
Chalkída, 100
Chalkis, 102
Chalkotheke, *23*
Chanià, 196
Chares of Lìndos, 189
Charièstratos, 107
Chàrites, 98, *99*
Chàvos, 130
Chersikrates, 54
Chìos, 82, 92
Chòra Tryfiliàs, 159
Christians, 28
Chrysaor, 54
Ciceros, 194, *194*
Cimmerian Bosphorus, 65
Cimon, 41, 90
City palace, 8, 198, *198*, 199, 200, 201, *201*, *202*, 204, *207*, *208*, 211
Claudius, Roman Emperor, 77
Cleopatra VII of Egypt, 50, 84
Cleopatra, 19, 65, *169*, *180*, 181
Clytemnestra, *132*, 137, *139*
Cocitos, 46
Colossus (of Rhodes), 189
Commagene, 41
Compitaliasts, 169, *169*, *171*
Concordia, 185
Constantine, 165
Constantinople, *81*
Copenhagen, Ny Carlsberg Glyptotek, *19*
Corcyreans, 52, 90
Corfu, 6, 54, *54*, 90

Corinth, 12, 113, 114, 118, 120, 121, 122, *122*, *123*, *125*, *126*, 148
Corinthia, 118, 162
Corinthians, 98
Cratero, 69
Cretans, 8, 210
Crete, 6, 8, *8*, 165, 170, 196, *197*, *208*, 210, 211
Cuma, 103
Cybele, 79
Cyclades, 166, 182
Cyprus, 211
Cyrene, 184

D

Damòphon, *161*, 163, *163*
Dàochos II, 97
Delians, 172
Delio-Attican League, 92, 170, 194
Delos, *5*, 6, 10, 92, 168, 169, *169*, *171*, 172, 173, *173*, 174, 175, *175*, *177*, *178*, *180*, 181, 186
Delphi, 10, 84, 88, *89*, 90, *93*, *95*, *96*, 97, 146
Delphi, Archaeological Museum, *14*
Delphic Amphictyony, 92
Demeter, 108, *108*, 111, 122, 163, *163*
Demetriàs, 57, 58
Democritos, 17, 82
Demosthenes, 41, 98, 104
Dervèni, cup, 70, *72*
Despoìna, 163, *163*
Dexìleos, 44
Diadoumènos by Polykleitos, 42, *169*, 175
Diana, *51*, 78, 79
Dimìni, 8, 58
Dimitsàna, 163
Dìon, *61*, 62
Dione, *30*, 52
Dionysus, 23, 37, 70, *72*, 98, 102, *102*, *103*, 106, 123, *125*, 142, 151, 155, 157, 162, 166, *169*, 177, 178, 182, *183*
Dionysus, house of, 67, 68, *68*, *180*, 181
Dionysus, theater of, *22*, 23, 34, *35*
Dionysus, villa of, *61*, 62
Dioscures, *169*, *180*, 181, 185
Dìpylon, 39
Dìpylon-Kerameikós, 39
Dirce, 98, *101*
Dìstos, 103
Dodecanese, 8, 186, 190
Dodona, 46, 51, *51*, 52, *52*, 84
Dorians, 8, 130, 164, 190
Droysen, J. G., 20
Dyrràchion, see Durres, 70

E

Echo, *151*, 154
Edessa, 66, *67*
Edict of Theodosios I, 28, 142
Edipsoù, 103
Eghìnio, 62
Eghìra, 148
Egnatia, via, 70, 73, 78, *78*, 80, 81
Egospotami, 90
Egypt, 8, 20, 50, 84, *183*, 190
Ekklesiasterion, *22*

Eleftherías, 189
Eléktrai, 100
Eleusinian Mysteries, *108*, 111
Eleusis, 16, 26, 33, 34, 97, 104, 108, *108*, *109*, *110*, *111*, 113
Eleutheraì, *112*, 113, *113*
Elipdios, bishop, 57
Elis, 148, 149, 158, 163
Emathìa, 62
Epaminondas, 160, 162
Epáno Englianós, 158
Ephebes, *183*
Ephebus, 14, *14*
Ephesus, *19*
Ephors, 164
Ephyra, 47
Epicuros, 62, *62*, 194
Epidamnus, 154
Epidaurus, 44, 142, *143*, *144*, *145*, 146, *147*
Epirots, 52
Epirus, 6, 46, 50, 56, 84
Erassinós, 106, *106*
Erechteion, 16, *23*, 32, *32*, 33, *33*, *110*
Erechtheùs, 32, 33
Eretria, 102, *102*, 103, *103*
Ermoù, via, 39
Erymanthos, 148
Eteocles, 98
Etolikó, 85
Etruscans, 88, 92
Eubea, 42, 103
Eumenes II, 26
Eupalinos of Megara, 194, *194*
Euridice, *63*, 64
Eurimedòn, 90
Europa, house of the rape of, 193
Europe, 8, 78
Eurotas, 165
Evans, Arthur, *208*
Evros, 77
Exechia, *12*

F

Farsala, 56
Fedríades, 88
Fere, 59
Filaco, *95*, 96
Filakopí, 167, *167*
First Persian War, 98
Focile, 88
Fontana Minoa, 172
Forbante, *68*
Fortuna, 123, 192
Ftia, 56
Ftiotide, 57, 98
Funerary Circle A, *132*, *134*, 135, *135*, *136*, *137*
Funerary Circle B, 141

G

Galatians, *92*, 94
Galerius, 70, *70*, 73
Gela, 154, 186
Gelon, 92, *92*
Gerousía, 164
Ghè, *51*, 88
Ghè-Thèmis, temple of, *51*
Ghenèleos, 194, *194*
Ghermenó, 113
Giant, 55, *96*
Gigantomachy, 31, 105
Gitiàdas, 165
Glà, 99
Glyptothek, Munich, *114*, 115, *117*
Gnósis, 69, *69*
Gonìes, 196
Gòritsa, *58*
Gòrtyna, 163, 196, *197*

Goti, 60, 160
Gournià, 211, *211*
Grànikos, 61
Great Gods, sanctuary of, *20*
Grota, 182
Gulf Saronikós, 114, 118
Gythion, 196

H

Hades, 47, 66
Hadrian, *22*, *25*, *36*, 37, *37*, *38*, 39, *40*, 122
Hageladas, 15, 157
Hagesandros, *186*, 188
Harpocrates, 178
Hector, *12*
Helen, 165, *165*
Helen, House of the rape of, *67*, *68*, 69, *69*
Helikòn, *93*
Helios, sanctuary of, 189
Hellanodikai, *128*
Hellas, 88, 150
Hellenism, 20
Hellenistic era, 20, *120*
Hellens, 8
Helots, 165
Hephaistos, 16, 32, 40, *40*, 105
Hera Akraìa, 54, 118, *118*
Hera Limènia, 118, *118*
Hera, 118, 138, *151*, 154, *154*, 155, *178*, 194, *194*
Heracles, 41, *51*, 52, 64, 70, 77, 91, 150, 157, 158, 162, 174, 192
Heraclides, 116
Heraìon, 178, 194, *194*
Hercules, 123
Hermaists, 169, *169*
Hermes Propylaios, *173*
Hermes, 66, 77, *151*, 155, 157, 169, *169*, 175, *176*, 177, *177*
Herodes Atticus, *25*, 34, *36*, 37, 124, 126, *151*, 154, *154*
Herodotus, 171
Herulians, *26*
Hesiod, 98
Hestia, *30*, 172
Hieron, 92, *92*
Hippocrates, 18
Hippodamus of Miletus, 13, 74
Hyerotytheìon, 189
Hygieia, 45, 161, 196
Hyperboreans, 97, 150, 171

I

Iàlysos, 186, 189
Ictinus, 16, 28, *28*, 158
Ideo, cave of, 196
Idi, mount, 196
Igoumenìtsa, 46
Ilyssòs, *30*
Imbrasos, 194
Indus, 19
Inopos, *169*, 178
Ioánina, 46, 51, 52, 56
Ionia, 19, 194
Ionian Sea, *5*, 149
Ionians, 8, 166
Iràklio, 196, *199*, 200, *200*, *203*, 207
Irèo, 118
Iron Age, 8, 148
Isis, *61*, 62, *178*, *178*
Ismaros, 82
Istanbul, 70
Isthmìa, 120, *120*, 121, *121*
Isthmian Games, 120
Isvòria, 66
Italy, 103
Itéa, 88

Ithaca, 54
Ithòmi, mount, 160, 161
Iulia Augusta Diensis, 62
Iulia, basilica, 124

J

Jerusalem, 73
Julia-Claudia, gens, 80
Julius Caesar, 56
Jupiter, 79, 122
Justinian, 50, 77, 81, 120, *120*

K

Kàdmos, 100, 101, *101*
Kaiafas, 158, *158*
Kaikos, battle of, 162
Kalamata, 163
Kallìchoron, 108, *109*
Kallikles, 66
Kallìmachos, 16, 27
Kalydòn, 86, *87*, 111
Kamàri, 184
Kanaláki, 48
Kanellòpoulos Museum, 42
Kapamà, 192
Karakónero, 189
Kardítsa, 56
Karneìai, 185
Karteia, 166
Karyès, *33*
Karystios, 177
Kàrystos, 103
Kassòpe, 48, *48*, 50
Kastalìa, sacred spring of, *95*, 96
Kastèli, 196
Kastrì, 47
Katagògion, 48
Katàra, 56
Kàto Zàkros, 211, *211*
Katochì, 85
Kavàla, 78, 81
Kea, 6, 166, *166*
Kefalòs, 192
Kefalóvrisso, 85
Kèkrops, 30, 32, 33
Kenchrèai, 120, 121
Kepheus, 162
Kephisodotos, 18
Kephisòs, *30*, 98
Keratòn, *169*, 170
Kèrkyra, 54, 90
Kiàto, 129
Killìni, 129
Kìmissis tis Theotókou, 98, 163
Kinch, tomba, 66
Kìssamos, 196
Kladiòs, 150, 153, *157*
Klazomènai, 82
Klein W., 21
Klèobis, *96*, 97
Kleòboulos, 186
Knossos, 8, *8*, 182, 200, *200*, 202, *203*, *204*, *205*, *207*, *208*, *209*, 210
Kokorètsa, 130
Kolòna, 116
Kolonós Agoréos, 40
Komotiní, 82
Kopaìda, 98
Kopaís, 98, 99
Kopanòs, 66
kòrai, 10, 11, 33, 44, 115, 182
Kore-Persephones, 108, *108*, 122
Kos, 6, 190, 192, 193, *193*
koùroi, 10, 11, 33, 97, 99, 101, 105, *111*, 182, *182*
Kráteia, 86
Krenìdes, *78*
Krestena, 158

Kritios, 14, *14*
Kroìsos, 42, *43*
Krònion, 150
Krònion, 150
Kymi, 103
Kynòs Kephalaí, 56
Kynthos, mount, *169*, 170, *176*, 178, *178*
Kythira, 165

L

Labyrinth, 170, 182
Laconi of Amyklai, 196
Laconia, 6, 158, 164
Laomèdon of Mytilène, 76, 77, 116
Làphria, 87
Lapiths, 66, 157
Larissa, 58, 59, *59*,
Lávrion, 106
Lawagetas, *159*
League of the "Free Laconians", 165
Lebanon, 34, 174
Lebenà, 198
Lèchaion, 121, 124, *125*, 126, *127*
Lefkàdia, 66
Lefkandi, 102
Lelantine War, 102
Lèlas, 102
Lèndas, 198
Leochares, 18, 155
Léon, 86
Leonidaíon, *151*, 153, *153*
Leonidas, 98, 153, 165
Lerna, 140
Leto, 88, 173, 174
Letòon, 173
Leucippos, 82
Libon of Elis, 156
Ligdami, 182, *182*
Limàni Litochòrou, 60
Lìndos, 186, *186*, *187*
Linear "A", 167
Linear "B", 101, *101*, 158, 204
Lissos, 196
Livia Augusta, 80
London, British Museum, *12*, 28, *30*, 33, 158
Loutrà, 103
Loutráki, 118
Lucius Aemilius Paulus, *89*, 92
Lucius Mummius, 122
Lycossoùra, 163, *163*
Lycurgus, *36*, 164
Lysicrates, *22*, 37, *37*
Lysippus, 18, 19, *19*, *20*, 69, 97, 128
Lyson, 66

M

Macedonia, 6, 19, *19*, 56, 59, 60, 62, 66, *72*, 74, 77, *77*
Macedonian Empire, 18, 20, 21
Macedonian Empire, 46, 67, *92*
Macedonians, 56, 66, 77, 98, 186
Machaon, 161
Maenads, 70
Maia, 169
Màllia, 210, *210*
Mandráki, 189
Mani, 165
Mantineia, 162, *162*, 163, *163*
Marathon, 90, 91, *106*, 107, *152*
Marcus Aurelius, 79, 80, 82, 108, *108*, *109*
Marcus Cossutius, 37
Mark Antony, 50, 78, 84
Markópoulo, 106

Marònea, 82
Mars, 50
Marseilles, *94*, 96
Mater Matuta, 192
Mavrommáti, 160, 161
Mediterranean Sea, *5*, 6, 90, 190
Medusa, Gorgon, 54, *66*, *72*, *103*, 116
Megàle Meter, 67
Megalòpolis, *162*
Megara Iblea, 154
Megara, 104, 113
Megarians, 98
Meidias, 17
Melanès, 182
Melantios, 69
Meleager, 86
Melíte, 85, *85* ,
Melqart, 174
Mènalon, 162
Menekràtes, 54, *54*, 55
Menelaos, 165, *165*
Mesopotamia, 19, 73
Messarà, 196
Messene, 160, *160*, *161*, 163, *163*
Messenia, 158
Messenians, *151*, 157, *157*, *161*
Messolónghi, 85, 86
Messopòtamos, 46, 48
Metapontium, 154
Meteore, 56
Metróon, *40*, 41, 154
Mètsovo, 56
Micale, 194
Michalítsi, 50, *50*
Midea, 141
Mieza, 66
Mikrothíves, 56
Milos, 6, 167, *167*
Miltiades, 90, *152*
Minerva, 79
Minos, king, 8, 196, *209*
Minotaur, 170
Minyàs, treasury of, 98, *99*
Mitropóleos, 182
Mnesikles, 16, 26, *27*
Modigliani, 8
Molossian dinasty, 46, 48
Monastirakìou, 39
Moschophòros, *43*, 44
Mourià, *154*
Mouseìon, *34*
Mouseìon, 41
Muses, 62, 88, *93*, 98
Museum of Cycladic Art and Ancient Greece, 42
Museum of the Agorà, *40*, 41
Mycenae, *7*, 8, *9*, 44, 99, 130, *130*, *132*, 133, *134*, *136*, 137, *137*, 138, *138*, 141
Mykonos, 169, *169*, 181
Myron, diskobolos by, *14*, 15

N

Nàfpaktos, 88
Nàfplion, 130, 138, 140, 141
Naples, 186
National Museum of Naples, *14*
Naukràti, 174
Naupactians, *151*, 157, *157*
Nàxioi, *169*, 170, 174, 182
Nàxos, 6, *89*, *91*, 92, 153, 170, 174, *175*, 182, *182*
Nèa Anchìalos, 56, *56*,
Nea Pleuron, 86, *87*
Nèdas, 149, 158
Nekromateìon, 46, *46*, 47, 49, 52
Nemea, *128*, 129, 130, 145
Nèmesis, 105, *106*, 107
Neolithic, 8, 57, *58*, 140, 167

Neoptolemus, 55
Neòrion, 172, *172*
Neptune, 50, 123
Nereid, *121*, 172
Nero, *191*, 192
Nesiotes, 14
Nessus, centaur, 158
Nestor, *135*, 158
Nike Alata, *20*, 157, *157*, 188
Nikias, 65, 171
Nikòpolis, 49, 50, *50*, 51
Nile, 174
Nymphs, 66, *188*

O

Odeíon of Agrippa, *40*, 41
Odeíon of Herodes Atticus, *22, 23*, 34
Odeíon of Pericles, *22, 23*, 34
Oedipus, 98
Oenomaus, 150, 157
Oiniàadai, 85, *85*
Olìgyrtos, 129
Olympia, 10, *12*, 13, 16, 145, *145*, 150, *151*, *152*, *154*, 157, *157*, 158
Olympia, Archaeological Museum, *12*
Olympia, Master of, 15
Olympiads, *36*, 37, 150, 153
Olympic Games, 13, 121, 154, *154*
Olympieìon, *36*, 37, *37*
Olympos, 59, 60, 173
Olynthos, 74, *75*
Orchomenos, 162
Orfeus, 77
Oropòs, 107, *107*
Ortagorids, 128

P

Pagasitikós, gulf, 57
Painter of the Dìpylon, 42
Paionios of Mende, 17, 157, *157*
Palaimon, *120*
Palaimónion, 120
Palàti, 182
Palatìtsia, 63, *65*
Paleà Episkopì, 163
Paleolithic, 8, 46,
Paleopolis, 54, *54*
Pàmissos, 158
Pamphilìdas, *186*
Pan, 175
Panachaikón, 148
Panaghìa Ahiropiìtos, , 73
Panainos, 17
Panathenaic Festival, 25, 31, *36*
Pandróseion, 33
Panhellenic Nemean Games, *128*, 129
Pantheon, 123
Pàrga, 46, 50
Paride, 69, *193*
Paris, Musée du Louvre, *20*, 44
Parnassòs, 88, 95
Parnònas, 164
Pàros, 92, 105, 111
Parrhasios, 17
Parthenon, 16, *16, 17, 22, 23, 26, 27, 27, 28, 29, 30, 31*, 40, *40*, 158
Parthenòpe, 186
Parthians, 124
pàthos, 18, 19
Patras, *128*, 148, *148*, 149, *149*
Pausanias, 6, 27, 33, 88, 91, *128*, 155, 165
Pausia di Sicione, *123*

Pegasus, 54
Peirene fountain, 124, *124*
Peisistratus, *109*, 170
Pèla, 66
Pèlla, 19, 67, *67, 68, 69*
Pelope, 150, 157, *157*
Pelòpion, *151*, 155
Peloponnese, 8, 118, 148, 150, 156, *158*, 164
Peloponnesian war, 16, 18, 26, 27, 77, 90, 106, 167
Peloponnesians, 120
Penthesilea, *12*
Perachòra, 118, *118*, *119*
Perdikovrìssi, 99
Pergamum, 21, 26, 41, *141*, 190
Pericles, 16, 25, 30, *37*, 41, 104, *109*
Perieci, 165
Peristerià, 158
Persephone, 47, 64, 65, *185*
Persia, 73
Persian Empire, 12
Persian Expiation, 26, 33, *43*
Persian Wars, 120
Persians, 26, 27, *33*, 66, *95*, 105, 107, 116, 194
Pètra, 59
Phaeacians, 54
Phaidyntai, *151*
Phaistòs, 198, *198*, 199, 210
Phàrsalus, 97
Phérai, see Fere
Phidias, 16, 17, 26, 29, *29*, 30, 33, 44, *152*, 153, 157
Phigáleia, see Vasses
Philip II of Macedonia, 18, 19, *19, 60, 63*, 64, 65, *65*, 66, 70, *72*, 74, 78, 98, *99*, *154*, 155
Philip V, 52, 56, 85
Philippeìon, *151, 154*, 155
Philippian Colonnade, 163
Philippoi, 78, *78, 81*
Philopappos, *22, 23, 34*, 40
Philopappos, Gaius Giulius Antiochos, *40*, 41
Phlegetontes, 46
Phocians, 98
Phoenicia, 178
Phoenicians, 184
Phthiotìdes Thèbai, 56
Phylakos, *94*
Phyle, 107, *107*, *112*
Phylos, 158, 159, *159*
Pidna, *92*
Pieria, 60
Pìndos, 46, *51*, 56, 60
Piraeus, 13, 16
Pirithous, 157
Pisistratids, 37
Plàka, *37*, 38, 167
Plateesi, 107
Plato, 18, 104
Plutarch, 98
Pluto, 65, 108
Pnyka, *34*, 41
Podalirius, 161
Poliorcetes, Demetrios, 57, 58, *58, 59*, 172
pòlis, 9, 10, 12, 13, 18, 20, 21, 46, 59, 90, 140, 148, 150, 194
Polygnotos of Thasos, 15
Polygnotos the Younger, 17
Polykleitos the Younger, 142, *143*, *144*, *145*, 146, 147, *147*,
Polykleitos, *14*, 15, 16, 122, 138, 175
Polykràtes, *178*, 194, *194*
Polymèdes of Argos, 97

Polyrrhènia, 196
Polyzelos of Gela, *14*, 15, 97
Pompeo, 56, 177
Portàra, 182, *182*
Poseidon, 16, *17*, 30, 32, *32*, 33, 42, *42*, *104*, 105, 120, *120*, 174, 185, 188
Poseidoniasts of Berytos, *169*, 174, *175*
Praxiteles, 18, *20*, *151*, 155, 157
Priam, 55
Propylaia, 16, *23*, 25, 26, *26, 27*, 108, *108*, *109*, *110*, *117*, *140*, *147*, 170, *173*, 198, 200, 203, 208
Pròsymna, 138
Protagoras, 82
Prusias, *92*, 94
Ptòion, 99, *99*, 101
Ptolemies, 172, *172*, *183*, 184, 185
Ptolemy II Philadelphus, 190
Ptòos, 99
Pyrasos, 56, *56*
Pyrgos, 150
Pyrrhus, 52
Pythagoras, 194
Pythagòrio, 194
Pythia, 88, 91, 94, 96
Pythian Games, 88, *93*
Pythokritos, 188
Python, 88, *89*, 91

R

Rampin Rider, 44
Ravenna, San Vitale, *81*
Rethymno, 196
Rhadamanthys, 66
Rhamnoùs, 105, *106*, 107
Rhodes, 6, 13, *20*, 186, 188, *188*
Rhoìkos of Samos, 194
Rhomàios, tomba, *6*, 64
Rhòmbos, *43*
Rodìni, 189
Rodopi, 60, 77
Roma, goddess, *23*, 32, 174, *175*
Romans, 56, 73, *125*, 186
Rome, 54, 62, 80, 167, *167*, 186, 192
Rome, National Museum, *14*
Rome, Templus Pacis, 39
Rotunda, 73
Roxane, 65

S

S. Omobono, 192
Sacred Band of Thebans, 98
Sacred Lake, 174, *175*
Salamìna, 108
Saloniki, *63, 65*, 67, 70, *70, 72*, 74
Saloniki, Archaeological Museum, *19*
Samii, 194
Sammicheli Loggia, 196
Samos, 6, *178*, 194, *194*
Samothrace, *20*, 82, 178, 188
Samothràkeion, 178
Santorìni, 6, 8, *9*, 44, 167, 183, *183*, 184, *184*
Saqqara, 101
Sàra, 130
Satyrs, 70
Scherìa of the Phaeacians, 54
Schliemann, Heinrich, *130*, 135, *135*
Sea Peoples, 8, 130, 166
Sebasteìon, *78*, 80, *160*
Seleucid dinasty, 41
Seleucus I Nicator, 41

Selinos, 154
Septimius Severus, 124, *125*
Serapeion, *169*, 178
Serapis, 62, 178
Sèsklo, 8, 58, *58*
Sibilla, 91
Sicily, 182
Sikyon, *14, 89*, 91, *128*, *128*, 154
Silenus, *35*, 178, 193
Silla, 34
Silvanus, *78*
Simis, 189
Simonides, 166
Sìndos, 70
Siphnos, *89*, 91, *96*
Skardanà, *169*, 177
Skòpas, 18, 44, 162, *162*
Slavi, 90
Smith, monte, 189
Soughià, 196
Sparta, 12, 18, 77, *89*, 90, *95*, 160, 162, 164, *164*, 165, *165*, 167
Sphinx, *91, 92*, 178
St. Leonidas Bishop, *127*
St. Lydia, 78
St. Paul, 78, *78*, 79, 80, 81
Stadium of Herodes Atticus, 22
Stefanovíkio, 59
Stephanos, architect, 57
Stoà dei Naxii, 171
Stoà of Antigonos Gonates, *169*, 172
Stoà of Attalus II, *22*, *40*, 41
Stoà of Eumenes II, *22, 23*, 34, *34*
Stoà of Philip V, *169*, *169*
Stoà of the Athenians, *89*, 91, 92
Stoà of the Attalids, *169*, *169*
Stoà of Zeus Eleutherios, *40*
Stràtos, 84
Strymonas, 76
Strymonas, 77
Stymphalian Marsh, 129
Susa, 69
Sybaris, 154
Sylànion, 44
Syracuse, *89*, 92, 150, 154
Syria, 19, *20*, 37, 178, 211
Syrian Divinities, *169*, 178

T

Tanàgra, 101
Tanit, 178
Taranto, *14*, 164
Taurokathápsia, *207*
Taygetos, 158, 164
Tegèa, *45*, 162, *162*
Telchines Street, 183
Telephos, 162
Telestérion, 34, 108, *108*, *109*
Tempe, 59, 60
Téos, 82
Thasos, 78
Thebans, 98, *99*
Thebes, 18, 57, 98, 99, 100, *100*, 101, *101*, 102, 113, 162
Thèmis, 52, 107, 145
Themistocles, 41
Thermopyles mountains, 98
Thermos, 84, 87
Thersìlion, 163, *163*
Theseíon, *40*, *40*
Theseus, 37, 39, 41, *68*, 69, 91, *103*, 170, 182
Thessaly, 8, 56, 59, 98

Thirty, tyranny of, 107
Thissìo, 40, *40*
Tholò, 158
Thorikòs, 106, *106*
Thorvaldsen, 116
Thrace, 6, 77
Thracian Knight, 79
Thrasybolos, 107
Timòtheas from Tegèa, 18, 44, *143*, 145
Tower of the Winds, 38, *38*, *39*
Trajan, 37
Treasure of Atreus, 99, *132*, 137, *138*
Treasure of the Athenians, *88, 89, 91*
Triánda, 189
Triarius, *169*, 177
Trichonìda, 84, 85
Trikala, 56
Tripitì, 167, *167*
Tripolis, 162, *163*, 164
Tritons, 175, *176*
Trojans, 66, *114*, 116
Troy, 31
Turkey, 70, *141*
Turks, *39*, 48
Tyche, *183*
Tylissòs, 196
Tyrannicides, group of, 14
Tyrins, 138, 140, *140*, 141, *141*, 158

U

Ulysses, 54

V

Vafèika, 82
Vafió, *164*, 165, *165*
Vài, 211
Valerian, *34*
Vasilóspito, 49
Vàsses, 16, 158, *158*
Velestìno, 59
Venus, 123
Verghìna, 19, 63, *63*, 65, 70
Vèria, 66, *66*
Vèrmio, 60
Vèrno, 60
Verres, Gaius, 194
Vistonìda, 82
Volimìdia, 159
Vólos, 56, 57, 58, *58*
Vourkàri, 166
Vràna, 107

X

Xánthi, 82
Xeròpolis, 102
Xerxès, 92
Xestè 3, 183, *185*

Z

Zagòria-Vìkos, 56
Zálongo, 48
Zànes, 154
Zeus Agoraíos, *40*
Zeus Hypatos, 32
Zeus Olympios, 13, *22*, *36*, 37, *151*, *152*, 153, 156, 157
Zeus Sotèr, 163
Zeus Stràtios, 84
Zeus, 30, 33, 37, 42, *42*, 52, 55, 60, *61*, 103, 150, 154, 185, *194*, 196
Zeus, sanctuary of, 62
Zeus, temple of, *12*, 15, 16, 51, *51*, 52, *128*, 129, 157
Zeuxis, 17, 19
Zipári, 192

PHOTOGRAPHIC CREDITS

Antonio Attini / Archivio White Star: pages 1, 2-3, 8, 52, 52-53, 75 bottom, 106 top and bottom, 106-107, 107 bottom left, 160 top, 160-161, 170, 170-171, 172 bottom, 172-173, 173 bottom, 174 bottom left, 174-175, 175 bottom right, 178 top right, 178 bottom, 179, 180-181, 181 bottom left, 182, 186-187, 188 bottom, 190 top, 190 left, 194, 194-195, 200, 201, 202 bottom, 204, 205 bottom left, 208 bottom left, 208-209, 216.

Marcello Bertinetti / Archivio White Star: pages 16-17, 28-29.

Alfio Garozzo / Archivio White Star: pages 9 left, 22-23, 24 bottom, 26-27, 29 top, 32-33, 34 bottom right, 35 bottom left and right, 36 top and bottom, 37 top and bottom, 38, 39, 40, 41, 46, 47, 48, 49, 50, 50-51, 53 bottom, 54 top, 54-55, 56, 57, 58, 59, 60, 61, 62, 63 top, 64, 66, 67, 70 bottom right, 74 top, 75, 76, 77, 78, 79, 80, 81, 82, 83, 84, 85, 86, 87, 90-91, 91, 92 top, 93 bottom left, 97 bottom, 98 bottom, 98-99, 99 top and bottom, 104, 105, 106 center, 107 bottom right, 108, 109, 110, 111, 112, 113, 118, 119, 120, 121, 122, 123, 124, 125, 126 top right and center, 126-127, 128-129, 129 bottom, 130, 133 bottom, 136 top, 140, 141, 148, 149, 151, 152-153, 153 top and bottom, 154 center and bottom, 154-155, 155 bottom, 153 top left, 156-157, 158 bottom left, 158-159, 159 bottom, 161 bottom, 162 left, 164 left, 164-165, 165 bottom right, 166 top, 166-167, 168, 171, 172 top, 174 bottom right, 175 top and bottom left, 176, 177, 178 top left, 180, 181 bottom right, 183, 184 top left, 186, 187 bottom, 188 top and center, 188-189, 189 top, 190-191, 191, 192, 193, 195, 196, 197, 198, 199 top and left, 200 left, 202-203, 203 top, 204-205, 208 top and bottom a right, 209 bottom, 210-211.

Giulio Veggi / Archivio White Star: pages 26 top, 28 top and bottom, 32 top and bottom, 32 right, 34 top, 34 bottom left, 34-35, 36-37, 88, 88-89, 92 center and bottom, 92-93, 93 bottom right, 94-95, 95 bottom, 114-115, 115 bottom, 117 top, 126 bottom, 128 top and bottom, 132 top right, 136-137, 137 center, 138 top, 139 bottom, 142 top left, 144, 144-145, 156 top right, 158 top left, 158 right, 162 right, 162-163, 163 top, 164 bottom left.

Agenzia Double's, Milano: pages 9 right, 16 top, 22 bottom, 31 center, 99 center, 184 top right, 145 right.

Agenzia Luisa Ricciarini, Milano: pages 11, 12, 43 left, 45, 72 bottom, 136-137 bottom, 150, 152 bottom, 157, 184 bottom, 184-185, 185 left, 203 bottom, 199.

Agenzia Luisa Ricciarini, Milano / Photo Nimatallah: page 29 bottom.

Agenzia Luisa Ricciarini, Milano / Emilio F. Simion: pages 132 top left, 206 bottom, 206-207.

Agenzia Luisa Ricciarini, Milano / Foto W. P. S: page 68 bottom.

AKG Photo, Berlin: pages 130, 156 bottom.

Giovanni Dagli Orti: pages 6-7, 14 left and right, 15 right, 18, 18-19, 19, 20, 27 top and bottom, 43 right, 44 left and center, 44 right, 54 bottom, 58-59, 63 bottom, 64-65, 65 bottom, 68-69, 71, 72 top, 72-73, 73 top right, 87 bottom left, 88 top, 91 bottom, 95 right, 96, 96-97, 100 top and bottom, 101 bottom right and left, 101 top left, 114, 135, 137 top, 138 bottom, 138-139, 146, 146-147, 147, 164 left, 166 bottom, 189 bottom.

Mauzy Photography: pages 142-143, 145 top.

Musee Louvre Paris, ASAP / The Bridgeman Art Library: page 21.

On Location / V. Constatineas: pages 150-151, 152 top.

On Location/ Loukas Hapsis: pages 102 top and bottom, 103.

On Location / Velissarios Voutas: page 154 top.

SCALA Group, Firenze: pages 14-15, 42-43, 142 top right, 199 bottom right.

SIME / Johanna Huber: pages 205 bottom right, 206 top, 207 bottom.

Henri Stierlin: page 4 bottom.

Studio Kontos / Photostock: pages 69, 70 bottom left, 73 bottom, 102-103.

Studio Koppermann / Staatliche Antikensammlungen und Glyptothek Munchen: pages 116-117.

The British Museum, London: pages 10, 13, 30 top, 30-31 top.

The British Museum, London / The Bridgeman Art Library: pages 30-31 bottom.

216 From the top of Mount Khyntos, you can enjoy the exciting view of the ruins of Delos and waters of the Aegean, which wash over the island.